PHILOSOPHY FOR A2: UNIT 4

Philosophy for A2: Unit 4 is the definitive textbook for students of the new AQA Advanced level syllabus introduced in 2008. Structured very closely around the AQA specifications for Unit 4: Philosophical Problems, this book helps students to engage with and understand the arguments of the five texts:

- Hume's *An Enquiry Concerning Human Understanding*
- Plato's *The Republic*
- Mill's *On Liberty*
- Descartes' *Meditations*
- Nietzsche's *Beyond Good and Evil.*

All chapters are helpfully subdivided into short, digestible passages, and include:

- quiz questions to test core knowledge
- discussion questions to deepen understanding
- 'going further' sections for advanced study
- text boxes highlighting key definitions and arguments
- cross-references to help students make connections.

In addition, a chapter on exam preparation contains a wealth of helpful hints and tips on revision and exam techniques. Written by an experienced philosopher and A level consultant, *Philosophy for A2: Unit 4* is an essential companion for all students of A2 level philosophy.

Michael Lacewing is Director of Research and Senior Lecturer in Philosophy at Heythrop College, University of London. He is founder of the company A Level Philosophy, and a consultant on philosophy at A level for the British Philosophical Association.

PHIL
A2: U

Philoso

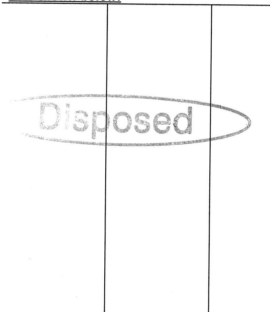

Michael L

Routledge
Taylor & Francis Group

LONDON AND NEW YORK

£15.19

First published 2010
by Routledge
2 Park Square, Milton Park, Abingdon, Oxon, OX14 4RN

Simultaneously published in the USA and Canada
by Routledge
270 Madison Ave, New York, NY 10016

Routledge is an imprint of the Taylor & Francis Group, an informa business

© 2010 Michael Lacewing

Typeset in Mixage by
Keystroke, Tettenhall, Wolverhampton
Printed and bound in Great Britain by
the MPG Books Group

British Library Cataloguing in Publication Data
A catalogue record for this book is available from the British Library

ISBN 13: 978–0–415–45823–8

CONTENTS

INTRODUCTION

Deepening philosophical ability

The AQA AS Philosophy syllabus aimed to introduce students to a number of philosophical issues. The aim at A2 is to build upon the knowledge and skills learned at AS, and to develop both a deeper critical understanding of philosophical theories and an ability to engage in discussions that are conceptually sophisticated.

Philosophical depth does not come easily. *Philosophy needs to be read slowly and, usually, more than once*. Each paragraph is intended to be taken as a thought to be considered, re-read, reflected on. You will probably find, in addition, that your understanding of any one part of a philosopher's views grow as you come to understand the other parts. And so, at the end of each chapter, you may feel that you need to return to earlier discussions, to think about them again in light of what you learned later.

How to use this book

Following the syllabus

Each of the five texts specified in Unit 4 is discussed in a separate chapter. Each chapter opens with a brief synopsis of what the chapter covers and what you should be able to do by the end of it, followed by the AQA syllabus for that issue. The discussion follows the AQA syllabus very closely. Many headings and sub-headings from the syllabus are used to structure the discussion, and each section is further divided by the main ideas, arguments and objections.

It is worth noting that, for each text, the syllabus identifies three issues from the text to concentrate on, for example, for Hume's *Enquiry*, they are 'empiricism', 'cause and effect' and 'free will'. Although the syllabus for each text is not itself divided according to the three issues, in this book each of the headings and sub-headings is arranged under one of these three issues.

Glossary

Philosophical terms are explained when they are first introduced, and there is a glossary providing definitions of the most important ones, so that wherever you start to read from, you can always look up the words you don't understand (words that appear in the glossary are in **bold**).

Features

Alongside the text, there are a number of features in the margin. There are definitions of key terms; further thoughts; references for quotations or to philosophical texts where the argument can be followed up; and questions that test your understanding and your abilities to analyse and evaluate the arguments. These are the kinds of questions you'll find on the exam. To get the most out of the book, stop and answer the questions – in your own words – as you go along.

Understanding is also about being able to make connections. So there are lots of CROSS-REFERENCES, not only to other discussions in this book, but also to topics in AS Units 1 and 2 and A2 Unit 3, so that you can follow up the links and see how arguments and issues connect up. Units 1 and 2 are discussed in the textbook *Philosophy for AS* (indicated by the icon), and Unit 3 is discussed in the textbook *Philosophy for A2: Key Themes in Philosophy* (indicated by the icon).

'Going further' sections provide discussions of more difficult ideas or take the arguments further. So they will broaden your knowledge, and help you 'go further' in your evaluation of the theories and arguments.

At the end of each discussion, there is a list of 'Key points', putting clearly the main issues the section has covered.

The final chapter provides advice on how to revise for the exam, and how to perform well on the day.

Companion website and further resources

You can find further resources, including book lists, helpful weblinks, PowerPoint presentations and material on the philosophical skills you need to argue well, on the companion website www.routledge.com/textbooks/philosophy.

The examination

Assessment objectives

The examiners mark your answers according to three principles, known as 'Assessment Objectives' (AOs). They are:

AO1: *Knowledge and understanding*: how well do you know and understand the central debates for a particular issue, the positions philosophers have defended and the arguments they use to defend them?

AO2: *Interpretation and analysis*: how well do you interpret and analyse relevant philosophical positions and arguments? Are you able select and apply relevant ideas, concepts, examples and arguments to support your account of an issue? Do you understand how the argument works and what the implications of a position are?

AO3: *Assessment and evaluation*: how well do you assess and evaluate arguments and counter-arguments? Are you able to construct arguments in support of a particular position, and defend it against objections? Do you understand whether an argument succeeds or fails and why? How well do you compare arguments and counter-arguments to weigh up what the most plausible position is?

In addition, you will be marked on your writing. Do you write clearly and grammatically, so that the examiner can understand what you mean? Does the way you write reflect a proper philosophical engagement with the issue? Are your points made coherently?

The structure of the exam

The exam for Unit 4 is 90 minutes long. It is divided into five sections, one for each text. You must choose **one** section to answer questions from. Within each section, there are three questions. You must answer the one compulsory question, and then one of the two other questions.

The compulsory question, worth 15 marks, tests AO1 (8 marks) and AO2 (7 marks) only. Here are two examples, from the specimen paper:

Text: Hume's *Enquiry*

Outline and illustrate the **two** kinds of knowledge distinguished by Hume.

Text: Mill's *On Liberty*

Explain why Mill thought there were dangers inherent in a democracy.

The essay questions, worth 45 marks, test all three AOs, with particular emphasis on AO3 (AO1: 10 marks; AO2: 11 marks; AO3: 24 marks). The two essay questions always come from two of the three issues identified for each text. Here are the specimen questions for Plato's *Republic*, in which the first question comes from 'Appearance and reality' and the second from 'Political rule'.

EITHER

5 Explore Plato's thesis that knowledge is of the Forms.

OR

6 Assess whether Plato was right to distrust democracy.

Acknowledgements

In preparing this book, I have drawn on two excellent reference works: the *Stanford Encyclopedia of Philosophy* (http://plato.stanford.edu/contents.html) and the *Routledge Encyclopedia of Philosophy* (http://www.rep.routledge.com). Thanks to Routledge for providing me with free access during this time.

Thanks also to Katy Hamilton, Gemma Dunn, Priyanka Pathak and Tony Bruce at (or formerly at) Routledge for encouraging this project, and to my colleagues at Heythrop College, for supporting my work with A level philosophy. A final and deep thank-you to Lizzy Lewis, without whom A Level Philosophy (the company) would not survive.

1

HUME *AN ENQUIRY CONCERNING HUMAN UNDERSTANDING*

Sections II–VIII and X

In this chapter, we examine Hume's text in the light of three key issues: his empiricism, including its application to the question of miracles, his views on causation and his theory of free will. Students should be able to explain Hume's views clearly and accurately and critically evaluate his arguments and objections to them. They should also be able to make connections between his theories and other views on the same topics discussed elsewhere in the syllabus.

All quotations and page references come from the AQA recommended edition from Oxford University Press (ISBN 0-19-875248-6).

SYLLABUS CHECKLIST ✔

The AQA A2 syllabus for this chapter is as follows.
Candidates should demonstrate an understanding of the following:

✔ the relation between impressions and ideas; what Hume means by these terms
✔ the principles of association and what they are intended to explain

✔ the distinction between relations of ideas and matters of fact (Hume's 'fork') – the scope of each

✔ the nature of belief and imagination and the difference between them

✔ the analysis of causation in terms of constant conjunction – the role of custom and repetition

✔ Hume's definitions of 'cause'

✔ the idea of necessary connection and the search for its origin – Hume's solution to the problem

✔ the attempt to reconcile free will and determinism; the diagnosis of the nature of the problem, Hume's account of what is meant by 'liberty' and 'necessity'

✔ past experience, rationality and probability in relation to belief in miracles.

Essay questions will focus on the following problem areas:

✔ empiricism

✔ cause and effect

✔ free will.

I. EMPIRICISM

Hume's empiricism

In *An Enquiry Concerning Human Understanding*, Hume is interested in what we can know and how. Philosophy as '**metaphysics**', he claims, has little of substance to it, but a wholesale rejection of philosophical investigation of human knowledge is rash and dogmatic. Instead, we must first understand the workings of the mind, an investigation of which will show that our minds are not 'fitted for such remote and abstruse [metaphysical] subjects' (p. 92). Hume's aim, then, is to come to understand the workings of the mind. A secondary aim is, using this knowledge, to demonstrate that **empiricism** is the only defensible philosophical position.

See METAPHYSICS AS SPECULATIVE NONSENSE p. 185.

See p. 10.

Review the distinction between rationalism and empiricism.

Essay on Human Understanding, II.viii.8

There's been a lot of debate about exactly what the terms '**rationalism**' and 'empiricism' mean. In Unit 1.1 REASON AND EXPERIENCE, we argued that the distinction essentially comes to this: Rationalists argue that it is possible for us to know something about how the world outside our own minds is without relying on sense experience. Empiricists argue that this is not possible, that all our knowledge of the outside world comes through our senses. That is to say, rationalists argue that there can be **synthetic a priori** knowledge; empiricists deny this.

Hume's empiricism shows itself in another way as well. He also argues that all our ideas are derived from sense experience, one way or another. It is this claim with which we start.

The relation between impressions and ideas (§ II)

Hume's theory of the mind owes a great debt to John Locke's ideas. Hume names the basic contents of the mind, and what we are immediately and directly aware of, 'perceptions', what Locke described as 'whatsoever the mind perceives in itself, or is the immediate object of perception, thought or understanding'. 'Perceptions' are divided by Hume into 'impressions' and 'ideas', the difference between the two being marked by a difference of 'forcefulness' and 'vivacity', so that impressions relate roughly to 'feeling' (or 'sensing') and ideas to 'thinking'. 'Feeling' here should be understood broadly, and Hume, again following Locke, divides impressions into those of 'sensation' and those of 'reflection'. Impressions of sensation derive from our senses, impressions of reflection derive from our experience of our mind, for example, feeling emotions.

Ideas are 'faint copies' of impressions, 'less forcible and lively' (p. 96). Think what it is like to see a scene or hear a tune; now what it is like to imagine or remember that scene or tune. The latter is weaker, fainter. (Thinking, for Hume, works with ideas as images in the same way as imagination and memory.) However, Hume immediately qualifies his claim about liveliness – disease or madness can make ideas as lively as impressions. This suggests that the distinction in terms of liveliness is incomplete. So Hume's claim that ideas are also *copies* of impressions is important. So just as there are ideas of sensation (e.g. the idea of a colour), there are also ideas of reflection (e.g. the idea of an emotion).

Hume later provides a third distinction between ideas and impressions: we are liable to confuse and make mistakes about ideas, but this is more difficult with impressions (p. 99).

The basic building blocks of all thought and experience are simple impressions – single colours, single shapes, single smells and so on. And to each there is a corresponding idea. We can also have more complex impressions, such as the colour and shape of something, for example, a dog. The corresponding idea we have of the dog can be made more complex by adding the idea of its smell or the sound it makes. To think of it as a 'dog' is still more complex, because it requires abstraction. The concept DOG doesn't correspond to any *one particular* set of impressions or any single dog. When we abstract, we ignore certain specific features and concentrate on others; so to develop the concept DOG, we ignore the different colours and different sizes dogs are, picking out other features, like four legs, tail, bark, hairy.

> When referring to the idea, rather than what the idea stands for, I capitalise the word.

> Outline and illustrate Hume's theory of the origin of ideas.

On complex ideas

The view that all ideas derive from sense experience is very appealing in many ways. However, there are complex ideas that seem to correspond to nothing in our sense experience, for example, UNICORN and GOD. (While many of us have seen a picture of a unicorn, *someone* had to invent the idea without seeing a picture.) So is it true that *all* ideas derive from sense experience?

Hume does not claim that *complex* ideas must be copies of impressions. It is only simple ideas that are copies of impressions. But all complex ideas are composed of simple ideas. This is easy to see in the case of unicorns: we have experiences of horses and of horns and of whiteness; if we put them together, we get UNICORN.

Hume argues that in creating new complex ideas, we can only work with the materials that impressions provide. *No* idea, no matter how abstract or complex, is more than a combination, alteration or abstraction from impressions.

Hume believes this is an **empirical** discovery, rather than a **necessary** truth, and presents two **arguments** for thinking it is true. First, all ideas can be analysed into simple ideas which each correspond to an impression. For example, in direct opposition to Descartes (see Objections, p. 192), Hume claims that the idea of God, based on ideas of perfection and infinity, is extrapolated from ideas of imperfection and finitude: 'The idea of God, as meaning *an infinitely intelligent, wise, and good Being*, arises from reflecting on the operations of our own mind, and augmenting, without limit, those qualities of goodness and wisdom' (pp. 97–8). We will challenge Hume's claim in Complex ideas again (p. 11).

> Explain and illustrate Hume's account of complex concepts.

> The origins of 'God' are discussed on pp. 132 and 149.

Outline Hume's arguments for the claim that all ideas derive from impressions.

Hume's second argument is that without having a particular type of experience, a person lacks the ability to form an idea of that experience. Thus, a blind man does not know what colour is and a mild man cannot comprehend the motive of revenge.

The missing shade of blue

Hume notes that there is an exception to his principle that all simple ideas are copies of impressions. If someone has seen all shades of blue except one, and you present them with a spectrum of blue with this one shade missing, using their imagination, they will be able to form an idea of that shade. This idea has not been copied from an impression.

Hume dismisses the example as unimportant, but it is not. If it is possible that we can form an idea of a shade of blue without deriving it from an impression, is it possible that we could form other ideas without preceding impressions? The reason the question is important is because Hume uses his 'Copy Principle' repeatedly in his philosophy, to reject ideas such as SUBSTANCE, the SELF and, in his discussion of causation, causal NECESSITY:

SELF and SUBSTANCE are discussed in COMPLEX IDEAS AGAIN, p. 11; NECESSITY is discussed in THE IDEA OF A NECESSARY CONNECTION, p. 42.

> All ideas, especially abstract ones, are naturally faint and obscure: the mind has but a slender hold of them: they are apt to be confounded with other resembling ideas; and when we have often employed any term, though without a distinct meaning, we are apt to imagine it has a determinate idea annexed to it. On the contrary, all impressions . . . are strong and vivid: the limits between them are more exactly determined: nor is it easy to fall into any error or mistake with regard to them. When we entertain, therefore, any suspicion that a philosophical term is employed without any meaning or idea (as is but too frequent), we need but enquire, *from what impression is that supposed idea derived*? (p. 99)

It is because impressions are more *reliable* in this way that Hume makes impressions the test for ideas.

But if we don't need an impression for the missing shade of blue, perhaps we don't need impressions for our ideas of substance, self or necessity either. Unless we can secure some version of the Copy Principle against the example of the missing shade of blue, Hume's mode of argument here is unfounded.

Explain the importance of 'the missing shade of blue' for Hume's philosophy.

Going further: amending the Copy Principle

There are two possible solutions that allow the exception in the case of the shade of blue, while maintaining the strong dependency Hume wants of ideas on impressions. The first solution weakens the Copy Principle: in the quote above, Hume argues that words get their meaning from ideas, and ideas get their meaning from impressions. The Copy Principle then becomes something like this: 'an idea only has meaning if it is derived from impressions of things that *have been* encountered in experience'. But the missing shade of blue shows that this is too strong. A weaker version claims that 'an idea only has meaning if it is derived from impressions of things that can be encountered in experience'. The missing shade of blue clearly meets this condition, whereas Hume argues that we have no impressions of self, substance or necessity (as we usually think of these).

The second solution keeps the Copy Principle, but explains how and why the missing shade of blue is an 'exception'. In such a case, the simple impressions of different shades of blue are not unrelated to each other, as they can be arranged in a sequence of resemblance. They are all determinate qualities (shades) of the same determinable quality (blue), and we have impressions of other determinates of this quality. From the arrangement, we can form the idea of the missing determinate, *drawing on other similar impressions we already have*. But this only works with this structure of relations between ideas. And substance, self and causal necessity are clearly not like this; they are not determinate qualities of some determinable. And so, as we have no relevantly similar impressions, we cannot form the idea meaningfully. This is the same reason that a blind man cannot form an idea of colour, and so it forms an integral part of Hume's theory.

> Can Hume successfully respond to the challenge raised to the Copy Principle by the missing shade of blue?

Complex ideas again

Hume argues that all complex ideas are constructed out of simple ideas, which are copies of impressions. We can therefore challenge him to give us his analysis of complex ideas, such as NECESSITY, SUBSTANCE or SELF. If he cannot give us a satisfactory analysis of how we derive these concepts from experience, that is a reason to think that the concepts derive from elsewhere – either they are

On these alternatives to the traditional empiricist theory of the origin of ideas, see pp. 12 and 29.

A Treatise of Human Nature, I.iv.vi

Personal identity is discussed in Unit 1.5 Persons. See especially PHYSICAL AND PSYCHOLOGICAL CONTINUITY II (p. 187) for discussion relevant to Hume's theory.

Explain Hume's analysis of the concept SELF. Is it possible that there are no 'selves', just thoughts and feelings?

innate, or they are reached using a priori reasoning. If this is right, then Hume's theory of the mind is very seriously wrong.

In fact, Hume argues that these three particular examples cannot be derived from experience. His response, for each of these examples, is that the idea – as we usually think of it – has no genuine application. In their place, he suggests clearer ways of thinking, using ideas that can be derived from experience.

Going further: self

According to our common-sense idea of the self, the 'I' is something that exists over time, persisting from one thought to another.

Hume argues that we never have any experience of such a self:

> when I enter most intimately into what I call myself, I always stumble on some particular perception or other, of heat or cold, light or shade, love or hatred, pain or pleasure. I never can catch myself at any time without a perception, and never can observe any thing but the perception.

The idea of the 'self' as a thing distinct from thoughts and perceptions doesn't survive the attempt to find the 'corresponding impression' that is the test of meaning. Hume suggests that the self is nothing more than a 'bundle' of thoughts and perceptions, constantly and rapidly changing. This is all that we have experience of. To come up with the idea of SELF as one and the same thing over time, we've confused *similarity* – the similarity of our thoughts and feelings from one moment to the next – with *identity* – the identity of a 'thing' to which such mental states belong.

We can object that there can't be a thought unless something thinks it. So the 'I' must exist in order to think thoughts. Hume can ask how we know this. As he has just argued, our experience doesn't confirm it. So is it part of the *definition* of thought that thinkers exist to think thoughts? This is hard to show.

We will look at objections to Hume's analysis of SELF in THE PRINCIPLES OF ASSOCIATION (p. 15).

SUBSTANCE

Hume makes a similar argument regarding (physical) substance. PHYSICAL SUBSTANCE is the idea of a physical object as something that exists independently of our experience, in its own right, and in three-dimensional space. Hume asks how we could have had an impression of such a thing. How can experience show us that something exists independently of experience? I see my desk; a few moments later, I see it again. If my two experiences are of one and the same desk, then the desk existed when I wasn't looking at it. But I can't know that my two experiences are of *one and the same* desk; I can only know that the two experiences are *very similar*. In coming up with the idea of physical substance that exists independently of my experiences, I have confused similarity with identity.

A Treatise of Human Nature, I.iv.ii

Discuss the concept PHYSICAL SUBSTANCE. Can we derive it from experience?

OBJECTIONS

We can object that Hume's theory makes most of our common-sense idea of the world wrong. This is unacceptable. Our ideas are coherent. The fact that we cannot derive them from experience only shows that they are innate (or known through rational intuition). We should really take Hume's arguments to show not that the ideas are wrong-headed, but that they have their origins elsewhere.

Second, is Hume's view that *all* ideas are derived from experience, or only that *all meaningful, coherent* ideas are derived from experience? He explicitly asserts the first claim, but then how can he account for 'incoherent' ideas? For instance, if we cannot have got the idea of something existing independently of experience from experience, where did the idea come from? – Because we most certainly have it!

Hume's answer regarding SELF and SUBSTANCE is that we have confused similarity with identity. How does this happen? Our perceptions of physical objects exhibit constancy: if I look at my desk and then shut my eyes and open them again, the desk looks exactly how it did before. On the basis of this similarity, the mind simply has a tendency, says Hume, to *imagine* that what I see after I open my eyes is not just similar but identical to what I saw before I close my eyes. The origin of the idea of identity – and with it, the idea of something that exists between and independent of perceptions – is the imagination. The ideas that the imagination works with in creating the idea of identity are similarity and unity (the idea of an individual thing, being 'one'), both of which we can derive from experience. We can distinguish between perceptions as different – so each has identity; and we can tell when two perceptions are similar. (A similar story applies in the case of the self.)

Assess Hume's theory that all ideas derive from impressions.

A final objection is that there is good reason to think that Hume's attempts at analysis will not work for all complex ideas, even if they do work for SELF and SUBSTANCE. For example, attempts to analyse philosophical concepts such as KNOWLEDGE, TRUTH, BEAUTY into their simple constituents have all failed to produce agreement. Perhaps this is because they don't have this structure.

Key points • • •

- Hume's aim in the *Enquiry* is to understand how the mind works, and to show that only empiricism is philosophically defensible.
- He calls the contents of the mind 'perceptions'. These are divided into 'impressions' and 'ideas', the former being more forceful and vivacious than the latter. Ideas are what we think with. Impressions are derived from sensation (sense experience) or reflection (experience of our minds).
- Hume argues that all ideas derive from impressions. Simple ideas are copies, while complex ideas are formed by various processes from simple ideas. He gives two arguments in support: that all complex ideas can be analysed into simple ideas; and that without the right experience (e.g. visual), someone can't form the corresponding idea (e.g. colour).
- Hume uses the claim that ideas are copied from impressions to reject traditional interpretations of the ideas of SELF, SUBSTANCE and causal NECESSITY. However, he accepts that in some cases – a shade of blue – an idea does not need to derive from an impression.
- We can make Hume consistent either by saying that an idea does not need to be copied from an impression, but that there is a possible impression it could be copied from; or by explaining why the shade of blue is a very specific exception that cannot be generalised.
- Hume argues that we do not have impressions of the self or physical substance. Instead, SELF and (physical) SUBSTANCE derive from a confusion between similarity and identity; we experience similarity, but we imagine identity.
- We can object that his analysis is implausible, and the ideas therefore have a source other than experience. Or we can object that, even if his analyses work in these cases, there are others, such as KNOWLEDGE or BEAUTY which cannot be analysed – and so his theory of complex ideas is false.

The principles of association and what they explain (§ III)

We have discussed Hume's theory of the contents of the mind (perceptions). Now, how does the mind work? Hume claims that there are three types of regularity that hold between perceptions. While impressions (merely) exhibit these regularities, it is *on the basis* of these regularities that our ideas pass through our minds in the sequences that they do.

The three regularities are:

a) *resemblance*, for example, moving from an impression of a picture, for example, of a dog, to the thought of the pictured object, the dog;

b) *contiguity* in time and space, for example, moving from the thought of an event, the Moon landing, to something else that happened at the same time, the presidency of John F. Kennedy;

c) *cause* and effect, for example, moving from the thought of a wound to thinking of pain.

It may seem implausible that just these three relations govern all transitions of thought. Hume discusses this at greater length in the *Treatise of Human Nature*, where he emphasises that we must explore the 'full extent' of the relations to see that they hold. Two apparently unconnected ideas will always, he claims, be linked by a third idea which is connected by a principle to both. He also develops the principle of cause and effect: for the ideas of A and B to be linked by this principle, it needn't be that A is the cause of B or vice-versa. Rather, they simply need to be connected by causation, for example, I might think of a cousin and then of another relation. The two are causally linked, by genetic ties, without one being a cause or effect of the other. Again, the object of the first idea need not be a cause of the object of the second, but may only cause some action or movement in it; or need only have the *power* to do so. So we might move from the idea of a judge to that of a criminal.

Hume presents his theory as an empirical discovery. Are there any other regularities? We must look and see, but he claims he cannot find any and that a consideration of literature and historical narrative support him. If we look at how these works are organised, we see that the events narrated form a kind of unity, and to create this unity, authors use the three types of connection listed.

We might, however, suggest an amendment to Hume's view. Hume intended these relations to hold between ideas in virtue of what they are about. But Sigmund Freud suggested that ideas could be connected through their

> Explain and illustrate Hume's three principles of association.

emotional significance. Hence one idea, which is accompanied by a certain emotion, might be followed by another, accompanied by the same emotion; and this is all the two ideas have in common.

We can also make a more radical objection: Hume has not included *logical* relations among his principles. But surely trains of thought can and do follow logical inferences. Of course, this will involve resemblance, but we can argue that resemblance doesn't capture the real relation between the thoughts.

The three principles are, according to Hume, natural functions of the mind. We do not *intend* to connect ideas in this way; this is just how the mind works. They are the foundation of thought. Without them, our ideas would remain isolated, unconnected, and we could not think about experience and reality at all. As we will see, Hume ascribes a particularly important role to the principle of cause and effect.

Finally, though he mentions it only briefly in § III, the regularities also account for complex ideas and for the overlaps between concepts in different languages: 'Among the different languages . . . it is found, that the words, expressive of ideas, the most compounded, do yet nearly correspond to each other: a certain proof that the simple ideas, comprehended in the compound ones, were bound together by some universal principle' (p. 23).

> In fact, Hume says the principles are all functions of 'imagination'. See THE NATURE OF BELIEF AND IMAGINATION, p. 18, where we also note the difficulties raised by the absence of logical relations.

> Explain the relation between complex ideas and the principles of association.

Going further: the principles of association and the self

We saw earlier (p. 12) that Hume argues that the self is nothing more than a 'bundle' of thoughts and experiences. So what is it that ties a particular set of experiences into the particular bundle that constitutes a self?

Hume appeals to the principles of association: the many thoughts and perceptions are related to each other by *resemblance*, for example, a memory resembles the original perception of which it is a memory, and *causation* – impressions cause corresponding ideas, experiences cause memories, beliefs cause other beliefs and so on. This provides a further explanation of how we have confused similarity for identity in forming the idea of SELF. It is because of these many links of causation and resemblance that we think of the self as an 'identity'. The imagination replaces our experience of them with a fictitious idea of something continuous and uninterrupted.

Hume's theory suggests a strange result: intuitively, we think that I might have had a quite different set of experiences from the set I have had. But if I am just a set of experiences, this isn't true! Hume could respond that this is a matter of degree. Because the self has many experiences, if just some of these were different, that would not be enough to make for a different self. So I can still be the same person, even if *some* of my experiences were different. But I wouldn't be the same person if a *great deal* of my thoughts and experiences, beliefs, desires, emotions and so on were different.

But this then leads to an even stranger result: many of your thoughts and experiences are related both casually and by resemblance to *mine*. For example, I say what I think, you then think what I was thinking. Are you now partly me? It doesn't seem quite right just to say that the only difference between two selves is the sheer *number* of these relations between mental states. Instead, we might want to say that *some* relations of cause and resemblance are constitutive of personal identity and not others. But Hume can't say this. We can't say that the relevant types of relations of causation and resemblance link together the mental states of the same person but not the mental states of different people, because this presupposes the idea of the 'same person'. But that is just the idea that we are trying to analyse - so where did that idea come from?

1. Assess Hume's account of the self.
2. What does Hume use the principles of association to explain?

Key points • • •

- Hume argues that three principles of association govern the working of the mind: resemblance, contiguity and cause and effect. Any sequence of ideas is regulated by these principles.
- Hume claims that these are the only principles of association, but we can challenge the absence of logical relations.
- The principles are the natural foundations of the workings of the mind, which Hume ascribes to the 'imagination'. Without them, our ideas would remain unconnected and we would be unable to think.
- They also explain how we form complex ideas and why different languages have words similar in meaning.

- The principles also explain how we can form complex ideas, such as SELF, which are not properly meaningful. We confuse the sequence of impressions and ideas related by resemblance and causation for the idea of an identity.
- Hume's theory of the self faces some strong objections. One is how we can distinguish between the ideas of one person and another – is the only difference between whether a thought is mine or yours the number of relations it has to other mental states?

The nature of belief and imagination (§§ III, IV and V.2)

Imagination

Hume has an 'imagistic' theory of thought – he thinks that thought uses images, derived from impressions. He therefore thinks of the imagination as working with images – but this covers all thought.

What makes the imagination important for Hume is that it *connects* up ideas, according to the principles of association: 'When the mind . . . passes from the idea or impression of one object to the idea or belief of another it is not determined by reason, but by certain principles which associate together the ideas of these objects and unite them in the imagination'.

Treatise, I.iii.vi

All three principles involve a movement to an idea, for which the impression is not usually present to the senses. When your mind moves from looking at a picture to thinking of the person in the picture (resemblance), that person isn't (usually) present, so you have an idea in mind of something not present to the senses. Again, when you move around a house, and your mind anticipates what is around the corner (contiguity) – this isn't yet something you can see. And when you experience some event and infer its cause, the cause itself is not something you are experiencing.

Why does Hume say the principles of association are principles of the imagination?

And so the imagination plays a crucial role in Hume's philosophy. The function of the imagination is not just 'imaginative' – creating scenarios and ideas which are not real. The imagination is the foundation of everything that is believed to be real as well.

So how do we distinguish between what we 'imagine' and what we think is real? We'll look at this next.

Belief

After a long discussion of our knowledge of matters of fact (see p. 25), Hume continues to develop his theory of mind in Chapter V, Part 2, where he raises and answers the question of how we distinguish between 'fiction' and belief. His claim is that a belief is an idea that is particularly forceful and vivid: 'belief is nothing but a more vivid, lively, forcible, firm, steady conception of an object, than what the imagination alone is ever able to attain' (p. 125). The same quality that distinguished impressions from ideas also distinguishes beliefs from ideas of memory and imagination.

We can imagine whatever we want; but we cannot believe whatever we want. Forming a belief is not under our control. Hume's account of belief in terms of vivacity explains this. Suppose I have an impression of the senses. My mind is immediately led to form the correlative idea, the 'copy'. Because of the close and immediate connection to a current impression, the idea gains much of the vivacity of the impression, and so I have a particularly forceful and lively idea – a belief. But when I imagine seeing something, my idea does not rely on an impression, so it cannot have the same vivacity.

The general principle here is that vivacity is transmitted from one perception to another by the principles of association. A copy of an impression both resembles the impression and is caused by it. When I look at a photo, I form an idea of the photo and then an idea of the person in the photo. I believe the person whose photo it is exists as a cause of the photo. The vivacity of the impression of the photo is transmitted to the idea of the person, so I believe the person exists. Or again, if I see a billiard ball strike another, I can imagine that the first ball will simply stop dead upon contact. But this doesn't have the same vivacity as my belief that the second ball will move away. This is because my belief is the effect of past impressions, while the imagined alternative is not.

What does Hume mean by 'belief'?

THE ROLE OF CAUSE-EFFECT

Where the relation of regularity between one perception and the next is cause–effect, vivacity can be transmitted so as to form beliefs (and this distinguishes belief from imagination). This is not so with resemblance and contiguity, because they link a perception to many different perceptions, which means that the 'vivacity' is dissipated, each connected perception only getting a small share of the original vivacity. But cause–effect connects a perception to just one other (the idea of the cause or effect of what is being thought about or experienced), and so that one perception receives all the vivacity of the first.

Treatise, I.iii.viii

Is this right? Do we never form beliefs on the basis of just resemblance and contiguity? Again, my thoughts turn from the photo to the person (resemblance) and form a belief; when I am near home, I think of it (contiguity), and form a belief.

But note that from the photo, I don't form the belief that the person is *present*, as the photo is present; from being close to home, I don't form the belief that home is *here*, because it is near to here. Rather I believe that the person and home *exist*, that they are *real*, not fictitious, as objects standing in relations of resemblance and contiguity to my thoughts.

But these beliefs about what is real are not formed by resemblance or contiguity alone. They depend on cause–effect. Our thoughts would not move from the photo to the person or from being near to home to home itself, Hume argues, unless we *already* have the beliefs that the person and home exist. And these beliefs were formed by cause–effect – the ideas of the friend and home being caused by the relevant impressions, or by ideas that are related as cause or effect to ideas caused by impressions.

To summarise: a belief is an idea that has a greater vivacity than the imagination can achieve. The source of this vivacity depends on two things: at some point, being derived from *impressions*, and not just by any principle of association, but by *cause–effect*. A belief may itself be caused by impressions, or it may be the idea of a cause or effect of what we have experienced. Resemblance and contiguity can add to the vivacity of a belief, but cannot create a belief out of an idea on their own. Whether or not his account of vivacity is right, this relation of belief to impressions and the role of cause–effect deserves serious consideration and illustrates Hume's empiricism.

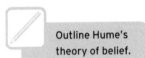

Outline Hume's theory of belief.

Going further: vivacity, belief and reason

Hume's theory of 'vivacity' is highly problematic, and is no longer taken seriously. He is trying to place on the single scale of vivacity all the differences between impressions, memories, ideas and beliefs. At one end, impressions, then beliefs, memories, imagination and other ideas.

1.   Is this scale even correct? Don't some daydreams have more vivacity than memories or abstract beliefs?

2. Do beliefs and memories have similar amounts of vivacity? But how do we draw these boundaries? Hume can't say.
3. Is it right to say that a memory could be turned into a belief or even an impression by a further increase in vivacity? Surely not. Memories and impressions are *logically different* kinds of mental state from belief. For example, a belief about the future can't become a memory of the future with an increase in vivacity! Nor can a belief become an impression, because an impression is given immediately by a particular sensory modality.
4. The idea of vivacity is linked to energy and force. Yet we have no clear conception of a distinct 'mental energy'. Is vivacity linked to neuro-physiological energy? We have no evidence to suggest so. We must reject the theory as, at best, metaphorical.

Hume's claim that beliefs, unlike fictions of the imagination, relate to impressions and cause–effect, also faces an objection. We normally take our beliefs to be a cognitive response to evidence. If the evidence gives us *good reasons* for a particular belief, we form that belief. Hume rejects this, as we saw in the quote above: 'When the mind . . . passes from the idea or impression of one object to the idea or belief of another it is not determined by reason', but by the principles of association. His theory has the consequence that we do not form beliefs on the basis of the reasons that justify them. Coming to have a belief is not a rational process.

Part of Hume's argument is that the formation of belief cannot be controlled by the will. This seems right; we cannot believe at will. (And this is a far better way of distinguishing belief from fiction!) But it doesn't follow, as Hume thinks, that beliefs are merely caused by non-rational factors (vivacity). What is missing is the idea of *judgement*, weighing up whether the evidence provides sufficient reason to believe. This process is not directly under the control of the will (although it has some element of agency – judging is something we *do*) and it is rationally directed.

A further objection is discussed in PROBABILITY AND BELIEF, p. 32.

Treatise, I.iii.vi

See CAN BELIEFS BE VOLUNTARY?, p. 164.

Discuss Hume's account of the nature of belief.

Imagination again

Having drawn the contrast with belief, we can say that there are two senses of 'imagination' in Hume. In the 'narrow' sense, imagination contrasts with belief. In the 'broad' sense, imagination includes and supports belief, because the principles of association, including cause–effect, that lead to the creation of belief are principles of the imagination. With this picture of the mind, Hume draws some startling conclusions about the basis of our knowledge, that is, that very little is secured by reason and almost all is secured by the imagination. It is difficult to appreciate the importance of the imagination, and how it functions, until we have seen its role in his theory of knowledge. That is our next topic.

> Discuss the nature and role of the imagination in Hume's philosophy.

Key points • • •

- The imagination, working from ideas derived from impressions, creates ideas of things not present to the senses.
- The three principles of association – resemblance, contiguity and cause–effect – are principles of the imagination. As a result, the imagination underpins our belief in what is real.
- Hume argues that belief is a particularly vivid idea, more vivid than can be achieved by 'imagining'. The vivacity of a belief is derived from impressions through the principle of cause–effect.
- Resemblance and contiguity can add to a belief's vividness, but cannot transmit enough vivacity to an idea to turn it into a belief without cause–effect.
- Hume's theory of vivacity faces severe objections. In particular, the differences between impressions, memories, beliefs and ideas are logical, rather than a matter of some quantity of mental energy.
- Hume argues that beliefs are caused by non-rational processes (the transmission of vivacity). We can object to the implication that evidence plays no rational role in the formation of belief.

The distinction between relations of ideas and matters of fact (Hume's 'fork'); the scope of relations of ideas (§ IV)

Empiricism denies that we can know anything about how the world outside our own minds is without relying on sense experience. In § IV, Hume argues that we can have knowledge of just two sorts of thing: the relations between ideas and matters of fact. He uses two related criteria to make the distinction.

First, he says that relations of ideas are known as 'intuitively and demonstratively certain' because '**Propositions** of this kind are discoverable by the mere operation of thought, without dependence on what is anywhere existent in the universe' (p. 108). A mathematical example: 'If A is longer than B, and B is longer than C, then A is longer than C.'

Second, he says that the negation of a (true) relation of ideas is a contradiction; the negation of a matter of fact is not. (A contradiction asserts both a proposition and its negation.) To say that vixens are not foxes is a contradiction in terms; it is to say that female foxes are not foxes. And so we can know for certain that vixens are foxes, because its truth depends on our thought (our concepts), not the world. By contrast, to say that foxes are pink is false, but not self-contradictory. It is through experience, not intuition or demonstration, that we discover the properties of foxes. As a first interpretation of Hume's criteria, we might say that we gain knowledge of relations of ideas through merely understanding concepts and through **deductive** inference.

> Explain and illustrate what Hume means by 'relations of ideas'.

Going further: relations of ideas in the **Treatise**

In the *Treatise* I.iii.i, Hume cites 'resemblance, contrariety, degrees in quality, and proportions in quantity or number' as relations between things that depend on the ideas alone. Of these, he says, the first three are 'discoverable at first sight', and it is only the last - mathematics - where we use demonstration. So the only form of reasoning that has complete certainty is reasoning about numbers.

In the *Enquiry*, Hume cites only mathematics as an example of relations of ideas. However, he retains the claim that relations of ideas can be *intuitively* certain, not just demonstratively. But he provides no explanation of what intuition is, or any examples of its use. The *Treatise* provides examples, but they are confusing. While Hume asserts that resemblance, contrariety, and degrees in quality are relations of *ideas*, he illustrates the relations by examples that come from *impressions*:

See Is CERTAINTY CONFINED TO INTROSPECTION AND THE TAUTOLOGICAL?, p. 37.

> When any objects resemble each other, the resemblance will at first strike the eye, or rather the mind . . . The case is the same with contrariety, and with the degrees of any quality. No one can once doubt but existence and non-existence destroy each other, and are perfectly incompatible and contrary. And tho' it be impossible to judge exactly of the degrees of any quality, such as colour, taste, heat, cold, when the difference betwixt them is very small: yet 'tis easy to decide, that any of them is superior or inferior to another, when their difference is considerable. And this decision we always pronounce at first sight, without any enquiry or reasoning.

But understanding that existence and non-existence are contrary is not at all the same thing as judging that one thing is hotter than another. Understanding that vixens are foxes is different from spotting a resemblance. What is immediately present to the senses is certain for quite different reasons from **analytic** judgements.

Development

If we leave Hume's distinction in terms of the two criteria he provides, then the history of philosophy is full of debate about what will count as a relation of ideas. Rationalists, such as Plato and Descartes, have argued that a great deal can be shown to be certain through (rational) intuition and demonstration, including the existence of the Forms and of God (Descartes even maintains that, although it is not obvious, to say 'God does not exist' is a contradiction). They have a much wider conception of the powers of reason to achieve certainty through intuition and demonstration than Hume.

Hume thinks these claims are false, and the 'mere operation of thought' cannot establish anything about what exists. But philosophers have also sought to make his distinction more precise. We can reinterpret it in terms of two distinctions: analytic/synthetic and a priori/**a posteriori**. Following the spirit of Hume's argument, rather than the letter of his position, we can say that Hume argued that all a priori knowledge (relations of ideas) is analytic, while all knowledge of synthetic propositions (matters of fact) is a posteriori. In other words, anything we know that is not true by definition or logic alone, every 'matter of fact', we must learn and test through our senses.

What is 'intuitive certainty'? Compare Hume's idea with Descartes' notion of CLEAR AND DISTINCT IDEAS (p. 157) and Plato's notion of 'nous' (see THE SIMILES OF THE CAVE AND THE DIVIDED LINE, p. 63, and EPISTEMOLOGICAL IMPLICATIONS OF THE THEORY OF THE FORMS, p. 66).

See KNOWLEDGE THROUGH A PRIORI INTUITION AND DEMONSTRATION, p. 31.

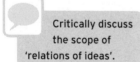

Critically discuss the scope of 'relations of ideas'.

Key points • • •

- Hume distinguishes between relations of ideas and matters of fact using two criteria: relations of ideas are 'intuitively and demonstratively certain', established by the mere operation of thought; and the negation of a relation of ideas is a contradiction.
- 'Demonstration' refers to deductive reasoning. It is unclear what Hume means by 'intuition', whether it is a form of understanding ideas or what we can tell immediately from impressions.
- Philosophers have developed Hume's distinction, using the analytic/synthetic and a priori/a posteriori distinctions. On this development, relations of ideas are analytic truths known a priori, and matters of fact are synthetic truths known a posteriori.

The scope of matters of fact (§§ IV, V.1 and VI)

Causal inference

We can say that, according to Hume, knowledge of matters of fact is always a posteriori and synthetic. We gain it by using observation and employing **induction** and reasoning about probability. The foundation of this knowledge is what we experience here and now, or can remember. Matters of fact beyond this are established by 'probable' arguments, not deductive proofs. Hume sets out 'to enquire what is the nature of that evidence which assures us of any real existence and matter of fact, beyond the present testimony of the senses, or the records of our memory' (p. 108). His answer is that such knowledge rests on *causal inference*.

If I receive a letter from a friend with a French postmark on it, I'll believe that my friend is in France – because I *infer* from the postmark to a place. I do this because I think where something is posted causes it to have the postmark of that place; and if the letter was posted by my friend, then I believe that he must be in France. In itself, this seems plausible enough. But it opens up a can of worms.

How do I know all the claims I assume when I infer that my friend is in France? I rely on past experience – in the past, I have experienced letters being posted, I have seen different postmarks, I have found that postmarks relate to

Outline and illustrate Hume's account of how we know matters of fact.

where you post something, and so on. I can't work out what causes what just by thinking about it. So causal inference rests on past experience.

But what, Hume then asks, is the basis of inferring from past experience to the present or future? We have experience that, in the past, whenever a cause of a particular type occurs, for example, one billiard ball strikes another, it was followed by an effect, the second ball moving; but why think that this succession will occur again?

The question is an important one. Much of what we think we know we haven't experienced. Either it lies in the past, but outside our experience (e.g. what happens in Australia when one billiard ball strikes another); or it lies in the future (what will happen when one billiard ball strikes another). Can we know about what we haven't experienced on the basis of what we have?

The objection to reason

There are two ideas connected with causation which we might think provided us with good grounds for thinking that causes *always* have the same effects; and so we can reason from the occurrence of the cause to the effect, whenever or wherever the cause occurs.

First, if a cause is *necessarily* connected to its effects, then if we perceive the cause occurring, we can logically infer the effect. But Hume points out, there is no *contradiction* in supposing that the second billiard ball won't move when struck.

Second, philosophers before Hume often thought that an effect must *resemble* its cause. For example, Descartes argues that only God could have caused the idea of God; Locke argues that only an intelligence could have caused intelligence. On this basis, knowing the cause, we could infer the effect. And again, we could reason that because the cause in this case is similar to causes in the past, the effect will be similar to effects in the past. This would justify knowledge of matters of fact outside our experience. But Hume rejects this. Anything *can* cause anything, and it is only through experience that we find out what causes what.

So far, Hume has argued that we cannot *deduce* effects from experiencing causes, or deduce causes from experiencing effects. We can back this up with a further argument. The relation between a cause and its effect is not a relation of ideas. The relation is not that of resemblance, nor is it a contradiction to think that, for example, a billiard ball will not move when struck. Nor can this claim be proven (by deductive argument) to be false. So, given an experience of a cause, we cannot deduce that the effect will follow. So we cannot deduce that the world outside our experience resembles (or will resemble) what we have experienced so far.

Why does Hume argue that we cannot deduce causes from effects or vice-versa?

The problem of induction

So how can we infer matters of fact we haven't experienced from ones we have? If it isn't through intuition or deduction, the inference must itself rest on matters of fact. The trouble is, establishing any matter of fact assumes just what we are trying to prove. Hume is calling the basis of induction into question.

Suppose I say that I know the billiard ball will move, because it has always moved in the past. It's true that in the past the billiard ball always moved. But why think it will move again now? On what basis do I think that the future resembles the past? Past experience can give me '*direct* and *certain* information of those precise objects only, and that precise period of time, which fall under its cognizance' (p. 114).

If I am to infer that the billiard ball will move when struck, I'm going to have to do so on the basis of the principle that 'the future will be like the past'. But this principle is in the same boat as my claim that the billiard ball will move when struck. It is not a contradiction to suppose that the future will *not* be like the past, so I can't prove the principle by deductive reasoning. But, of course, I can't prove it by appealing to matters of fact, since I am trying to establish a matter of fact by appealing to the principle! If I say, 'but in the past, the future was like the past', this still gives me no basis on which to infer that 'in the future, the future will be like the past'.

Explain Hume's challenge to inductive reasoning.

Hume argues that our belief that the future will resemble the past is not based on reason at all. He remarks that children are capable of learning from experience, and yet here we are, professional philosophers, struggling to produce the reasoning which we suppose the child easily employs (p. 118)! We can't produce the reasoning, because the inference is not based on reasoning at all. Hume has argued not just that there isn't a reason on the basis of which we make our causal inferences, he has argued that there is no *type* of reason which could serve.

The positive account

Hume's account is this: on the basis of our past experience in which the cause is repeatedly followed by the effect (which Hume calls 'constant conjunction') when we perceive the cause (or effect) again, our minds immediately infer the effect (or cause). From seeing one billiard ball strike another, we immediately believe that the second will move. From receiving a letter with a French postmark, we immediately believe the letter was posted in France. We draw the inference without reasoning or argument, but on the basis of a principle of association by which the imagination has bound the two ideas – of the cause and of the effect – together in our minds: 'When the mind . . . passes from the idea or impression of one object to the idea or belief of another it is not determined by reason, but by certain principles which associate together the ideas of these objects and unite them in the imagination'.

This movement of our minds repeats a previous sequence of thought, originally, our experiences of the repeated conjunction of cause and effect. And so Hume calls the principle that governs it 'custom', without pretending that such a label explains it at all. Custom is not a reason or principle of reasoning. It is not that we *think* 'this object has constantly been conjoined to this second object, so the second will occur again'. We don't even need to *notice* the constant conjunction; our experience of it is enough for our minds to move from the impression of the cause to a belief in the effect. Custom is a natural instinct of the mind, a disposition we simply have in the face of experience of constant conjunction. Without custom, we would be unable to draw causal inferences, and so we would have no knowledge of anything beyond what was present to our senses and memory.

Is Hume's account 'sceptical'?

Hume's attack on reason, and his resulting account of induction and causal inference, has traditionally been understood to produce **scepticism**. Since there is no 'reason' to believe the future will be like the past, then any belief about what the future will be like is equally unsupported. So we have no rational justification for our causal inferences, and our knowledge of matters of fact is limited to what we have directly experienced.

But more recently, philosophers have argued that this was not Hume's intention. A passage of particular importance is this:

Treatise, I.iii.vi

It is unclear whether 'custom', as a principle of the mind, is just another name for the cause-effect principle of association. If not, then it is very closely related.

? What is 'custom'? Why does Hume argue that it is the foundation of our knowledge of matters of fact?

See also DO RELATIVISM AND CONTINGENCY INVITE INERTIA IN CERTAIN FIELDS OF HUMAN ACTIVITY?, p. 209.

> Though we should conclude . . . that . . . in all reasonings from experience, there is a step taken by the mind which is not supported by any argument or process of the understanding, there is no danger that these reasonings, on which almost all knowledge depends, will ever be affected by such a discovery. If the mind be not engaged by argument to make this step, it must be induced by some other principle of equal weight and authority. (p. 120)

Hume asserts that our knowledge of matters of fact does not rest on reasoning, but he is not sceptical about inference from experience or its use. He calls custom a principle of *equal weight and authority* and is happy to continue speaking of *knowledge* depending on it. Again, he calls custom:

> the great guide of human life . . . Without the influence of custom, we should be entirely ignorant of every matter of fact beyond what is immediately present to the memory and senses. We should never know how to adjust means to end, or to employ our natural powers in the production of any effect. (pp. 122–3)

He clearly implies that we do know how to adjust means to end. Induction is a normal function of the mind, and our only (and best) guide to how reality is. We can conjecture that he calls § V a 'Sceptical solution' only because he rejects the view that the foundation of knowledge of matters of fact is reason, and not because he doubts that we have such knowledge.

> Discuss Hume's account of our knowledge of matters of fact.

Going further: custom and reason

In support of the claim that Hume is not a sceptic about matters of fact, we should note that he is willing to talk of 'good' and 'bad' causal inferences. During his argument against reason, he indicated that we cannot say that the billiard ball will move when struck rather than stay still. Anything is *possible* – the ball could move, it could stay still, it could vanish . . . But his argument is that we cannot decide between these options *on the basis of reason*. Having introduced the principle of custom, we can reliably infer that the ball will move; any other belief is not equally well supported by custom.

In fact, despite having drawn such a strong contrast between reason and custom, Hume sometimes talks as though causal inference is a form of reasoning. We could say that Hume uses the term 'reasoning' with more than one meaning. In its narrow sense, it applies only to deductive reasoning, and should be contrasted with induction, which rests on custom. In its broader sense, it covers inductive reasoning, so custom is a form of reasoning.

But there is a deeper issue here. If custom is *just* a natural principle of the mind, it is hard to see how we can say that it can be *better* or *worse*, that causal inferences can be *justified* or *unjustified*. Yet we obviously can say this, for example, 'My grandfather smoked all his life and didn't get cancer; so smoking doesn't cause cancer' is a bad inference. Yet to talk of 'justification' is to talk about reasoning. Perhaps we can say that while custom, not reason, is the foundation of our ability to draw causal inferences, actually drawing such inferences can count – at least in many cases – as a genuine type of reasoning.

See the objection raised in THE NATURE OF BELIEF AND IMAGINATION, p. 20.

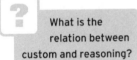 What is the relation between custom and reasoning?

Going further: the return of scepticism?

The conclusion that Hume is not a sceptic is too quick. At the end of the *Enquiry*, in § XII, Hume appears to endorse a sceptical reading of his arguments about causal inference. He displays his conclusion that all matters of fact, beyond what we have directly experienced, rest on custom – 'which it is indeed difficult to resist, but which, like other instincts, may be fallacious and deceitful' (p. 206). In this chain of reasoning, the sceptic has 'ample matter of triumph', 'shows his force', and 'seems, for the time at least, to destroy all assurance and conviction'.

But he does not endorse this reading. Hume sought to understand the nature of the mind, not to draw a sceptical conclusion from his discoveries. So he argues, in this passage, that to be sceptical about matters of fact *has no point*. There is no real doubt cast on our knowledge, because as soon as we have to act, or make some causal inference in life, scepticism of this kind disappears. Hume adopts what he calls a form of 'mitigated scepticism', which he endorsed as his aim in § I, that is, 'the limitation of our enquiries to such subjects as are best adapted to the narrow capacity of human understanding' (p. 208).

See MITIGATED
SCEPTICISM, p. 149.

Key points • • •

Is Hume a
sceptic?

- Hume argues that the foundation of our knowledge of matters of fact is what we have directly experienced. We use causal inference and reasoning about probability to know about what we have not experienced.

- Hume argues that causal inference does not rest on reasoning. We cannot deduce from a cause what effect will follow. We cannot say that the usual effect *must* follow the cause; nor that the effect must resemble the cause. The relation between cause and effect is not a relation of ideas – that the effect will not follow the cause is not a contradiction.

- Causal inference, therefore, rests on past experience. But how do we know that what we have not experienced will be like what we have experienced? Past experience can provide knowledge only of what has happened in the past.

- Our belief that the future will resemble the past, Hume argues, is not based on reason, but on 'custom' – the principle that governs the mind to immediately infer the effect from the cause, once we have repeatedly experienced the two together.

- Hume calls custom a 'principle of equal weight and authority' as reason, and 'the great guide of human life'. Belief based on custom is therefore no less knowledge than belief based on reason.

- Hume also writes as though causal inferences can be justified or unjustified. This makes such inferences very like reasoning, if not a form of reasoning.

- However, Hume also suggests that his arguments could be read sceptically. But he says such scepticism would have no point.

Past experience, rationality and probability in relation to belief in miracles (§§ VI and X)

Probability and belief

Hume says that matters of fact are 'probable', as opposed to the certainty of relations of ideas. In § VI, he discusses the way we use probability in forming beliefs about matters of fact. Our beliefs about matters of fact are formed by repeated exposure to the facts. So Hume talks of 'degrees of belief' being exactly matched to how frequently something occurs in our experience. It is as though the mind keeps track of how often or how reliably something occurs (e.g. snow in January in northern Europe), and automatically adjusts how strong it infers and assents to the claim regarding the same thing happening again. The principle governing this automatic process of adjustment is custom.

Two points are worth noting about Hume's account. First, in light of the discussion of custom and induction above, it is worth noting that Hume refers to forming judgements of probability as a 'process of thought or reasoning' (p. 131). And yet in § V, he contrasts custom and reason; and he says that forming a belief is not a rational process.

Second, Hume suggests that the idea that we form the belief that something will or will not occur through repeated exposure helps to explain the nature of belief. A belief is an idea with great vivacity; it could have accumulated this degree of vivacity from the numerous impressions of its object. If it repeatedly snows in January (impressions), then I come to believe that it will snow in January.

But in this argument, Hume has confused two senses of 'degree of belief'. He seems to think I can only believe that it will snow in January or that it will not. The probability of the occurrence is represented by the strength of belief (itself a matter of vivacity). But, of course, I can believe with great certainty that there is an 80 per cent chance of snow in January. The probability of the occurrence is part of *what* I believe, and not given by the strength of my belief. Hume's theory doesn't seem to allow for this possibility. This is another reason to think that his account of belief is mistaken.

See THE NATURE OF BELIEF AND IMAGINATION, p. 20, for discussion.

Discuss the role of probability in Hume's theory of how we form beliefs about matters of fact.

Miracles

In § X, Hume uses his views about our knowledge of matters of fact to reject belief in miracles. Before looking at his argument, it is worth noting that there are different ways to define what a miracle is. Three important definitions are:

1. an event that has religious significance;
2. an event caused by God;
3. an event that violates (or is otherwise not in accordance with) the laws of nature, caused by God.

The appeal of the first definition is that people do talk of events as miracles even when the event isn't outside the laws of nature. However, whether an event has 'religious significance' or not may be a matter of subjective interpretation. An event can qualify as a miracle for one person and not another, even when both are religious believers.

The second definition rules out subjective interpretation, as miracles are only those events that are *in fact* caused by God. But it says that *every* act of God is a miracle, for example, God's continuous creation in sustaining the existence of the universe or all genuine religious experience.

The third definition has been most common with philosophers. Aquinas says a miracle is 'beyond the order commonly observed in nature', and it is the sense that Hume discusses.

> Explain the differences between the three definitions of a miracle.

Hume's argument against miracles

Hume defines a miracle as 'a violation of the laws of nature', or more fully, 'a transgression of a law of nature by a particular volition of the Deity' (p. 173). He then argues that it can't be reasonable to believe that a miracle has occurred: 'as a firm and unalterable experience has established these laws [of nature], the proof against a miracle, from the very nature of the fact, is as entire as any argument from experience can possibly be imagined' (p. 173). By definition, a miracle goes against our very regular and extensive experience of how the world works. Therefore, on the basis of experience, the probability that a miracle has occurred must always be less than the probability that it hasn't. Because it is rational to believe what is most probable, we never have a good reason to believe that a miracle has occurred.

> Explain Hume's appeal to probability in his attack on belief in miracles.

Hume is joining a debate about miracles that was going on at the time, about whether historical reports of miracles, for example, in the New Testament, could be believed, and what role they had in the foundations of Christian faith. So he considers the issue of testimony, that is, other people saying that they witnessed a miracle. (We will come back to the question of what it is reasonable to believe if you (think you) experience a miracle yourself.)

Testimony is very important in forming our beliefs. We experience so little of the world directly, so we rely on what other people tell us. This is reasonable, because we have discovered that testimony is generally reliable. However, we rightly distinguish between more and less reliable testimony, for example, depending on whether some witnesses say one thing, others another; how many people were witnesses, how they report what they experienced, and so on. These judgements are important in court, for instance. One factor in believing testimony is whether what is reported is probable or extraordinary. You're more likely to believe a friend who says they saw your mum in the street than one who says they saw a pig flying! So to believe testimony rationally, it needs to be more likely that the testimony is true than not; and there are many factors that affect this.

When it comes to miracles, then, to rationally believe someone who claims to have witnessed a miracle (a violation of the laws of nature), it must be less probable that the testimony is false than that the miracle occurred. But this, Hume argues, can never be. The miracle is extremely improbable: *all* our experience of matters of fact supports the belief that laws of nature are not violated. So Hume argues that the evidence against the belief that a miracle has occurred is *always* stronger than the evidence from testimony that it has occurred. And when the evidence against a particular belief is stronger than evidence in its favour, then we should not hold that belief.

We can compare miracles to unexpected events. After all, these *also* go against our experience, so do we ever have good reason to believe some unexpected event has occurred? Yes, says Hume, on two conditions: first, there is widespread, consistent agreement that the event occurred; and second, there are 'analogies' of the event in our experience. Our experience leads us to expect the unexpected, *within limits*. These may vary from person to person; Hume presents the case of an Indian who, never having lived anywhere cold enough, refused to believe that water turned into ice (p. 172). Hume thought he was right to do so until he was shown that the testimony was very strong. If we hear of someone coming back from the dead, we would be in a similar situation, and should not believe it.

> **?** What is it important to consider when judging whether to believe someone's testimony?

Furthermore, he continues in § X, Part 2, the testimony for miracles is not very good evidence as testimony goes:

1. There is no miracle attested to by people of good sense, education, integrity, and reputation, where the miracle is witnessed by many such people (the attributes listed describe people we can trust not to be easily fooled and to tell the truth without exaggerating).
2. Human nature enjoys surprise and wonder, which gives us a tendency to believe unusual things even when the belief isn't justified.
3. Tales of miracles are common among ignorant peoples, and diminish in civilisation; and the tales of miracles are often given in explanation of everyday events, such as battles and famine, that don't need a miraculous explanation.

However, Hume's later remarks show that his first argument is his main objection. If there were reports of miracles in contemporary society, and they were attested to by people of integrity and education, 'the absolute impossibility . . . of the events' (p. 181) is reason enough not to believe the reports. No matter how strong the testimony is,

> It is experience only, which gives authority to human testimony; and it is the same experience, which assures us of the laws of nature. When, therefore, these two kinds of experience are contrary, we have nothing to do but subtract the one from the other . . . this subtraction, with regard to all popular religions, amounts to a total annihilation. (p. 184)

So even if the evidence mounts up, we should not believe that a *miracle* has occurred; we should try to find what the natural cause of the event is. The only rational response is scientific discovery, not religious belief.

Discussion

THE LAWS OF NATURE

It is important to interpret Hume's definition of a miracle correctly. A miracle is not a violation of something we *believe* to be a law of nature, but a violation of what *is* in fact a law of nature. For instance, it may turn out that what appears to violate the laws of nature simply demonstrates that we were wrong about

> Why does Hume argue that testimony supporting miracles is unreliable?

> Hume adds a fourth point against supporting religious belief by appeal to miracles, that is, that every religion proclaims miracles, but not all religions can be true. So the force of each claim to miracles destroys the force of the others, and it is rational not to believe any claim.

> Outline and illustrate Hume's argument rejecting belief in miracles.

what the laws of nature are. Being able to transmit the sound of someone talking over thousands of miles may once have seemed miraculous; but radio waves enable us to do that. It is not a miracle – even if someone thinks it is a miracle.

When faced with an event that challenges the laws of nature as we believe them to be, we will change our beliefs if we are able to repeat the event and if we are then able to explain it by reformulating the laws of nature. For Hume, this is always a path we must explore first. He is not arguing that events that *seem* to be miracles are impossible; he is arguing that it is unreasonable to believe that they are genuine miracles.

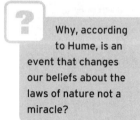

Why, according to Hume, is an event that changes our beliefs about the laws of nature not a miracle?

EXPERIENCING MIRACLES

Suppose we have good evidence for considering a miraculous event to have occurred, and we investigate it and are unable to find any natural causes that would explain it. Can't we reasonably conclude a miracle had occurred? According to Hume, we have only two choices: reject the claim that the event happened or look for a natural cause of it. But does experience support his claim? Is there *no* experience that could support a belief in a non-natural cause?

Hume does not discuss experiencing a 'miracle' oneself. But we can adapt his arguments regarding testimony. He could claim that no *experience* is evidence for a non-natural ('miraculous') explanation, because we never experience a *non-natural cause*. To suppose that God caused some event will always be speculative, because we have no experience of God. So even if we don't find a natural cause, we can only conclude that *we don't know* what the cause is, not that the cause is non-natural.

On Hume's account, if I personally witness someone undoubtedly killed before my eyes get up, wounds healing and walk off, I *still* shouldn't think there is a non-natural cause of this. All the rest of my experience casts doubt on the belief that what I am seeing is actually taking place. Is it not more likely that I cannot trust my eyes? To have good enough reason to believe the event actually happened as I experienced it, it must be analogous to the rest of my experience. But if it is analogous, then it will probably have a natural cause. If it is not analogous, then can my current experience be trusted?

We may argue that it can. For instance, if I am not the only witness (so I wasn't hallucinating or going mad), and everyone else who witnessed it are reliable witnesses, and there is simply nothing in current scientific understanding that relates to what happened, then perhaps it is reasonable to think a miracle has occurred.

See MIRACLES, p. 320 for further discussion.

This conclusion doesn't justify many people believing in miracles! It also doesn't mean that miracles have ever occurred.

Is Hume right to argue that the evidence from experience against miracles will *always* outweigh evidence in favour of a miracle?

Going further: are miracles violations of the laws of nature?

A different response to Hume is that his definition of a miracle is wrong; and as a result, his argument from probability doesn't work. If we say a miracle is a violation of the laws of nature, we risk *defining* miracles out of existence (not just showing that it is unreasonable to believe in them). Here's how: a statement is only a law of nature if it is true, general (or universal) and **contingent**. It must be general to be a law, and it must be contingent to be a law of *nature* rather than a law of logic ('all bachelors are unmarried' is true and general, but not a law of nature!). However, the occurrence of a natural event that violates the law makes the statement either not true or not general. But if it is not true or not general, it is not a law. Any statement that is a law of nature cannot be violated while remaining a law. Therefore, by definition, there can be no violations of a law of nature; if a miracle is a violation of a law of nature, then a miracle is a contradiction in terms. But this is wrong. Miracles are not *logically* impossible.

So what is a miracle? If we say that miracles are violations of what *we think* the laws of nature are (discussed above), then whether an event is a miracle or not depends on what we believe about the laws of nature. We have rejected this view.

An alternative definition is this: a miracle is an event, caused by God, that is *outside or not in accordance with* the laws of nature. This definition preserves both the idea that miracles are somehow 'at odds' with the laws of nature, and the idea that they are still laws. How? The laws of nature only apply to *natural* events. If an event is caused by God, it is not a natural event. So the event doesn't *violate* the laws of nature, it just falls outside them. (You aren't *breaking* the US speed limit of 55 mph if you drive at 60 mph on the motorway in England.)

We can now reply to Hume. The evidence against a miracle occurring, from our experience of natural events, is *irrelevant*, because miracles are not

Explain the difference between the definition of a miracle as a violation of the laws of nature and as not in accordance with the laws of nature.

natural events. Our experience shows that events thought to be miracles (say, coming back from the dead) do not happen *as natural events*. But since miracles are non-natural events, this doesn't undermine belief in miracles.

Hume can reply that we now need good evidence to suggest that an event is non-natural rather than natural. And on this matter, his arguments about experience and testimony still apply.

Assess Hume's argument against belief in miracles.

Key points • • •

- Hume argues that matters of fact are 'probable', and that we form judgements of probability on the basis of how frequently or reliably something has happened.

- The probability of some belief being true, Hume says, is matched by the vivacity and certainty of the belief. On this account, we can't have a certain belief that there is an 80 per cent chance of something happening.

- Hume defines miracles as 'a violation of the laws of nature'. By definition, it goes against our 'firm and unalterable' experience of matters of fact.

- Hume discusses only evidence from testimony, and argues that because testimony in favour of miracles goes against experience, we must reject the testimony.

- Furthermore, testimony in favour of miracles is not strong. In particular, no miracle has been testified to by many people who we can know are reliable.

- An event that violates what we believe the laws of nature to be, and which then shows that our beliefs about the laws of nature are false, is not a miracle.

- If we experience an event that appears to violate the laws of nature, our experience on this occasion is probably less reliable than all our experience that suggests the event is impossible. And we can never know that the cause of the event is not natural. However, we can object to Hume that under certain conditions, we could have good enough evidence to believe that an event not in accordance with the laws of nature has happened.

- We can also object that Hume's definition of miracles makes them logically impossible, which they are not. It is better to define miracles as outside the laws of nature.

II. CAUSE AND EFFECT

The analysis of causation in terms of constant conjunction – the role of custom and repetition (§ IV)

As we saw in THE SCOPE OF MATTERS OF FACT (p. 25), Hume's investigation of causation occurs in the context of thinking about what and how we can know about 'matters of fact'. He argues that it is on the causal relation alone that all such knowledge is founded. So how do we arrive at knowledge of causes and effects?

Hume argues that we can't deduce what something will cause from examining it alone, 'if that object be entirely new to [someone], he will not be able, by the most accurate examination of its sensible qualities, to discover any of its causes or effects' (p. 109). You might think that you could tell, for example, that one billiard ball colliding with another would move it. But you are being swayed by your experience here. In the absence of *any* experience of 'what happens next', imagining that the second ball moves is arbitrary; there are so many other things it could do, for example, stay still and the first ball bounce off it. From this perspective, just considering the qualities of the 'cause', the effect that follows must seem completely arbitrary.

So from examining the first object, we can't infer the thought that it *causes* 'what happens next'. The idea of causation is the idea of a *relation* between the two objects or events. We must use experience to find the causal relations between events. But what kind of experience will give us this knowledge? If we witness just one instance of an event being followed by another – a ball striking a second, the second ball moving off – we can't, from this single experience, infer that the first event caused the second. We have seen that the second *follows* the first; but to say that it is an *effect* of the first is to claim much more. The second event follows many events, for example, your eye blinking as you look at the two balls, someone sneezing outside the room. Perhaps either of these is what caused the second ball to move . . . How do you know? You have only had experience of this one occasion.

Hume's argument is not just that we cannot gain knowledge of what causes what on the basis of single objects or single instances. It is that we cannot even form the *idea* of causation from these sources. The idea of causation is more than the idea of one object being followed by another. But surely all that we actually *experience* is one object following another in time. So how do we form the idea of causation?

> Explain and illustrate Hume's argument that we cannot infer the cause or effect of some object simply from examining the object.

> Hume's argument for this doesn't appear in § IV, but in § VII, in relation to THE IDEA OF NECESSARY CONNECTION (p. 42).

> Explain and illustrate Hume's argument that we cannot infer that two events are causally related from a single experience of those two events together.

Constant conjunction and custom

The idea of causation enables us to *infer* an effect from a cause or vice-versa. That is, if we know how an event (one ball striking another) operates as a cause, we can infer its effects. You say 'I know what happens next'. You can't make this prediction on the basis of one experience. Instead, you need *repeated* experiences of the same event following the first. The basis for our idea of causation and our causal inferences, claims Hume, is *constant conjunction*. When I *repeatedly* observe one object following another, I begin to infer, from perceiving just the first object, that the second object will come about. Once I've seen enough times one billiard ball strike another, and the second move, when I see a billiard ball moving towards another, I immediately believe that the second one will move when it is struck.

So the idea of causation is derived from our experience of constant conjunction. This experience is, of course, past experience. Now we saw in THE SCOPE OF MATTERS OF FACT (p. 28), that Hume argues that our use of past experience to make inferences about the future – for example, what will happen next when one ball strikes another – is not based on reasoning. Instead, it is based on *custom*, that principle of the mind that associates cause and effect, so that whenever we experience an event which has had particular effects in the past, we immediately think of the effect now. What sets up this 'customary' movement of the mind is our experience of constant conjunction.

Again, it is important to note that we do not *infer* the effect by saying that because there has been constant conjunction in the past, this new instance (of a billiard ball moving towards another) will conform to it. Rather, the simple *fact* that we have experienced constant conjunction sets up the link between cause and effect in our minds. We can give two points in support of this claim:

1. We often don't, and don't need to, call on our memory when making the inference; for example, when seeing a body of deep water, I immediately think that it could drown me, without calling to mind past experiences of this.
2. Animals are clearly capable of making these causal inferences (p. 118), but animals don't construct arguments with general principles such as 'there has been constant conjunction in the past'.

> Explain the roles of repetition and custom in establishing causal inference.

Objection

Is Hume right that we must always have *repeated* experience in order to associate cause and effect? At the end of § IV, he gives the example of a child feeling pain when putting its hand in the candle flame, and learning not to put its hand near the candle (p. 118). But how many times must a child do this before becoming cautious? If Hume is right, after being burnt just once, the child will *not* be cautious – not even a little bit, because without repeated experience, custom will not have set up the anticipation of being burnt again. We can test this claim (a bit unethical, but possible!). I would predict that children burnt just once would be cautious. If I am right, Hume's account that the inference of effect from cause depends on repeated experience must be wrong.

This would mean that the mind can identify a cause after just one instance. It can identify and select the *relevant* event (hand in candle) preceding the effect (burnt hand) as the cause, despite the many other events occurring at the same time. For example, as Hume notes in the *Treatise* (I.iii.ii), we expect the cause to be *contiguous* to the effect. If the pain is in my hand, then I expect what causes the pain to be near my hand. Only the candle flame fits the bill.

Hume can reply that even if we can, in some cases, infer that one event causes another from a single instance, we nevertheless need experience of constant conjunction to form the *idea* of causation in the first place. (For instance, where does the expectation that a cause is contiguous to its effects come from?) The *general* claim that causal inference is based on custom, and custom is based on constant conjunction, would remain, even if in certain instances we can make a *particular* causal inference from experiencing just one instance of cause–effect.

> Is Hume right to say that we can *never* infer cause or effect from a single experience of an event? Does this inference depend on reasoning?

> For an argument that the idea of causation is innate, see CONCEPTUAL SCHEMES AND THEIR IMPLICATIONS II, p. 41.

Key points • • •

- Hume argues that we can't make causal inferences on the basis of examining the cause in isolation. Nor can we do so on the basis of a single experience of two events, one following the other.
- Instead, both the idea of causation and causal inference is based on our experience of constant conjunction.
- This experience sets up a movement of the mind, so that whenever we experience the cause (or effect), we infer the existence of the effect (or cause). Custom is the principle of the mind that forges this connection between the two events.

- We can object that we do not always need repeated experience to make a particular causal inference; in some cases, just one instance will do.
- Hume can reply that if experience of constant conjunction is not needed for each particular causal inference, it is nevertheless the origin of causal inference, and the idea of causation, in general.

The idea of necessary connection and the search for its origin – Hume's solution to the problem (§ VII)

See DETERMINISM DEFINED and DETERMINISM DEVELOPED, pp. 352 and 367.

Explain the idea of causal necessity.

Hume has not yet given us a complete analysis of the idea of causation. To say that one event causes another, we commonly think, is not just to say that the second follows the first, but that the second *must* follow the first. Hume first refers to this idea in § IV – 'the supposed tye or connexion between the cause and effect, which binds them together, and renders it impossible, that any other effect could result from the operation of that cause' (p. 111). (Hume takes this idea of necessary connection to be equivalent to the idea that the cause has the *power* to bring about its effects. We shall not discuss this assumption, but focus just on necessary connection.) Experience shows us what follows what; but, Hume argues, experience does not show us that the effect *must* follow. Since we have this idea of a necessary connection, Hume must explain its origins in accordance with his theory of ideas. What is the impression from which the idea is derived?

The search

If it were true that the effect *must* follow the cause, then we could infer, by reasoning, that the effect will follow. But we have already seen (p. 26) Hume's argument that this inference relies on custom, not reason.

Hume begins with our experience of the events themselves. There is no impression of the 'necessary connection' deriving from our sense experience of the objects. If there were, then even in one instance of seeing an event cause its effect, we would immediately have the sense that the second event had to follow. But, he has argued, we don't. There is no impression that the effect *had* to occur just as it did.

How about constant conjunction? Could we gain an impression of necessary connection through repeated experience? This can't be right either. Surely everything we can experience that belongs to the objects is there, present, on just one occasion. Repeating the succession of events doesn't change the objects *themselves*. So we don't derive the idea of a necessary connection from looking to the objects.

If it is not an impression of sense, could it be an impression of reflection (see p. 8)? Hume considers and rejects the suggestion that the idea derives from our experience of willing (pp. 137–40). The necessary connection would connect one's will as the cause to its effects, for example, moving part of one's body. But we have very little sense of what connects our will to its effects; we just will and the effect follows. *How* the two are connected, we have no impression of. We experience only a succession of events.

Hume then turns (p. 141) to the philosophical theory that the connection between cause and effect is the will of God. It is God who brings about the effect when the cause occurs. But if we have no idea of the connection between the cause and the effect, we certainly have no idea of the will of God! The theory is unpersuasive and certainly no explanation for the origin of the idea of necessary connection.

The idea of necessary causation is part of the idea of causation, and this, Hume has argued, derives from the relation of constant conjunction. This relation, as already argued, doesn't change the objects or our sense impressions of them. But the experience of constant conjunction *does* change the mind. What has changed is

> that after a repetition of similar instance, the mind is carried by habit [custom], upon the appearance of one event, to expect its usual attendant, and to believe that it will exist. This connexion, therefore, which we *feel* in the mind, this customary transition of the imagination from one object to its usual attendant, is the sentiment or impression, from which we form the idea of power or necessary connexion. (p. 145)

So Hume claims that the idea of necessary connection, an essential component of the idea of causation, derives from an impression of reflection. When we experience constant conjunction between objects or events, our minds develop a tendency to move automatically from the experience of one to a belief in the occurrence of the other, the principle of the imagination being 'custom'. We experience this automatic movement, and it is the *feeling* of this movement that is the impression from which we form the idea of necessary connection. The imagination has connected the two events; and the movement of mind from one to the other happens automatically, outside our will. We thereby come to believe that the events themselves are necessarily connected.

> Outline and illustrate Hume's argument that any impression of a necessary connection does not derive from the two objects/events that are causally related.

> Explain Hume's account of the origin of the idea of necessary connection.

The implication

To say that two objects are necessarily connected, Hume argues, can have no other meaning than that they have acquired this association in our minds. We have a tendency to form the belief that the *objects* resemble our *impressions* of reflection. We 'project' onto the objects what actually originates in our minds. We can have no reason to suppose objects themselves are necessarily connected. If the property of necessary connection were in the two objects, we would be able to infer causes and effects from a single instance. This result does not mean that we should abandon all talk of necessary connection as mistaken. But it does mean that we must recognise that this way of talking is an expression of our experience, not a description of objects as they are independent of our experience of them.

> Hume argues that this tendency is widespread. It occurs with secondary qualities, aesthetic properties and moral properties. We think objects are themselves coloured or beautiful, that actions are right or wrong; but in each case, the idea (colour, beauty, right) derives from an impression of reflection, not sense.

Going further: is Hume's account circular?

Experiencing constant conjunction leads the mind to set up a connection in imagination between the two events. So, is the new habit of the mind an *effect* of experiencing constant conjunction? In the *Treatise* I.iii.xiv, Hume explicitly says that it is. Given that he is trying to analyse causation, is this a problem? Doesn't he have to *assume* the idea of causation in his explanation of the idea of causation?

We can reply that we can analyse his claim that experience of constant conjunction causes us to connect the events by custom using his account, that is, that experience of constant conjunction is *constantly conjoined* to our minds connecting the events experienced, and that on experiencing (or reflecting on) constant conjunction, our minds move automatically to the idea of a transition of the mind (custom).

We might well doubt this! It has taken a lot of hard work on Hume's part to demonstrate the connection between experience of constant conjunction and custom – hardly an automatic transition. What this shows is that the discovery of certain causal connections – and many examples from science suggest themselves, for example, smoking and cancer – is not itself automatic, but depends on much thought and investigation. Hume's theory does not deny this. He claims that the *idea* of cause originates, in part, in something that does happen automatically, and that *in coming to believe* that two events are causally related, our minds move from one to the other automatically. But Hume does not comment on how the production of this belief may, in some cases, require reflection on our experience. This again highlights how causal inference can, in many cases, operate as a form of reasoning (see p. 30).

Is Hume's account of how experience of constant conjunction gives rise to an impression of necessary connection coherent?

Key points • • •

- Constant conjunction is not a complete analysis of causation. We also have the idea that the cause and effect have a 'necessary connection', so that the effect must follow the cause. But where can we find the impression of 'necessary connection'?
- Hume argues that it is not an impression of sense – we do not find it in our experience of the cause alone, nor in a single instance of experiencing two events in sequence. Nor is it an impression derived from our experience of willing.
- The impression of necessary connection is the feeling we have of the customary transition of the mind from one event to the other, in response to experience of constant conjunction.
- The necessary connection between the events is therefore a connection forged by the imagination, and nothing between the events themselves. We are not wrong to talk of the events being connected; but this is all we can mean.
- Our experience of constant conjunction causes the imagination to forge the connection between events. Hume can make this claim without his account of causation being circular, because he can replace the reference to causation by his account itself.

Hume's definitions of 'cause' (§ VII)

Hume ends his discussion in § VII by providing two definitions of 'cause': one that refers to the relation between the objects themselves, the other that relates the objects to the mind of the observer. It is worth quoting the passage in full to try to understand why he gives two definitions not just one.

> Similar objects are always conjoined with similar. Of this we have experience. Suitably to this experience, therefore, we may define a cause to be *an object, followed by another, and where all the objects similar to the first are followed by objects similar to the second*. Or in other words, *where, if the first object had not been, the second never had existed*. The appearance of a cause always conveys the mind, by a customary transition, to the idea of the effect. Of this also we have experience. We may, therefore, suitably to this experience, form another definition of *cause*; and call it, *an object followed by another, and whose appearance always conveys the thought to that other*. (p. 146)

These two definitions of 'cause' are not equivalent. The first definition of cause picks out an objective relation between the objects; the second picks out a relation between the objects and our minds. Two objects could stand in the relation of constant conjunction without anyone knowing it – so the appearance of one does not convey thought to the second. Or again, our thought may be conveyed from one to the other – because they have been conjoined in our experience so far – even though the two objects are not constantly conjoined, and in unobserved cases come apart.

Does Hume intend that something is a cause only if it satisfies *both* conditions? He does not say so. Judging from the context of discussion, we can say instead that Hume is giving us two views of causation. To understand causation, we must take into account both what goes on in the world, and our experience of that. Either without the other would miss out an essential part of our concept of cause.

> Compare and contrast Hume's two definitions of 'cause'.

Objections

However, both definitions are problematic. The first definition is that of 'constant conjunction'. It reduces causation to simple 'regularity', the regularity of one event following another. But this faces two objections.

First, Hume refers to causes being 'similar'. But he does not, at any point, give us guidance on what counts as similar. And judgements of similarity are famously dependent on the mind of the observer. But if what counts as 'the same thing as' this object is subjective, then the relation of causation will be subjective. Yet the first definition clearly intends to pick out causation as it applies to objects (not our experience of them). Hume's only available response is to argue that similarity is not always subjective, that some objects just are objectively similar to each other, and that real causal relations are the ones that hold between these objects. But this is not a very Humean idea.

Second, there is a difficulty in distinguishing between constant conjunctions that are *accidental* from ones which are genuinely causal. For example, it just so happens that you and I both finish work at 5.00pm. I set the alarm on my computer to go off at this time. And so it occurs that every time my alarm goes off, you stop work. But my alarm has not *caused* you to stop work.

We can reply that we only need to introduce the idea, present in the *Treatise*, that the objects related as cause and effect are *contiguous* to each other as well. But, in fact, Hume does not claim that cause and effect must be *spatially* contiguous, only temporally. Even if we did introduce spatial contiguity, there are counter-examples to this. For example, night follows day; but day does not cause night.

> Is causation more than regularity? If so, what else is involved?

Going further: the counterfactual analysis of causation

In response, Hume can appeal to the supplementary sentence, that 'if the first object had not been, the second would never had existed'. This is a **counterfactual** analysis of causation (very popular among philosophers today). This does answer the objection - for instance, it is not true that if my alarm hadn't gone off, you wouldn't have stopped work. But this is a completely different idea from mere regular succession, and not one that Hume has addressed in any part of his discussion so far.

The counterfactual analysis itself continues to face problems. When is it true to say that 'if the water hadn't spilled, the table would be dry', and does this always capture the cause? Suppose, in the actual situation, I am trying to balance the water glass and a wine glass; and if the water hadn't spilled, this would be because I had taken my concentration off the wine glass to steady the water, and so the wine would have spilled - so the table would be wet. The counterfactual turns out false, and yet it is obvious that the water spilling is the cause of the table being wet in the actual situation.

> A counterfactual is a **conditional** statement, in which the first clause picks out a state of affairs that is contrary to fact, for example, 'if the water hadn't spilled, the table would be dry', which implies that the water *did* spill.

The second definition faces a different kind of problem, namely, that it is circular. To rephrase: a cause is an object, followed by another, whose appearance causes the mind to think of that other. To avoid the circularity, we must understand the appearance of cause within the definition in terms of the first definition. In other words, a cause is 'an object, followed by another, whose appearance to the mind is followed by the idea of the second object, where all the objects similar to the first are followed by a similar transition in the mind to objects similar to the second object'.

This means that the second definition cannot stand on its own, but is dependent on the first. The objections to the first definition therefore become all the more important, because Hume's whole definition of causation depends on it.

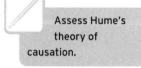

Assess Hume's theory of causation.

Key points • • •

- Hume gives two definitions of cause: *'an object, followed by another, and where all the objects similar to the first are followed by objects similar to the second'* and *'an object followed by another, and whose appearance always conveys the thought to that other'*.
- The two definitions are not equivalent. One refers to a relation between objects, independent of the mind; the second refers to a relation between objects and the mind. We can argue that Hume is giving two views of causation, both needed to get the complete picture.
- We can object to the first definition that judgements of 'similarity' are subjective; and that it does not distinguish between constant conjunctions that are accidental and ones that are properly causal.
- Hume's qualifying statement to the first definition is that 'if the first object had not been, the second never had existed'. This is a counterfactual analysis of causation which can help answer the objections raised, but Hume never discusses this analysis.
- The second definition is circular, since the definition of a cause refers to the experience of constant conjunction causing the mind to forge the connection between events. This circularity can be avoided by relying on the first definition.

III. FREE WILL

The attempt to reconcile free will and determinism; the diagnosis of the nature of the problem, Hume's account of what is meant by 'liberty' and 'necessity' (§ VIII)

In § VIII, Hume claims that the history of philosophy contains many examples of debates in which each side is using its terms with different meanings; and so the two sides misunderstand each other, neither persuades the other, and so the debate continues. The debate over whether we have free will or whether our actions and choices are determined is like this. In fact, Hume claims, all that is needed to end the debate are 'a few intelligible definitions' (p. 149). He aims to provide these definitions, of necessity and of liberty; to show that no one has ever disagreed that we are both free and yet our actions follow necessarily; and so end the debate. So he defends a form of COMPATIBILISM.

See pp. 359 and 378.

Human action and causal necessity

His account is very closely dependent on his theory of causation. He begins by reiterating his claim, defended in §§ IV, V and VII, that our ideas of necessity and causation arise from our experience of constant conjunction and the resulting inferences we make. He says that if anyone produces an analysis of causation which differs, or does not include the idea of necessity, he will give up the whole debate (p. 159).

From constant conjunction of two objects and inference from one to the other, then, we conclude that a necessary, causal relation holds between the two. At least, we do when it comes to material objects. We seem less willing to do so in the case of voluntary human action. But, in consistency, we should not, because we experience constant conjunction and make inferences here as well. So we must accept that actions and choices are both caused and necessarily follow from motives.

Constant conjunction: the same motives always produce the same choices and actions. History shows us nothing new; in fact, the point of doing history is 'to discover the constant and universal principles of human nature' (p. 150). Of course, we need to make allowance for the diversity of characters, prejudices, opinions that people hold, so that the actions of different people will differ somewhat. But this is usual in the material world as well: uniformity in *every* particular detail isn't found anywhere in nature. If we can't find a uniformity of motive and action, the cases differing from one person to the next, this isn't proof against the point. As philosophers and scientists, we recognise that there is such a variety of different possible 'minute or remote' causes. So it is very likely that where the effect differs, this isn't because the relationship between cause and effect is contingent rather than necessary, but that different causes are involved. And this seems to hold true about human action: people who know someone best, who know every particular of their character and situation, can often account for the most unexpected and irregular decisions. So we should conclude that human choice and action is as regular and uniform, involves constant conjunction just as much, as any part of nature.

Furthermore, we continually draw inferences on this basis. We act and plan our actions in ways that demonstrate our expectations that others will, in their *voluntary* actions, act in very specific ways. For example, in taking goods to market, I expect others to come, to want to buy and so on. And in our plans, we don't make any distinction between how natural causes and others' predictable actions will affect us. For example, a prisoner planning his escape reckons with the problems of jailors as much as with bricks and mortar. Finally, to the objection that, when thinking of other people's actions, we can say 'but he might change his mind, and in an unpredictable way', we should note that we make analogous claims regarding natural causation as well – that something could happen that we just didn't anticipate, for example, an earthquake. So, human action is as subject to causation and necessity as natural events: 'A man who at noon leaves his purse full of gold on the pavement at Charing-Cross, may as well expect that it will fly away like a feather, as that he will find it untouched an hour later' (p. 156).

> Outline Hume's argument that human motives display the same causal relation to actions as natural causes have to their effects.

Objections

Hume argues that 'the conjunction between motives and voluntary actions is as regular and uniform, as that between the cause and effect in any part of nature' (p. 154). This is highly controversial, and it is not entirely clear how Hume wants to handle the objection that it is false.

On the one hand, he says that we must not expect everyone in the same circumstances to act in the same manner – we must allow for differences of character and so on. This suggests that the conjunction between motives and actions only holds at a fairly high level of generality, for example, if someone is hungry, they will seek food. But, as Hume immediately acknowledges, taken as a causal law, this is false; there are many exceptions (e.g. the person is fasting or dieting or dislikes the food available and so on). Certainly, we have no sense of *necessity* here; hunger and seeking food are not so conjoined in our minds that we believe the one *must* follow the other – our expectation is not that strong. So far, the conjunction is *not* as regular and uniform as, say, expecting spilled water to fall towards the ground rather than up towards the sky.

This leads to his second approach, that is, that these many differences (between people and situations) that lead from the same motive to different actions can all be accounted for if we take into account every detail of character and circumstance. And this is exactly parallel to how we treat complex natural events, such as the weather or the operations of the human body. In our experience of these, there seems to be some variation in the effects that flow from some event, for example, taking medicine doesn't always lead to cure. But we don't think that the relation between taking medicine and its effects is contingent; we assume there are other causal factors we need to take into account. The same can be said about human action.

But there is a difficulty here. If we must take every detail of character and circumstance into account, then in what sense can we say that the conjunction of motives and actions is *regular and uniform*? For every character and every circumstance is different; how will we gain the requisite experience of *constant* conjunction that supports causal inference?

Hume faces a dilemma: the level at which we can speak of constant conjunction between motive and action is a very general level, where the conjunction is not so strong that it brings with it the sense of necessity; if we try to refine our description of how motive and action are conjoined, to avoid exceptions and generate the sense of necessity, then each situation we describe is different, and we have lost uniformity and constant conjunction.

Do we not face the same problem with causation in objects? How do we solve the problem of complex causes there? We can make two suggestions. First, there is more uniformity – we can and do replicate complex causes (as in Hume's case of the watch, p. 153), and are able to find every cause that operates; and this supports our belief that a variety of effects is the result of the interaction of many causes. Second, even when we cannot do this (as in the weather), we judge that we are dealing with the same *kind* of thing, namely, natural objects and events, in these cases as we are in cases in which we can successfully identify the 'hidden' causes. So again, our belief that all differences in effect spring from differences in causes is supported, in this case by analogy. In all of this, we are supported by the progress of science in the explanation of natural objects and events.

We can argue that these options for dealing with complex causes are not available to us with people. Motives are not the same kind of thing as natural events; and we know far less about the operations of the mind than about some natural objects, so we can never be sure that we have identified every cause that may operate. Psychology has not had similar success in discovering the 'hidden' causes in human motivation, and so has no more 'exceptionless' laws now than in Hume's day.

> Assess Hume's claim that 'the conjunction between motives and voluntary actions is as regular and uniform, as that between the cause and effect in any part of nature'.

Resistance to necessity

In presenting his account, Hume doesn't think he has said anything controversial. So if causation, and the idea of necessity it contains, derives from just such experiences of constant conjunction and inference, why do we not immediately accept that human actions are as necessary as natural events? Hume identifies two sources of resistance.

MISUNDERSTANDING NECESSITY

The first is that we mistakenly think that there is a difference in the operation of causation in natural events and in human actions. We may think that our actions are uncaused. Or we may think that there is at least no necessity in the relations between motive and action, while there is necessity between cause and effect in natural events. We think that investigation of natural events will reveal this, but we know we do not experience any such connection between their motives and their actions. So we suppose there is a distinction between natural events and human actions. It is the idea of *necessity*, the idea that we have no 'freedom' in bringing about our actions, given our motives, that feels threatening.

Can we conclude that there are two types of causation: one involving necessity, which applies to material objects, and one that does not, which applies to human action? Hume thinks the whole line of reasoning starts on the wrong foot:

> as long as we will rashly suppose, that we have some farther idea of necessity and causation in the operations of external objects; at the same time, that we can find nothing farther in the voluntary actions of the mind; there is no possibility of bringing the question to any determinate issue. (p. 157)

The point is that we make causal inferences as readily about human actions as we do about natural events. There just is *nothing else* to our idea of causal necessity than constant conjunction and inference. The idea of necessity is a result of custom, the movement of our minds that supports causal inference. Finding an absence of necessity between motive and action 'from the inside' is therefore unsurprising. But there is nothing additional in the case of objects. If we accept that material objects are subject to causal necessity, we must accept that human agency is as well. So there is no distinction to be drawn.

We have argued above that there *is* such a distinction to be drawn (and give another argument below). Hume is right that, at a *general* level, we make causal inferences about human actions. But this is not supported by the kind of necessary connection at the individual or particular level that we believe present in natural events. On the individual level, our experience and investigation of natural events and human actions differs. (This reply makes no special reference to finding an absence of a necessary connection in reflection, in one's *own* acting, but applies to our experience of human action in general.)

> Is Hume right to think that there is nothing to the idea of causal necessity except constant conjunction and causal inference?

Going further: the feeling of liberty

In a footnote (p. 158), Hume develops his comment that we do not feel necessity when we are in the process of actually *deciding* what to do. Quite the opposite – we actually have a feeling of liberty, that our action is *not* fixed or determined, that it is not true that the motives we have *must* lead us to act in one way rather than another. As already noted, this is unsurprising if necessity is not part of the cause and effect themselves, but arises from an impression of reflection. The impression of necessity occurs when we are *considering* a causal relation, it is only apparent from the *third-personal* point of view. It is not a feeling which occurs – or can occur – from the first-personal point of view.

Hume is therefore led to dismiss the lack of a feeling of necessity in agency as unimportant. It is a 'false sensation', since a spectator can successfully infer what we will do from knowing our motives. But we can take the argument in a different direction.

There are experiences people can have of being causally forced to do something – but in such cases, they feel that they are *not agents*, but *objects* subject to external forces. There is no experience of *agency* which involves the impression of causal necessity. There is the thought 'Knowing me, I will do this', which is clearly neither first nor third personal. At first sight, though, this is an acceptance of *constant conjunction* and even *inference*, but it still lacks the idea of necessity.

With natural events, we can have only a third-personal point of view. Given Hume's doctrine of the origin of ideas, and account of our experience of natural events, understanding causation between natural events as necessary is entirely appropriate. However, with events involving motives, we have both third-personal and first-personal points of view. From a first-personal point of view, agency does not involve necessity. So we have a *different experience*, for we experience the causal relation from a first-personal perspective as well, and from this perspective, there is no necessity. It would not be unjustified to form an idea of agency – causation involving a mind – which lacks the idea of necessity.

The idea is this: the experience of constant conjunction is sufficient to create the transition of the mind from cause to effect and impression of necessity in the case of natural events. However, it is not sufficient in the case of agency, because against it we place the absence of an impression of necessity in our experience of agency. It is not that something *more* is needed to account for necessity in causation between natural events. It is rather that this effect of constant conjunction upon the mind is *defeated* in the case of agency.

This account is highly speculative. Nevertheless, it is not completely implausible.

For a different discussion of the place of causal necessity in our understanding of human action, see FREE WILL AS COMPATIBLE WITH DETERMINISM, p. 380.

Discuss the significance of our first-personal experience of 'liberty' when making choices.

Liberty and choice

Hume's discussion of the definition of liberty is much more brief. He remarks that, given the evidence from constant conjunction and inference, liberty clearly doesn't mean 'unconnected to motives with uniformity'. It must therefore mean just '*a power of acting or not acting, according to the determinations of the will*' (p. 159). So I act as I do because I choose to act that way. If I had chosen not to act that way, I would not have done so. This allows, in fact, it requires says Hume, that my actions are caused by my motives. According to this definition, then, liberty is compatible with our actions being caused.

But it is also possible that we mean something else by liberty: that liberty is not a power of acting, but a power of *choosing*. If I can do what I want, but *I can't choose what I want*, then perhaps I am not free. This is a stronger sense of freedom. It is not enough to say that I *would* have acted differently if I had chosen to do so. We also need to say that I *could* have chosen to act differently.

The modern debate regarding free will has centred around this question: I must want to want what I want, or just doing what I want isn't enough for freedom. A common example is that of an addiction which I want to give up, for example, smoking. I may want a cigarette, but I don't want to want a cigarette – and this is why addictions leave us unfree. For Hume, to want a cigarette and smoke is to be free, even if you want not to want a cigarette. But if our desires and choices are like addictions, we are not free. Hume's definition of liberty would say that we are. Liberty must therefore be more complex than he allows.

Hume considers the idea that if our actions are subject to causal necessity, then there is a chain of causes reaching back to the beginning of everything: our actions are caused by our motives, our motives by, say, our experience and our genetic inheritance, each of these has preceding causes too, and so on. That would mean that our actions are 'pre-ordained and 'pre-determined' (p. 162). This doesn't sound like free will, and is the basis of an objection to compatibilism. Hume doesn't answer the objection in this form, though he concludes that reason overreaches itself in attempting to consider these issues.

The argument from moral responsibility

The debate about free will and necessity has not been just about the metaphysical question of causation. It has always involved a moral dimension, that is, what is required for us to be morally responsible for our actions? Hume argues that we must accept both that actions are caused and that they are free, in the sense defined, in order to attribute moral responsibility.

If our actions were not caused by the motives of the person, in what way could we hold that person morally responsible? An action is only someone's if it is caused by their motives, that is, the cause is 'within' them, part of them, rather than external to them. And if the act is not caused at all, then the person

> Explain and illustrate the difference between doing what one wants to do and choosing what one wants to choose.

> **For further discussion** of COMPATIBILISM, pp. 359 and 378.

> **For further discussion** of moral responsibility, see THE IMPLICATIONS OF DETERMINISM, pp. 363 and 382.

? Does Hume successfully defend his compatibilist theory of free will?

can't be held responsible. We are only morally concerned with actions insofar as they indicate someone's character and motives. They therefore can't arouse praise or blame in us unless they derive from these.

Key points • • •

- Hume argues that our actions are both free and caused, and that we only need to define these terms clearly to understand this.
- Constant conjunction and causal inference are the origin of our idea of causal necessity. But constant conjunction and causal inference apply to human motives and actions just as much as to natural objects, and therefore, so does causal necessity.
- Where there is a difference in action, this is because there is a difference in motive, not because actions are not caused. And we constantly plan what to do assuming other people's actions are predictable.
- We can object that the regular connection between motives and actions only holds at a general level. Because this allows exceptions, we don't think a particular action *must* follow from a particular motive. If we try to take all details into account, then the connection between motives and actions is not regular and uniform.
- Hume dismisses our 'feeling' of liberty when we decide how to act as unimportant. Causal necessity arises only from a third-personal point of view, when we consider the relation between cause and effect.
- We can object that there is no good reason to privilege the third-personal point of view in our account of causation. Because agency does involve the first-personal feeling of liberty, perhaps agency involves a kind of causation that does not involve necessity.
- Hume defines liberty as 'a power of acting or not acting, according to the determinations of the will'.
- We can object that liberty is not just the power to do what I choose, but the power to choose what I want to choose.
- To the objection that we are not free because our motives are caused, and what causes them is itself caused and so on, Hume responds that we cannot properly reason about these ideas.
- Hume argues that his compatibilism is necessary for moral responsibility. We must be able to act as we choose. But also our motives must cause our actions – if our actions were not caused, we couldn't be responsible for them.

PLATO *THE REPUBLIC*

Book I 336b to 367e, Book V 474c to Book VII 521b

2

In this chapter, we examine Plato's text in the light of three key issues: the relationship between appearance and reality and Plato's theory of the Forms; the relationship between knowledge and virtue, including Plato's account of morality; and Plato's claims that philosophers should be political rulers. Students should be able to explain Plato's views clearly and accurately and critically evaluate his arguments and objections to them. They should also be able to make connections between his theories and other views on the same topics discussed elsewhere in the syllabus.

All quotations are from the AQA recommended edition of Lee's translation (Penguin Classics, ISBN 0-140-44914-0).

SYLLABUS CHECKLIST ✔

The AQA A2 syllabus for this chapter is as follows.
Candidates should demonstrate an understanding of the following:

✔ the nature of morality (justice)
✔ knowledge is virtue
✔ the theory of the forms, metaphysical, epistemological, ethical and political implications

✔ knowledge, belief and ignorance (divided line), reasons for making the distinctions
✔ the objects of knowledge and belief
✔ the philosopher ruler and his qualities; his suitability to rule
✔ democracy, the philosopher's present status, similes of the ship and the beast
✔ the form of the good, its role and status, similes of the cave and the sun.

Essay questions will focus on the following problem areas:

✔ appearance and reality
✔ political rule
✔ knowledge and virtue.

I. APPEARANCE AND REALITY

The theory of the Forms; metaphysical implications

From sense experience to the Forms

In Book V (476f.) of *The Republic*, Plato argues that all objects we experience through our senses are particular things. We don't ever sense anything 'abstract', but always some individual thing or other. For example, we only ever see this particular beautiful thing or that particular beautiful thing, but we never see 'beauty'. But, obviously, more than one thing can be beautiful. Beauty is a property that more than one thing can have. So, Plato claims, if many different things can be beautiful, then there is something they share in common, namely, beauty. So there must be something which is 'beauty', even though we never experience beauty itself through our senses. This idea of a universal, a property that more than one thing can have, is a first approximation to the idea of a Form. The Form of Beauty manifests itself in all the different things, in all the different ways, we call 'beautiful'.

But why should we agree that just because many different things can be

See UNIVERSALS AND PARTICULARS, p. 178.

beautiful, there is some *thing* which is 'Beauty'? Because, Plato goes on to argue, Forms exist independently of particular things. All particular beautiful things could also be destroyed, yet that won't destroy Beauty itself. So Beauty must be a separate thing, existing in its own right. So, he concludes, particular things 'share' or 'participate' in the Forms, but these exist independently.

Plato gives another **argument** for this claim, relating to the nature of knowledge, which we will return to in the next section.

> Outline and illustrate Plato's argument for the existence of the Forms.

Metaphysics of the Forms

In arguing that Forms exist independently of the particular things that 'participate in' them, Plato constructed an original and controversial **metaphysics** (one that Aristotle, for example, rejected). Plato discusses several essential properties of the Forms:

1. Self-predication: the Form of Beauty is itself beautiful. But this is different from the way in which all other beautiful things are beautiful. Every other beautiful thing is beautiful because it 'participates in' the Form of Beauty; but the Form simply *is* beautiful. It is what it is in virtue of itself. This also provides an explanation of why things that participate in Beauty are beautiful: participating in Beauty makes a particular thing beautiful because the Form is itself beautiful. Beauty is 'transmitted' to particular things that participate in it.
2. Independence from particulars: it follows from (1) that each Form is its own essence. Because this is what a Form *is*, we can understand *why* it is that Forms (can) exist independently of whether any particular object participates in them. Because it is its own essence, it is what it is regardless of whether particulars participate in it; it is not essential to its existence that it is exemplified in particulars. A Form, therefore, also does not exist in time or space (either at a particular space/time or as distributed across all particulars exemplifying it).
3. Perfection: a Form is the perfect example of itself. Nothing can be more beautiful than the Form of Beauty, and there is no way in which the Form is not beautiful. This is sometimes suggested as an important difference between 'participating in' and 'being' Beauty: all particular things only approximate to the property of beauty, which is only perfectly possessed by the Form.

4. Permanence: Forms do not change. The Form of Beauty cannot become not beautiful, nor can it have ever been not beautiful. If it changed, then by the new Form of Beauty, the previous Form would not have been perfectly beautiful; by the previous Form, any change would be a change away from being beautiful. As this is impossible, Forms do not change.

5. Simplicity: Plato repeatedly says the Forms are 'one'. Each Form has just the one property of which it is the Form: the Form of beauty is only beautiful (and the only thing which is only beautiful). However, Plato also suggests that each Form is good, and that the Form of the Good is the Form of Forms (see THE FORM OF THE GOOD, p. 71). Furthermore, Plato attempts to give a full account of each Form that explains what it is. For example, in *The Republic*, Plato argues that justice is doing one's own job (433a). This equates justice to a particular set of properties, so it is not simple or just 'one'.

> Explain and illustrate *two* properties of the Forms.

In contrast to Forms, particulars are complex, changeable and imperfect. These important differences suggest that the way Forms and particulars *exist* is different, and that the existence of the Forms is superior: they *are* in a way that particulars are not. Forms exist independently, but particulars only exist through participating in the Forms. Plato speaks of 'two worlds': the world of Forms and that of particulars. But if they are so different, how can particulars 'share' or 'participate' in the Forms *at all*?

One suggestion is that the properties particulars have are 'copies' of the Forms. The beauty of this rose is a copy of the Form of Beauty. While particulars are material (made of matter), they can possess properties that are copies of the Forms. Unlike the Forms, a particular can lose its properties (e.g. its beauty) and even cease to exist as that particular (a rose can become ash). A particular is what it is in virtue of the properties it has (e.g. a rose, beautiful, etc.). But its properties are how it participates in the Forms. So a particular only exists by participating in the Forms.

> Outline the different types of existence Forms and particulars have.

Key points • • •

-   Plato argues that many particular objects can have the same property, for example, beauty. These properties can exist independently of the particular objects, as shown by the fact if we destroy all beautiful things, we haven't destroyed beauty.

- We don't detect these abstract properties through sense experience.
- These properties are Forms. Forms are self-predicating, exist independently of particular things (and therefore outside space and time), and are perfect, permanent and (perhaps) simple.
- The existence of Forms is of a different and superior kind to the existence of particulars. Particulars exist by participating in the Forms. One understanding of this is that particulars possess (for a time) copies of the Forms.

Knowledge, belief and ignorance

Reasons for making these distinctions

KNOWLEDGE AND THE FORMS

Plato's second argument for separating the Forms from the particular things we experience with the senses relates to the nature of knowledge. Particular things will always be both X – have some property, for example, beauty or largeness – and not-X, either at different times, or to different observers, or in different contexts. And so 'can we say that any of these many things *is*, any more than it *is not*, what anyone says it is?' (479b).

Plato argues that because particular things are what they are (beautiful, large, etc.) only *relatively* and *transiently*, there cannot be *knowledge* of them. Knowledge needs more permanence and certainty. He argues that we cannot know what is not true; knowledge is about truth, about what is. So if something both is and is not X, then we cannot *know* that it is X.

In contrast to particular beautiful things, the Form of Beauty is beautiful under all conditions, to all observers, at all times. The Form of Beauty is pure beauty; it alone is not both beautiful and not beautiful. It is therefore possible for us to acquire knowledge of the Forms. (As noted above, we can't *experience* Forms through our senses. We have this knowledge through reason.) Because we can have knowledge of the Forms, but not knowledge of particular objects of sense experience, the Forms must be separate from particular things.

> Outline Plato's argument that we can only have knowledge of the Forms.

THE OBJECTS OF KNOWLEDGE AND BELIEF

Plato's argument relies on making a distinction between knowledge (*epistémé*) and *doxa*, translated as 'belief' or 'opinion'. Just before giving the argument above, he argues knowledge and opinion are different 'faculties' for two reasons (477a–478e):

a) Knowledge is infallible – you cannot know what is false. Opinion, however, can be mistaken. So opinion cannot be knowledge.

b) Knowledge is only of what is real. We cannot have knowledge of what is not real or does not exist. Knowledge is 'about' what is real. By contrast, ignorance relates to what is not real, what does not exist, that is, 'nothing'. If you are completely ignorant of something, you don't think of it at all; if you don't understand it, you can't form an opinion about its reality. If there is something between what is real and what is not real (which Plato argues there are, that is, particular things, which are both X and not-X), then there must be something between knowledge and ignorance. We know from (a) that opinion is not knowledge; but opinion is obviously not ignorance either, because opinions are always 'about' something or other. And opinion does seem to be between complete ignorance and knowledge.

According to (a), knowledge and opinion must have different powers. According to (b), knowledge and opinion must have different objects (what is real versus what is between what is real and what is not real). Therefore that about which we have opinions cannot be the same thing as that about which we have knowledge. Plato argues that opinion relates to the world of the senses, knowledge to the world of the Forms. So Forms must exist separately from particular things.

1. **Explain and illustrate *three* features of knowledge which distinguish it from opinion.**
2. **Outline Plato's argument that the Forms are more real than the objects of sense experience.**

Key points • • •

- Plato argues that particular things are always both X and not-X, depending on context, observer, time and so on. So it cannot be said to *be* X rather than not-X. By contrast, the Form of X is always X.
- Knowledge is of what *is*. So if something is both X and not-X, we cannot have knowledge of it. But we can have knowledge of the Forms.
- Knowledge is different from opinion for two reasons. Knowledge is infallible, opinion is fallible. Knowledge is of what is real, ignorance is of what is not real, while opinion is of what is between what is real and what is not real.
- Forms are real, and so objects of knowledge, but particular things, being both X and not-X, are between what is real and what is not real, and so objects of opinion.

The similes of the Cave and the Divided Line

Plato's arguments mean that acquiring knowledge involves turning away from the world of the senses, which can only ever produce opinion, towards the Forms and the world of the intellect. He uses metaphors and analogies to help us understand his theory.

The Divided Line

We may divide the world into the realm of the 'sensible' – what we detect through our senses – and the realm of the 'intelligible' – what we discover using the intellect (see THE SIMILE OF THE SUN, p. 69). Opinion relates to the former, knowledge to the latter. As we saw above, our epistemic states can be divided into two, and aligned with what is real. We can think of these states as lying on a line (see *Plato's Republic*, p. 236 for a diagram), knowledge as one half, opinion as the other. Plato goes on to divide each half of the line again, making four divisions in total.

Opinion is divided into belief (*pistis*) and illusion or imagination (*eikasia*). Illusion, the lowest form of epistemic state, is characterised in Plato's discussion by shadows and reflections. These things, and our thoughts about them, are very changeable and unclear. But Plato means more than just physical shadows and reflections. He also means the sorts of second-hand, uninformed views that people hold, not finding out for themselves about the world, but just believing what they are told, for example, in the newspapers; and in the last book of the *Republic*, Plato implies that art and poetry fall under 'illusion' as well.

One step up, our common-sense views on the physical world, and on other matters such as morality, fall under 'belief'. In the *Timaeus*, Plato also includes the natural sciences under belief, since they deal with the changeable, physical world. Unlike 'illusion', belief is informed by a direct study of the world, and it is more stable and a little clearer. But it still takes the world as it appears for reality, so it isn't yet knowledge.

Knowledge also has two divisions, *dianoia*, which we can translate (in this context) as 'reasoning', and *noésis*, which we can translate as 'intelligence' or 'full understanding'. Both relate to the Forms, but *dianoia* relies on assumptions and imagination (images from the realm of the sensible) while *noésis* does not. A good example of *dianoia* is geometry. In studying triangles, for example, in proving that the three internal angles add up to 180°, students of geometry

> **Explain and illustrate the two divisions of 'opinion'.**

don't study the actual, imperfect triangles they draw; they create proofs using the idea (the Form) of a triangle. They

> make use of and argue about visible figures, though they are not really thinking about them, but about the originals which they resemble; it is *not* about the square or diagonal which they have drawn that they are arguing, but about the square itself or diagonal itself . . . The actual figures they draw or model . . . these they treat as images only, the real objects of their investigation being invisible except to the eye of reason. (510d)

And that is why *dianoia* relates to the realm of the intelligible, not the sensible. But this type of knowledge works with unproven hypotheses, for example, about different types of angle (obtuse, acute, right), and it uses images from the realm of the sensible to help its investigation.

Noésis is a 'purer', more perfect knowledge of the Forms, which doesn't use images and which treats the assumptions of mathematical reasoning *as assumptions*. We acquire this knowledge of the Forms, of the very first principles 'of everything' (511b), using *nous*. By engaging in dialectic – philosophical argument – we finally reach a vision or insight of the Forms directly, without relying on sensory images or assumptions. By seeking first principles, *nous* does away with the need for the 'hypotheses' that it takes for granted when using *dianoia* (*nous* can be said to include *dianoia*, but goes beyond it). When the first principle has been reached, *nous* can reason through the consequences to generate further knowledge, *noésis*, 'moving solely through Forms to Forms' (511c). When we know the Forms in this way, we understand what the objects of mathematical study, and all other Forms, truly are. This type of knowledge has the greatest clarity, and its objects (the Forms understood directly) have the greatest truth.

Plato has not yet told us exactly *how* we can gain direct knowledge of the Forms. We will return to this question below.

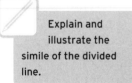

What does Plato mean by *dianoia*? How does it differ from 'belief'?

Explain and illustrate the simile of the divided line.

The Cave

The Divided Line informed us of the different *types* of epistemic state we can have, and what they relate to. The simile of the cave gives us a story about *moving* up the line, from illusion to intelligence, and the consequences of doing that.

In the cave, prisoners are chained to face a wall. Behind and above the prisoners, people carry objects along a road. Beyond the road, there is a fire. The fire casts shadows of the people onto the wall in front of the prisoners; so images is all the prisoners see. If a prisoner is freed, and forced to turn around, he will see the people on the road and then the fire. If he is then 'dragged' outside the cave – and he must be dragged, or drag himself, because the process will be painful as he won't be used to the light – he will experience reality as it is, not as it seems in the cave.

The simile of the cave

The cave	The world of the senses
Prisoners	People who believe 'second-hand'
Images on the wall	Illusion (*eikasia*)
The fire	The (physical) sun; more generally, what enables us to have sense experience
Seeing the fire and the people on the road	Belief (*pistis*)
Outside the cave	The intelligible world – reality
The prisoner dragged outside the cave	The philosopher
Objects outside the cave	The Forms
Looking at reflections of objects outside the cave	Reasoning (*dianoia*)
Looking at objects outside the cave	Intelligence (*noésis*)
The sun	The Form of the Good

What does the simile of the cave illustrate?

Going further: the difficult ascent

The simile of the cave is about gaining knowledge. But it is also the beginning of Plato's focused argument that only philosophers should rule. Plato uses the analogy to argue that for society to be a just society, the rulers must be educated as philosophers, so that they acquire knowledge of the Good, but then they must be forced 'back down' into the cave, to rule.

This is discussed further in THE PHILOSOPHER RULER'S SUITABILITY TO RULE, p. 85.

See also THE
PRESENT STATUS OF
PHILOSOPHER, p. 90.

Discuss Plato's
argument that
philosophers will not be
welcomed by people
generally.

Plato emphasises that moving from being a prisoner to eventually being able to look directly at the sun itself will be a difficult and painful process. This fact also explains why philosophers, having achieved knowledge of the Forms, will not want to be rulers; and why people (the prisoners) would not welcome philosophers or recognise that what they say is true. Philosophers, having finally got used to sunlight, will not want to go back into the cave, and will (at least at first) find it very difficult to see properly in the darkness. Meanwhile, people who can *only* see the images cast on the wall by the fire will believe that those images are reality, and dismiss claims about a 'world outside the cave' as madness. Since the philosopher has difficult seeing, they will also argue that 'the visit to the upper world had ruined his sight, and that the ascent was not even worth attempting' (517a).

Key points • • •

- The Divided Line divides into opinion, relating to the world of the senses, and knowledge, relating to the intelligible world.
- Opinion divides into 'illusion' (including second-hand views) and 'belief' (direct study of the physical world). Knowledge divides into 'reasoning', which uses assumptions and physical images to assist it, and 'intelligence', which is direct insight into the Forms.
- The simile of the cave (see table above) provides an analogical account of how we can gain knowledge and why it is difficult.

Epistemological implications of the theory of the Forms

How can we acquire knowledge of the Forms?

Those people in Plato's republic who eventually acquire knowledge of the Forms are those guardians who become philosophers (see ETHICAL IMPLICATIONS OF THE THEORY OF THE FORMS, p. 72). The guardians are trained in arithmetic, geometry and astronomy to bring them to *dianoia*. But to achieve *noésis*, the guardians must be additionally trained in dialectic, or philosophical argument.

Using the simile of the cave, Plato argues that to gain knowledge of the

Forms, a person must be 're-oriented', away from being concerned and caught up in the world of the senses: 'the mind as a whole must be turned away from the world of change until its eye can bear to look straight at reality, and at the brightest of all realities which is what we call the good' (518c). The final step in the philosophers' education is not so much about imparting knowledge, and but turning the mind towards the Forms. However, the question still remains *how* dialectic leads to an understanding of the Forms.

In fact, Plato doesn't say. One theory is that, as shown in Plato's *The Republic* and other dialogues, dialectic establishes both the existence and the nature of the Forms. Another relates to the fact that the Forms are 'one-over-many'. A Form is unitary and simple, but many particular things can participate in it. There is only one Form of Beauty, but many things can be beautiful. Mathematics helps us to understand the idea of 'one-over-many', and helps us understand how the 'one' is the real essence that the many share in. For example, mathematics establishes the necessary properties that all triangles must have in common. And all existing triangles are triangles because they share the essential properties of the Form of the Triangle. Dialectic helps us understand this more generally, or abstractly, because it searches for a unifying account of each and every thing. Dialectic asks 'What is justice?' or 'What is courage?', and so we think about the abstract ideas, the Forms, of Justice and Courage.

> For more on the importance of unity-over-difference, see THE FORM OF THE GOOD, p. 71.

Assessing Plato's theory of knowledge

KNOWLEDGE AND REALITY

Many philosophers reject Plato's claim that knowledge must match something 'real' in the sense that Plato means, namely, things that don't change and perfectly exemplify some property. Plato might be right that knowledge cannot change (*it* can't go from truth to falsehood), but that doesn't mean the *object* of knowledge can't change. For example, I can know (it seems) that a particular object of sense experience – this book – has a particular property, for example, it is a certain size, even though its size can change – if you burn it, for instance. What I know is that the book is this size *now* (at a specific moment in time), and this truth won't change even if the size of the book changes. Plato seems to have confused a property about knowledge with a property about the object of knowledge.

From this, we can see that even if knowledge and opinion are different faculties because knowledge is infallible and opinion is not, that doesn't mean

> [?] Can we have knowledge about things that change?

Questions about the relation between knowledge, justification and certainty are discussed in KNOWLEDGE, BELIEF AND JUSTIFICATION, p. 159.

Outline and illustrate Plato's conception of the relation between knowledge and the Forms.

that they have different objects. There is no need for the object (particular thing, Form) to match the epistemic state (opinion, knowledge). We can make the distinction in some other way, for example, knowledge is always *true* and *justified*, whereas opinion can be false and unjustified.

KNOWLEDGE AND CERTAINTY

Plato controversially sets the standard for knowledge very high, which has perhaps inspired sceptics ever since. Because knowledge by definition cannot be false, it seems he believes that knowledge must involve certainty. If we cannot be certain, we cannot know. Plato argues we can have certainty about the Forms, and so know them, because they are unchanging; but we cannot be certain of, or have knowledge of, particular objects of sense experience. But we can reject the claim that knowledge requires certainty, and argue instead that it requires only justification. In fact, Plato put forward an argument of this kind in the *Theaetetus*.

For further discussion, see ARE ALL CLAIMS ABOUT WHAT EXISTS ULTIMATELY GROUNDED IN AND JUSTIFIED BY SENSE EXPERIENCE?, pp. 17 and 29.

Going further: Plato's rationalism

Plato's conclusion is that only *nous* delivers knowledge of reality. However, we have seen that his account of how *nous* works, how we finally achieve *noésis*, is not clear. After all, unlike in the case of sense experience being caused by physical objects, Plato didn't claim that the Forms *cause* our knowledge of them. So what is the means by which *nous* knows the Forms?

Hume argues, indirectly, that there is no such thing as *nous*. There are only two sorts of knowledge: what reason can demonstrate (**a priori** knowledge), and what we confirm through the senses (**a posteriori** knowledge). But, Hume argues, reason can only demonstrate **analytic** truths. It can't provide 'insight', that is, it cannot prove **synthetic** truths. It is not surprising that Plato cannot give us a clear account of how *nous* works if there is no such thing!

Plato's best form of defence is probably attack. He could argue that unless we allow that there is such a thing as rational insight, we will fall into **scepticism**. For example, the first knowledge of the Forms we have is through mathematical reasoning. If he can argue successfully that this knowledge is based on reason, but isn't analytic, then his theory is supported – even if he can't then give us an account of *how* we have knowledge of the Forms. In other words, Plato can argue that we need rational insight to account for mathematical knowledge. If the argument from mathematical knowledge doesn't work, Plato could try the same argument in some other area of knowledge, for example, moral knowledge.

On moral insight, see How is knowledge of moral truth possible?, p. 227.

Key points • • •

- To acquire full knowledge of the Forms, we must be trained in philosophical argument. This is not about imparting information, but 'turning the mind' towards the Forms.
- Mathematics may help us acquire this knowledge, as it helps us understand the idea of 'one-over-many' and that the one abstract thing is the essence of the many particular things. Dialectic develops this knowledge by searching for a unifying account for each thing.
- Philosophers have objected that Plato's claim that the objects of knowledge must be 'certain' or unchanging for knowledge to be possible is based on a confusion. Opinion and knowledge can be about the same objects, although knowledge cannot be false, while opinion can. We may also object that Plato is wrong to think knowledge requires certainty.
- Plato's theory of *nous* remains unclear. However, if reason is incapable of insight, if it is limited to establishing analytic truths, then we may fall into scepticism.

Discuss Plato's claim that true knowledge is of the Forms.

II. KNOWLEDGE AND VIRTUE

The Form of the Good, its role and status; the simile of the Sun

The simile of the Sun and the Form of the Good

Plato introduces the simile of the sun after arguing (503–4) that philosophers must be prepared to undertake the difficult task of study he describes. Their studies will not be complete until they achieve the highest form of knowledge,

knowledge of the Form of the Good. It is from the Good that 'things that are just and so on derive their usefulness and value. . . . Is there any point in having all other forms of knowledge without that of the good, and so lacking knowledge about what is good and valuable?' (505a–b). And so Adeimantus and Glaucon ask Socrates what the Good is, and he responds with this simile.

The simile of the sun

The visible world	The intelligible world (the Forms)
The sun	The Form of the Good
The eye	The mind (reason)
Sight	Intelligence
To see	To know
Light	Truth
Growth	The being (reality) of the Forms

Unless there is light, our eyes cannot see, even though they have the power of sight, and objects that we can see exist and have colour and shape. It is only in the presence of light, which comes from the sun, that we can see. The sun also causes growth and, Plato says, it is a cause of sight. This last claim is difficult to understand; Plato thinks of sight as a power that the eye gets from the sun (the eye is 'sunlike', he says), as though eyes actually make what they see 'visible' in a way similar to how the sun makes things visible. However, the sun is not sight and it is not light; it is different from them, and because it is their cause, it is 'higher' than them.

The Form of the Good plays the same role in the intelligible world. We cannot come to know anything without the Form of the Good. Just as the sun is the source of light and the source of sight – together necessary to see anything – the Form of the Good 'gives the objects of knowledge [the Forms] their truth and the knower's mind the power of knowing' (508a). Both intelligence and truth have their source in the Form of the Good. And, just as the sun is the cause of growth, the Form of the Good is the source of the very being of knowable objects: 'The good therefore may be said to be the source not only of the intelligibility of the objects of knowledge, but also of their being and reality' (509b). And as we noted above, Plato says that everything derives its value from the Good (505b). Finally, just as the sun is not light nor sight nor growth, the Form of the Good is not intelligence nor truth nor the reality of the Forms, but 'beyond it, and superior to it in dignity and power' (509b).

Explain and illustrate the simile of the sun.

The Form of the Good

It is obvious from these remarks that the Good is not just one Form among others. But what *is* the Form of the Good? Socrates says he cannot say (506e), and offers the simile of the sun instead. We know that the Good is *not* intelligence, truth, knowledge or the reality of the Forms; and we know that it is the source of all these. Plato doesn't say any more, and we do not even know *how* the Good is the source for all of this. But we can speculate somewhat to fill out an account of what the Good is.

The Good is sometimes said to be the Form of the Forms. But we have listed at least five characteristics of all Forms (see THE THEORY OF THE FORMS, p. 58), and Goodness will not be all of these. The obvious characteristic of the Forms that is related to Goodness is perfection; Forms are purely and perfectly their own essence. By contrast, particular things fail to be completely their essence (hence their existence is inferior to the type of existence enjoyed by the Forms).

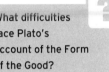

What difficulties face Plato's account of the Form of the Good?

> ## Going further: the Form of the Good and harmony
>
> But this doesn't solve the puzzle. If the Good is *just* each thing exhibiting its own essence, the Good would seem to be different in each case, since it is dependent on what a thing *is*. However, in accordance with the rest of his theory of the Forms, Plato assumes that the Good is the same thing in every case. One suggestion is that if the Good is *coherence* or *harmony* or *unity-over-difference*, this would make sense of a great deal of Plato's theory of the Forms, and so it is worth taking seriously:
>
> 1. Mathematics leads to knowledge of the Good as it is through mathematics that we understand the account of the one over the many.
> 2. The Good is superior to other Forms, not just another Form alongside others, since it is the unity or coherence of other Forms.
> 3. It is the Form of Forms, and other Forms owe their being to it, since they are good in being unities (of that which participates in them) and in being part of a unifying and coherent order.
> 4. Unity and harmony play a very important role in the ethics and politics

of *The Republic* – both the good state and the good soul are said to be harmonious.

This interpretation is also supported by a passage from the *Phaedo*, where Plato says 'that the truly good . . . binds and holds everything together' (99c).

How does this relate to the idea that the Good is each thing exhibiting its own essence? Plato repeatedly argues in *The Republic* that when each person plays their role in society, harmony is achieved. More generally, then, it seems he believes that when each thing exhibits its essence, harmony – the Good – is achieved.

However, Plato clearly thinks of the Good as not just a *property* that the Forms have, but a force from which reality emanates. If the Good is unity and harmony, it is also the first principle of everything – the standard by which everything is what it is, that has an existence and power all of its own.

> Discuss the view that the Form of the Good is unity or harmony.

Key points • • •

- Plato has Socrates say that he cannot say what the Form of the Good is. He offers the simile of the sun (see table above) to explain that the Good is the source of truth, intelligence, knowledge and the being of the Forms. As the cause of all this, it has an existence superior to that of the Forms 'in dignity and power'.
- If the Form of the Good is something like harmony or unity-over-difference, we can explain many aspects of Plato's theory, including one central idea of *The Republic*, that when each person in society or each part of the soul plays its proper role, exhibits its essence, the result is a good, harmonious society or a good, harmonious soul.

Ethical implications of the theory of the Forms

Plato clearly believes that there is MORAL TRUTH. We can have moral knowledge, knowledge of the Good. However, knowledge and the Good are more closely related to this.

See p. 213.

First, there is a close relation between reality (which is what knowledge is of) and goodness. The Forms are perfect and more real, whereas particular objects are imperfect, and derive their existence from the Forms. But the Forms in turn derive their being from the Form of the Good, which is the first principle of everything.

So, second, knowledge of what *is* is related to knowledge of what is *good*. To knowledge what something is is to understand its essence. Exemplifying its essence is what it is for that thing to be good. So if we understand something's essence, we understand what it is for it to be good (of its kind). This is a clear example of the way in which the Form of the Good is the source of knowledge.

Third, the Good and all the Forms do not change, which is why they can be known. Since the Good does not change, the good person will also not change. There is one absolute standard for being good. (Plato's account of the good person is discussed in THE NATURE OF MORALITY (JUSTICE), p. 74.)

> Outline and illustrate the relation between reality, the Forms and the Good in Plato.

'Turning the soul around'

In other works, Plato famously argues that virtue is knowledge: if you know what the good thing is, you will be good. We will discuss his claim that knowing the Form of the Good will make you good in more detail in THE PHILOSOPHER RULER AND HIS QUALITIES (p. 79). In this section, we will look at how coming to know what is good involves becoming virtuous.

During his discussion of THE SIMILE OF THE CAVE (p. 64), Plato says that the prisoner, when freed, must be turned around to face the fire and then the outside world. So, he infers,

> our argument indicates that the capacity for knowledge is innate in each man's mind, and that the organ by which he learns is like an eye which cannot be turned from darkness to light unless the whole body is turned; in the same way the mind as a whole must be turned away from the world of change until its eye can bear to look straight at reality, and at the brightest of all realities which is what we call the good. (518c)

The philosopher, Plato argues, will not be concerned with or distracted by things of this world, but only with the Forms, and, above all, with the Form of the Good. His *whole* mind must be turned around. He has to be this focused in order to acquire knowledge of the Good. But then, having achieved knowledge of the Good, what motivations could a philosopher have for not *being good* himself? The usual temptations won't be there, because as a philosopher, he is just not interested in money, fame and so on. He is only interested in the Good. So to know the Good is to be good.

However, the philosophical temperament necessary to acquire knowledge of the Forms is very rare (503b–d). So Plato's theory of the Forms, and the Form of the Good, means that most people will never achieve knowledge of what is good. This, of course, can be challenged. For example, Kant, while agreeing that ethical understanding depends on rationality, argues that everyone is sufficiently rational to understand the good. Christians would argue similarly that everyone has a conscience. To agree with this universal knowledge of the good, if we do not reject Plato's theory of the Forms altogether, we must reject his stringencies on what is required to acquire knowledge of them and produce a different story about the development or nature of reason.

Why does Plato think that coming to know the Good involves becoming virtuous?

See MORAL DECISIONS, p. 258.

Key points • • •

- Knowledge and the Good are closely related. What is real (which is the object of knowledge) also has more goodness than what is not real. To know what something is is to know its essence, which is also to know what it is for it to be good. We need to know what is Good in order to organise a good state. And what is Good, like knowledge, does not change.
- To come to have knowledge, the whole soul must be 'turned around', away from the world of the senses. The philosopher will become interested only in the Good, and so will not be tempted not to be good.

The nature of morality (justice)

For other conceptions of JUSTICE, see p. 104.

The official topic of *The Republic* is justice. Everything we have discussed so far is part of Plato's answer to the question 'What is justice?' The ancient Greek idea of justice – *dikaiosuné* – applied in the first instance to law-abiding behaviour, but with the sense of not wanting or taking more than one ought to. As with our notion of justice today, it primarily refers to external acts, but also marks a state of mind or desire. Plato built upon and deepened both aspects of the concept. His discussion, however, is not just about justice, but also about morality as a whole.

The challenge

The discussion begins with a challenge from the Sophist Thrasymachus, who argues, in essence, that might is right. Justice or morality, so-called, is nothing more than obeying the rules that those who are strong make and impose on others (the weak). Because the strong make the rules in their own self-interest, then 'justice' is simply what is in the interests of the strong.

Socrates, as Plato's mouthpiece, points out that these two definitions – obeying the laws and what is in the interests of the strong – are in tension with each other. What if the rulers mistakenly make laws that are *not* in their self-interest? Then is it just to obey the laws or to do what is actually in the interests of the strong (339d)? Given the challenge to our normal conception of justice, this is a quibbling objection, and Thrasymachus says as much. The essential idea is that rulers impose laws that are (mostly) in their self-interest, and that these laws determine what we would conventionally think of as 'morality'.

If this is all there is to morality, then our usual conception of morality is very mistaken. For instance, why should we be moral? It only serves the self-interest of the strong! Thrasymachus draws precisely this conclusion: there is no reason for people who can get away with being immoral (unjust) not to be immoral. '[T]he just man always comes off worse than the unjust' (343d). Since they are making the rules, the strong are in a very good position not to punished for disregarding the interests of others while pursuing one's own. Acting unjustly is always in one's own interest, while acting justly is always in the interest of the strong (344a–c).

Socrates replies that this cannot be so. Justice is a virtue, and virtues help us live well. So it is the just that are happy. But Thrasymachus replies that injustice is the virtue, not justice (348e). Thrasymachus has, of course, specified that the unjust man must 'get away with it' to be happy; and he has noted that the law-makers get away with it – for who can challenge them? He would be quite willing to agree that for the weak, the ruled (most of us!), to act unjustly (not in accordance with the laws) would bring unhappiness, since we won't get away with it. But this is only to advocate prudence, not justice per se. There's no value in being just.

We may doubt now, in a democracy, whether rulers really can 'get away with it'. If so, there is some point to being a just ruler, that is, making genuinely impartial laws that give each their due. But Thrasymachus would reply that it would be better to aim to get whatever one can, compromising where necessary (the corruption of politicians comes to mind). Where the rulers are not 'the

Explain and illustrate Thrasymachus' definition of justice.

See Unit 1.3 Why should I be moral?, p. 87.

What are the implications of Thrasymachus' definition of justice?

strong' and the people are not 'the weak', then 'justice' (at best) will be nothing more than social compromise, between groups or individuals with competing interests.

Some notable philosophers, including David Hume and John Rawls, have endorsed forms of this, but placed a positive spin on it by adding an initial premise of equality between people. Social compromise, when it secures law and order, and thereby enables citizens to go about their lives without fear of others, is very valuable. Hume argues that understood like this, and given our need for society, it is easy to see how justice is in our self-interest. Rawls defines justice as that set of principles for designing the structure of society that everyone would agree upon, on completely self-interested grounds, if they did not know what position in society they occupied. As justice serves self-interest, broadly understood, in the conditions of rough equality, justice will make us happy.

An Enquiry Concerning the Principles of Morals, § 3

A Theory of Justice, pp. 11f.

Compare and contrast the relation between justice and self-interest according to Thrasymachus and Hume/Rawls.

Justice as a virtue

But Hume and Rawls are still open to the objection which Glaucon, who wants Socrates to be right, presses: no one would act justly if they could get away with cheating (359b). He tells the story of the ring of Gyges, a ring that made Gyges invisible whenever he put it on. Gyges is able to steal, murder and seduce without detection. Who wouldn't use the ring that way? Again, although justice may be of benefit to society (your acting justly benefits me and vice-versa), justice offers no benefit to the just person. It is better to be narrowly self-interested and prudent.

Plato's argument against this claim forms a substantial part of *The Republic*. The claim is, intuitively, plausible. If justice conflicts with self-interest, then we do better to act unjustly when we can. Plato needs to show that acting justly – not because you avoid punishment, not because people then treat you well, but for its own sake – is in one's self-interest. In developing the argument this way, it seems that Plato makes an assumption to the effect that unless justice can be shown to appeal to the possessor, it has no 'real' value. Underlying this questionable assumption is the thought, common in ancient Greece, that virtues must, by definition, contribute to the happiness (or good life) of the virtuous person. If justice does not, it is not a virtue; and if it is not a virtue, on what grounds can we recommend it?

In fact, Plato had already put the point in these terms in an earlier response to Thrasymachus. After Thrasymachus argues that injustice is a virtue, Socrates responds that it cannot be. One reason he gives is that the unjust cannot co-operate for their own good. They must at least act justly towards each other. Justice enables people to cooperate more effectively. But he also says (352a) that injustice leads to *internal* conflicts in the individual, so he becomes less capable of acting well even on his own.

It is plausible that justice between people enables their cooperation – and so justice is a 'social' virtue. But why injustice should lead to internal conflict is very unclear when Plato first says it. But it forms the essence of his response to Glaucon. Glaucon presses the point that justice is not thought to benefit its possessor. It is thought to be a cost to the individual, though a benefit to society. Any benefits the just man receives are through reputation and social rewards.

Critically discuss Glaucon's description of justice.

Going further: Plato's answer

This is the point (367e) at which the syllabus leaves the discussion. Plato's attempt to demonstrate that injustice leads to inner conflict and that justice leads to inner harmony is very lengthy. However, it is worth discussing briefly, both for the sake of a better understanding of Plato's view of what justice is, and in light of the many connections to his arguments regarding the virtue of philosophers.

See THE PHILOSOPHER RULER AND HIS QUALITIES, p. 79.

To show that justice makes its possessor happy, we must first under-stand what justice 'in the soul' is. In this exploration, Plato develops and extends the idea that justice involves not wanting more than one's share. He argues, from the common experience of internal conflict between what we want and what we believe is good, that there are different parts of the soul (436b). Desires are distinct from the 'spirited' part of the soul, and both are distinct again from reason. When reason rules the soul, the person is wise; when the spirited part has its appropriate strength, the person is courageous; when all parts of the soul collude in the rule of reason, in particular with desires being restrained and not unruly, the person is temperate; and thus justice consists in each part functioning as it should, being contented to make its contribution and accepting the contributions of the others (444d). Plato talks of 'friendship' between the parts of the soul (589a). Justice, then, brings wisdom, courage and temperance with it.

This leads to the conclusion that the just person will be happy, the unjust person unhappy. A life without inner conflict is a happier life than one in which parts of the soul fight each other for supremacy. In Books VIII and IX (543–80), Plato describes the life of people with various desires in charge (money: encourages licentiousness; satisfaction: with no overall desire in charge, unnecessary desires grow in strength; lust: uncontrollable desires grow in strength, the soul becomes fearful and full of regret). When ruled by a desire or by spirit, how we conceive of what is good is skewed, and we lack a true conception of the good. Rule by desires, therefore, cannot provide happiness as securely as rule by reason. It is essential for Plato's argument that only the rule of reason can secure the absence of inner conflict, and the pursuit of the truly good, that is the mark of true happiness.

Objections

These charges all depend on his view that desires are incapable of self-regulation, that they are, in an important way, 'blind'. This description seems to fit bodily desires and obsessions (e.g. with money) better than others (e.g. those involved in friendship and compassion). One line of response Plato can make is that desires, as desires, do not involve consideration for the person as a *whole*; however, this is precisely the kind of reflection that reason provides (442c).

But we can object that the kind of reason needed is prudential, not moral. An immoral person needs to think about how to act in their self-interest, and this can involve reasoning. But why think this reasoning will lead them to act morally? Plato assumes that having reason in control automatically means acting morally. This is because he believes that if we reason well, we will realise that acting morally is truly good. But that still doesn't mean it is in my self-interest. As the argument stands, a *prudential* immoral person could be happiest.

Plato can respond that with reason in charge, desire is appropriately directed or restrained, so the person will not be greedy or narrowly self-interested; spirit has strength and is likewise appropriately directed, so the person will not flinch from the difficulty of pursuing justice. Finally, reason recognises moral demands, and so, if it rules, directing desires and spirit rightly, the person will produce moral behaviour.

Outline and illustrate Plato's argument that the just man will be happy.

Does Plato succeed in showing that justice leads to greater happiness for the individual than injustice?

Key points • • •

- Thrasymachus argues that justice is nothing other than obeying the laws that the strong create in their self-interest.
- This gives us no reason to be moral, if we can get away with being immoral. Injustice, not justice, is a virtue.
- Hume and Rawls argue that justice is a social virtue. Because we all have an interest in society running smoothly, justice is in our self-interest. Plato likewise argues that justice enables cooperation, while injustice leads to conflict.
- Plato adds that injustice leads to inner conflict – but does not say why until much later.
- His answer is that there are parts of the soul, each with its own task. When reason rules the soul, desires are restrained and spirit provides courage. When the parts treat each other justly – each content to play their role – the person has inner harmony.
- Injustice in the soul occurs when reason is not in charge. Desires, without the guidance of reason, have no concern for the soul as a whole, and so lead to conflict.
- We can object that what is needed is not justice, but prudence.

The philosopher ruler and his qualities; knowledge is virtue

The philosopher's love of truth

When Plato has Socrates first introduce the idea that the rulers of the republic should be philosophers, Socrates does so with hesitation and in recognition that the view is somewhat ridiculous. But in fact, it was not so unheard of as might be thought; there were a number of city-states in which men of learning were the rulers. More to the point, however, is Glaucon's warning (473e) that Socrates would be punished for the proposal. Not long before, Athens, under the rule of Socrates' associates, had lost a war with Sparta, and very anti-democratic reprisals had followed which Athenians still resented. Plato therefore takes pains to distinguish the true philosopher from people who would pretend to be philosophers and have a false confidence in their wisdom.

A philosopher, by definition, loves wisdom. Plato conceives this as a form of real love; and as love, must love the whole of the object – so philosophers

See THE PHILOSOPHER RULER'S SUITABILITY TO RULE, p. 85.

love all learning. Glaucon suggests that many people love new experiences, and seek out new sights and sounds. But that isn't enough to be a philosopher. People who love sights and sounds don't have a genuine passion for truth and knowledge. They rest content with discovering and experiencing the many particulars; they don't search for the reality behind the appearances.

Plato then begins his discussion of the difference between particulars and the Forms, to explain his claim that experiences of particulars is not knowledge, but opinion, and to think otherwise is to mistake appearances for reality. Only someone who has a passion for knowledge, who will not rest with experiences of particular things, can be called a philosopher. Only philosophers, he argues, can see the distinction between opinion and knowledge, because only they keep searching to attain true knowledge – of the Forms. Lovers of sights and sounds have only opinions, not knowledge (480a); whereas philosophers see that what others think of as 'knowledge' is just opinion, what others think of as 'reality' is just appearance.

See THE THEORY OF THE FORMS, p. 58 and KNOWLEDGE, BELIEF AND IGNORANCE, p. 61.

How are true philosophers different from other people, according to Plato?

The other qualities of philosophers

Plato does not pretend that philosophy is easy. It is, in fact, very difficult, and the 'true philosopher', someone who loves all learning, is very rare. This is in part because we 'can't expect anyone to have much love for anything which he does with pain and difficulty and little success' (486c). So there are a number of traits that philosophers need to have 'naturally', to equip them with the ability and temperament to love learning. A philosopher needs an ability to learn, a good memory, a sense of proportion, a breadth of vision and a quick mind.

Knowledge of the Good and virtue

We will see (THE PHILOSOPHER RULER'S SUITABILITY TO RULE, p. 85) that Plato's argument that philosophers should rule is that they have both the knowledge and virtue required of a good ruler. He argues that the height of their knowledge, 'the greatest study' (503e), is knowledge of the Form of the Good. They are 'experts' on the Good, so they know what makes human life go well.

But are they also virtuous? The love of wisdom is a passion that subdues one's other passions: 'if a man's desires set strongly in one direction, they are correspondingly less strong in other directions' (485d). A person who desires knowledge will take pleasure in the things of the mind, so physical pleasures won't be tempting. He will be self-controlled, not greedy about money, broad-minded and generous, and not fear death, and so be courageous. Anyone who doesn't show these traits, Plato suggests, can be dismissed as not a true philosopher.

So philosophers are virtuous because of their *love* of wisdom. Does their knowledge of the Good, when they achieve it, also help? Plato argues that it does, because you cannot stop someone 'assimilating himself to anything with which he enjoys dealing . . . So the philosopher whose dealings are with the divine order himself acquires the characteristics of order and divinity so far as a man may' (500d). So a philosopher who knows the Form of the Good will make himself good, that is, virtuous.

See also the discussion of the virtuous person in THE NATURE OF MORALITY, p. 77.

Explain Plato's argument that philosophers will be virtuous.

Assessing Plato's argument

Plato's argument that *knowledge* of the Good (not just love of wisdom) will help make philosophers virtuous is left very vague. The idea of 'assimilation' is unclear. Suppose being good is a matter of character: How is it that knowledge could transform someone in the way Plato suggests? Suppose being good is a matter of acting morally: Plato never says the very abstract, theoretical knowledge of the Good could be applied to everyday life and help someone make the right decisions about what to do.

One possible response draws on the connection between THE FORM OF THE GOOD (p. 71) and harmony, and the idea, discussed in THE NATURE OF MORALITY (p. 77), that the good (virtuous) soul is in a state of harmony. Perhaps Plato means to suggest that knowledge of the Good enables the philosopher to recognise and implement this harmony in his soul. But this suggestion still doesn't tell us how this is possible.

If we turn from knowing what is good to wanting to be good, we face similar problems. Why should knowledge of the Good on its own create the *motive* to be good oneself or to bring about goodness in society?

Plato is highly sensitive to the possibility that the guardians may become corrupt. He remarks that a philosophical nature is particularly prone to corruption (491d, 495a), that philosophical examination of moral principles is dangerous for young people, as they are not yet stable enough to cope with uncertainty (539d), that the rulers must be highly vigilant and weed out any guardian being trained to rule who shows signs of corruption.

Could knowledge of the Form of the Good help someone be good in everyday life?

'Plato's claim that philosophers assimilate themselves to the Form of the Good tells us nothing about how knowledge produces virtue.' Discuss.

See POLITICAL IMPLICATIONS OF THE THEORY OF THE FORMS, p. 83.

See THE PRESENT STATUS OF PHILOSOPHERS, p. 90.

Assess the connection Plato makes between knowledge and virtue.

Does this suggest that studying philosophy is not particularly effective at encouraging virtue? Plato could respond that in people who become corrupt the passion for wisdom is not sufficiently strong to reign in their other passions. But this begs the question: does the acquisition of philosophical knowledge help this self-restraint?

Going further: producing virtue

In Plato's perfect state, philosopher rulers are selected from the wider ruling class, called 'guardians'. Only the best guardians are selected for training as rulers. In his description of this selection process, Plato suggests that those guardians who *don't* show the character traits that he lists as marks of the 'true philosopher' can be judged not to be philosophers. The guardians who are selected to be educated as philosophers must not only show a natural ability for doing philosophy, but must also have stable, reliable characters (503c).

However, Plato's argument that love of wisdom produces virtue cannot only appeal to those cases that confirm the claim. Common sense and experience would suggest that philosophers are just as lacking in virtue as anyone else. Plato's argument, that love of wisdom suppresses physical pleasures, the desire for money and fear of death, lacks empirical backing. His own argument that philosophers are particularly prone to corruption seems to assert that love of wisdom is not enough. In a democratic society, the naturally gifted philosopher will be influenced by popular praise and blame and become corrupt. So a love of wisdom only produces virtue in a society that supports and encourages a love of wisdom. Becoming virtuous depends on being trained and encouraged to be virtuous, not just on philosophy.

Key points • • •

- Only philosophers love learning, and will enquire deeply enough into reality to acquire knowledge of the Forms.
- Because of their love of learning, philosophers are not susceptible to any

vices, but are self-controlled, just, broad-minded, generous and courageous. Furthermore, because of their knowledge of the Good, they will become like the Good.

- Plato never says how it is that knowledge of the Good will make a philosopher virtuous. In fact, he seems concerned that philosophers may even be particularly prone to corruption.
- One suggestion is that the Good is harmony, and the virtuous person has a harmonious soul. But it is still unclear how abstract knowledge of harmony could bring about psychological harmony.
- Plato's remarks about training and selecting philosophers to rule suggests that becoming virtuous is not about knowledge, but about the formation of character.

III. POLITICAL RULE

Political implications of the theory of the Forms

Plato's argument in *The Republic* as a whole develops an account of what the perfect state would be like. How would it be organised? In the next section, we will see that Plato argues that in the perfect state, philosophers must be rulers. This is the main political implication of the theory of the Forms. But to understand it, we need to understand the type of state that they are to rule.

The perfect state has, by definition, all the virtues. Plato accepts the idea that the four main virtues are wisdom, courage, temperance or moderation (being self-controlled about pleasure) and justice. If he can describe a state that has all these, he will have described the perfect state (427e).

The state has its origins in the fact that human beings are not individually self-sufficient, so we naturally group together. First, Plato assumes that we are also naturally disposed to different types of task, we each perform well in different areas of life (370b). This needs to be respected in a successful city, so we need a division of labour. Second, to defend itself against attack, or to launch attacks in order to become more prosperous, the city will need professional soldiers, 'guardians'. By the division of labour, these will be separate people from the farmers and traders. Good soldiers need to be both fierce in battle and gentle towards their fellow citizens. Third, the city's leaders, who should be selected from the guardians, will obviously need intelligence, and they will need to know what is good for the state as a whole. So they will be educated as philosophers, so that they come to have knowledge of the Good.

Plato then argues this state is perfect. Wisdom lies with the rulers – their knowledge benefits the whole city; courage lies with the guardians; temperance, involving traits of restraint and self-control, Plato understands as the acceptance of the social order – all parts of society are in agreement about who should rule (432a). Justice must, by elimination, be the remaining organising principle of the city (427e); and this is the assumption that got us started – that everyone does their own job, making their own distinctive contribution to the good of the whole, functioning as they should, and not interfering with the functions of the others (433a). So a perfectly good society is one in which everyone fulfils their task, which creates harmony.

We should note three points about this account. First, philosophers again turn out to be fully virtuous. They have wisdom, courage (because they were first trained as guardians), temperance and justice, as they accept their role as rulers and preserve the just organisation of society.

Second, in the case of understanding how a good state is organised, we need to understand the role that each person in the state needs to play. A good citizen is someone who plays their role in the good state. So we need knowledge of the Good in order to know how to organise a state (this argument is discussed in the next section).

Third, the Good and all the Forms do not change, which is why they can be known. Since the Good does not change, the state will also not change. There is one absolute standard for being good, and the purpose of politics is to bring about the good state. Once this is achieved, the purpose of politics is just to maintain that state, not to allow it to keep changing.

> **Outline Plato's account of the perfect state and why he claims it is perfect.**

> **Discuss how the theory of the Forms, in particular Plato's account of the Form of the Good, relates to Plato's political theory.**

Key points • • •

- Plato argues that we each perform best in different areas of life. So the best state needs a division of labour. One division will be those who protect and expand it, soldiers, 'guardians'. Rulers will also need intelligence.
- The perfect state has all four virtues: wisdom, courage, temperance and justice. Wisdom lies with the philosopher rulers, courage with the guardians, temperance with all citizens, accepting the social order, and justice with everyone doing their proper task.
- Philosophers also have all four virtues as individuals.

- Knowledge of the Good is needed to know how to organise the state; and because the Forms don't change, the standard of the good state remains the same.

The philosopher ruler's suitability to rule

Plato's discussion of knowledge – how and why it is different from belief, his theory of the Forms, his similes of the Sun, the Cave and the Divided Line – is part of a discussion about the education of selected guardians to become the rulers in his perfect city. Just before these discussions, Plato says that the only way the republic can come about is if philosophers become rulers or rulers become philosophers (473d). And after discussing the simile of the Cave, he says that 'a necessary consequence of what we have said [is] that society will never be properly governed . . . by the uneducated, who have no knowledge of the truth' (518c).

The ultimate purpose of a philosophical education, in the perfect republic, is to gain knowledge of the Form of the Good. Until this has been achieved, the education is not complete. The rest of knowledge has little point, especially if you are a ruler, unless you know what is useful, valuable and good.

The argument and challenge in outline

Pappas identifies Plato's central argument for philosopher rulers as follows:

Plato's The Republic, p. 111

1. The good state is possible if and only if virtuous and expert rule by its leaders is possible (484d).
2. Virtuous and expert rule is possible if and only if the rulers are philosophers.

As (1) is relatively uncontentious, the rest of the argument offers support to (2):

3. Philosophers, as lovers (*philo-*) of wisdom (*sophia*), love every kind of learning (475c).
4. No one else loves every kind of learning (475c–480a).
5. The love of every kind of learning produces knowledge of ethical matters.
6. The love of every kind of learning produces virtue (485d).

7. Therefore, the love of every kind of learning makes one a virtuous and expert ruler.
8. Therefore, since only philosophers love every kind of learning, only philosophers can be virtuous and expert rulers.

Each of these premises, (3)–(6), need further defence, and this is the challenge Plato faces in making his case for the philosopher ruler. We have seen the arguments for these premises already, in THE PHILOSOPHER RULER AND HIS QUALITIES (p. 79). First, philosophers and only philosophers love every kind of learning. Second, *knowledge of the Good is needed for good rule*; without it, a ruler does not know what is useful or valuable (505a), so he cannot think coherently about the good plan for human life. But only philosophers have knowledge of the Form of the Good. This defends premise (5) and links – if only in an abstract way – philosophers' knowledge and the justification of their rule. Third, Plato defends (6) when he argues that the love of wisdom and knowledge of the Good produce virtue (p. 81). So philosophers are both experts (they have the knowledge necessary to rule) and virtuous (7). Only philosophers have both the necessary knowledge and virtue; so only philosophers should rule (8).

So Plato's argument that philosophers should be rulers depends on his arguments about how knowledge and virtue are linked. We have, however, seen the objection (p. 81) that it is not certain that studying philosophy and the Forms will make someone virtuous. A second objection is to the alleged link between knowledge and virtue in ruling.

> **Why does Plato claim that the good state is only possible if ruled by philosophers?**

Knowledge of the Good

Is Plato right when he argues that philosophers have the knowledge necessary to rule? His argument is that they have knowledge of the Form of the Good, and knowledge of what is good is necessary to rule. But is knowledge of the Form of the Good knowledge that helps with the *practical* matter of politics? We do not have an account of how knowledge of the Form of the Good could help with practical affairs of state, which requires knowledge of how a good life for people should be organised. When Plato talks about the Form of the Good, it is as the source of all knowledge, truth and reality. How is *this* helpful in knowing how to make good practical decisions?

Plato is not unaware of the gap between the knowledge philosophers gain and the practical world. It emerges in the simile of the cave; when the philosopher returns to the cave, he is initially blinded, unable to make things out. But Plato suggests this will only last a while, and argues that his knowledge will be useful in the cave. But he never argues *how*, except to say that knowledge never loses its power (519a).

In our earlier discussion of knowledge and virtue (p. 81), we suggested the solution that the Form of the Good is related to harmony, and in the previous section, we saw that the virtuous state is in harmony. Knowledge of the Good, then, may enable the philosopher to bring about harmony in the state. But it is unclear how abstract knowledge of the Good could help the philosopher to achieve this harmony, or even recognise it in real life.

> **Assess Plato's claim that only philosophers possess the knowledge needed to rule well.**

Do philosophers want to rule?

A further objection to Plato's theory is suggested by a particular claim of Plato's which indicates that, even in the perfect republic, philosophers may not be completely virtuous. At the end of his discussion of the simile of the cave, he remarks that 'a necessary consequence of what we have said [is] that society will never be properly governed . . . by those who are allowed to spend all their lives in purely intellectual pursuits . . . the intellectuals will take no practical action of their own accord' (518c). Plato says philosophers would prefer to spend their time engaged in philosophy – after all, they love wisdom! However, they will rule because the law compels them to, and it is for the greater good of the city. Compelling them to rule is not an injustice, since justice relates to the harmony of the whole.

If true philosophers are virtuous, why won't they be *motivated* to rule, that is, to fulfil their role in society, which is what justice consists in? Doesn't virtue involve being motivated by the demands of justice, not just submitting to them? Yet perfectly virtuous philosophers lack this motivation independently of the requirements of law.

> **Is philosophers' love of wisdom in conflict with their sense of justice?**

Going further: knowing justice and acting justly

What is the source of virtue in philosopher rulers? In Plato's account of the education of the rulers, there is much discussion of how to best form the characters of the guardians to make them virtuous. We could argue that justice is a character trait, and so the motive to be just – if not the knowledge of what justice is – is created through this early education. This childhood training creates the right balance between the parts of the soul, so that, when the person comes to know what justice is, his spirit and desires are ready to obey his reason. All the guardians, the ones who don't become philosophers as well as the ones who do, are motivated to act justly, that is, to do their particular task in the city. There is no need, then, for a separate account of why philosophers would be motivated to be just. Knowledge of justice (which only philosophers have) plays no special role.

However, if being motivated to be just is not the result of knowing what is just, Plato can still argue that knowing what is just is still necessary for the virtue of justice. To be just, one must also know what justice is. And to know what justice is, Plato has argued, involves knowing the Form of Justice. So philosophy is relevant for knowing what justice is. This isn't the same as being motivated to act justly, so philosophy doesn't produce virtue in the sense of motivating someone to be just. But Plato can argue that it is only philosopher rulers who have *both* qualities, the motivation from their training as guardians and knowledge from their training as philosophers. So he can still argue that it is only philosopher rulers who should rule the republic.

'To know justice is not to act justly.' Discuss with reference to Plato's *Republic*.

Going further: doing two things at once

Plato argues that justice consists in each person doing their own specialist thing (433-434a). But there is an obvious tension with suggesting that philosophers should rule, that is, that this involves one person being both philosopher and ruler, thereby doing *two* things. If philosophy and ruling are two separate tasks, according to Plato's principle of justice, they should be done by different people.

Plato must argue that these two things *necessarily* go together, and we have seen his argument that philosophy is necessary for knowledge of the Good, and knowledge of the Good is necessary for expert and virtuous rule.

However, we have questioned whether Plato succeeds in connecting the very abstract knowledge of the Good to political expertise. Furthermore, the education that philosophers receive must be sufficient for them to become good rulers; but we have also questioned whether there are really *two* types of education necessary – one to make them virtuous and practical (their education as guardians) and another to make them philosophers. This again suggests that ruling and doing philosophy are separate tasks. Finally, the fact that philosophers are reluctant to rule and would prefer to do philosophy also suggests philosophy and ruling are two distinct tasks.

Assess Plato's claim that philosophers should rule.

Key points • • •

- Philosophers' expertise in ruling comes from their knowledge of the Form of the Good; without it, a ruler does not know what is good or useful. Furthermore, the love of learning and knowledge of the Good makes philosophers virtuous.
- Plato has not shown how knowledge of the Form of the Good helps with the practical matter of politics. One possible response is that knowledge of the Good (as harmony) helps the philosopher recognise and bring about harmony in the state. But this is unclear.
- And even when fully educated, philosophers may not be motivated to rule, even though it is just.
- We can argue that the motivations required in a virtuous person may, instead, be produced by upbringing. Plato can respond that what is also required for virtue is knowledge. Because philosophy is required for this knowledge, philosophy is required for (full) virtue.
- Plato faces the objection that doing philosophy and ruling are two separate tasks, and so according to his principle of justice, should be done by separate people.

The present status of philosophers; the simile of the Ship

Plato is very aware that his suggestion that philosophers become rulers will not be taken seriously by most people. Adeimantus objects that most people who study philosophy too much are 'very odd birds, not to say thoroughly vicious', and that even the best of them become completely useless to society (487d). This, then, is their present status – and it does not recommend making them rulers! Plato responds to the charge of uselessness by the simile of the ship, and then tackles the issue of corruption in philosophers. His argument is that the present status of philosophers says a lot about society, but little about true philosophers.

The simile of the Ship

The simile of the ship (488a–489a) is intended to describe politics in a democracy. Politicians each seek to gain power, and they admire those able to help them do so. They do not know, and are not concerned with, what is good for the state – which is what politics *should* be about. They even argue that such knowledge is impossible. A philosopher, who spends time acquiring this knowledge, will be little help with how to influence other politicians. Unless his expertise is recognised, he will appear to be completely useless. But this is not because there is anything wrong with philosophers, but because politicians fail to *make use* of them. If philosophers seem useless, this is the fault of politicians, not philosophers.

> **?** How does the simile of the ship explain the apparent uselessness of philosophers?

The simile of the ship

The ship	The state (under a democracy)
The captain	The current ruler
The crew	Politicians
The art of navigation	The art of politics (what is good for a state)
The true navigator	The philosopher

Are philosophers vicious?

What about Adeimantus' objection that philosophers are vicious (not virtuous)? Plato's response is again to blame the *situation*, and not a training in philosophy. Plato argues that the natural qualities of the philosopher, in the wrong situation, become a source of corruption. Someone who is gifted will be sought after by other people, who will try to influence him. He will be 'swamped by the flood of popular praise and blame, and carried away with the stream till he finds himself agreeing with popular ideas of what is admirable or disgraceful' (492c). His training in philosophy, to seek the truth, will not be strong enough to withstand the constant pressure to do what people want. In fact, rather than sticking with philosophy, being gifted, he will become a leader (494b) and, winning popular praise, will become full of pride.

So, Plato argues, people with the ability to become true philosophers are corrupted by bad society, and end up agreeing with popular opinion. They may abandon philosophy to become politicians, and the corruption of their character will go further. In this situation, who actually practises philosophy? 'Second-rate interlopers', says Plato, people who are not naturally gifted nor love truth, who will be corrupt because they do not have the natural character to be virtuous.

If there are any true philosophers left in such a political state, they will be very few, and only remain true philosophers through some sort of miracle. And seeing the situation, 'they will live quietly and keep to themselves' (496d).

> How does society lead to the corruption of philosophers?

> Assess Plato's claim that the low status of philosophers in society reflects badly on society.

Key points • • •

- The simile of the ship describes, by analogy, the nature of politics in a democracy.
- It explains why philosophers will look as though they are useless, namely, because no one recognises the knowledge they have.
- Philosophers also seem not virtuous because most truly talented philosophers will be corrupted by society, while most of those who continue to do philosophy lack the talent and the love of truth, so they lack the natural character to be virtuous. Any remaining true philosophers will live quietly and not be noticed.

Democracy, simile of the Beast

Plato's simile of the ship (above) not only provides an account of the status of philosophers, but also accuses democracy of being a form of government which is disordered and harmful: the crew turn the voyage into a 'drunken pleasure-cruise'. Democracy is rule by ignorance, because politicians have no knowledge of what is good for the state as a whole; and rule by ignorance will be bad for everyone. Later in *The Republic*, Plato also argues that democracy is based on freedom of a particular kind – the freedom to do what you want. But if you don't know what is good for you, then this kind of freedom is actually harmful (555b–558c). Politicians who just do what they want harm the whole state.

> Discuss the simile of the ship as a criticism of democracy.

The simile of the Beast

Plato illustrates both these points, about ignorance and the difference between what we like and what is good for us, in his simile of the beast. He compares people in a democracy to a powerful beast, and rulers in a democracy to the animal's tamer. The rulers govern by giving people what they want, and pretend that this is a science, something to be taught and studied by politicians. But it completely misses the question of what is *good*. The tamer (politicians) 'would not really know which of the creature's tastes and desires was admirable or shameful, good or bad, right or wrong; he would simply use the terms on the basis of its reactions, calling what pleased it good, what annoyed it bad' (494b–c).

> Outline and illustrate the argument Plato expresses in the simile of the beast.

The simile of the beast

The large and powerful animal	The people
The animal's tamer	Politicians in a democracy
Knowledge of the animal's moods and desires	Political 'science' as democrats think of it

Plato's argument against democracy

In his two similes, and his arguments about why philosophers should be rulers, Plato makes a number of assumptions about the nature of politics.

First, he assumes that politics should be an attempt to bring about the common good. For example, a ship has a purpose for its journey. This purpose, and so what is good for the ship, is independent of the desires of the crew. Again, what an animal wants does not tell us whether what it wants is good. Likewise, what is good for the state as a whole is not determined by what people want.

Second, Plato thinks there can be knowledge about what this common good is and how to bring it about – the true navigator must study the art of navigation. Likewise, rulers need to have knowledge of the Good in order to rule well.

If Plato is right, why think that democracy is going to be good rule? People are so often incompetent and irrational. In general elections, the way people vote is swayed by all sorts of irrational or personal desires and prejudices; thinking hard about what might be good for everyone is very rare, despite the fact that there is information available. How many people even bother to read party manifestos, let alone research the possible impact of different policies? Politicians – rulers – need many skills, knowledge and insightful judgement; they need to understand economics, psychology and motivation; they need intelligence, an enormous capacity for work, a good memory, attention to detail and excellent people skills. (Many of these skills Plato has argued are the natural talents of the true philosopher.) We won't get the best politicians by letting incompetent and irrational people vote. We'll get people who are willing to give the people what they want. But people don't *know* much about what is good for society as a whole. And people *care* most – perhaps only – about getting the things *they* want for *themselves*. So if politicians give people what they want, they won't be governing by what is best for the state.

Plato argues that only philosophy gives us true and proper knowledge of what is good. It is philosophers, then, who ought to rule. Legitimacy is determined by what is good and just, and not by consent. Since people don't know what is good for them, consent can only tell us what they want, not what is good. Choice, freedom, consent in the absence of knowing what is truly good is not valuable. What is valuable is to choose what is good. And to choose what is good, we first need to know what the true good is. Philosopher rulers will organise society so that it is truly good.

Why does Plato object to democracy?

Assessing Plato's argument

Winston Churchill said that 'Democracy is the worst form of Government except all those other forms that have been tried from time to time.' So even if there is some truth in what Plato says, he might not be right to reject democracy. It is worth noting that Plato argues in favour of democracy in his more practical political work, *The Statesman*. There he says that democracy is resistant to the tyranny that could come about if rulers become corrupt.

ARE PHILOSOPHER RULERS A GOOD IDEA?

In THE PHILOSOPHER RULER AND HIS QUALITIES (p. 79) and THE PHILOSOPHER RULER'S SUITABILITY TO RULE (p. 85), we discussed two objections to the assumptions Plato makes in criticising democracy. First, does studying philosophy provide you with the other qualities, especially virtue, that a good ruler needs? Given that even Plato is worried that philosophers will be corrupted, avoiding tyranny is a good reason to adopt democracy. Second, does knowledge of the Form of the Good really give you the practical knowledge you need to make good political decisions? Even if democracy is, as Plato claims, rule by ignorance, this is not a powerful criticism unless it is possible for there to be rule by knowledge.

KNOWLEDGE OF THE GOOD

We may take this point further, and question whether there is such a thing as knowledge of the Good. In saying that there is, Plato argues that there is moral truth. But there are many philosophical arguments against this claim. If there is no moral truth, there is no knowledge of what is good. But then democracy is not rule by ignorance: ignorance requires there to be some knowledge that the person doesn't have; but if there is no knowledge of what is good, no one can be said to be ignorant of it.

See THE DENIAL OF MORAL TRUTH, p. 233.

WHAT IS THE GOOD?

Plato's criticism of democracy is that it gives people what they want, but not what is good. But according to utilitarianism, what is good is what makes people happy, understood either as pleasure or as what people want. So knowledge of what is good for society *just is* knowledge of what people want (or what gives them pleasure). A utilitarian would argue that, in Plato's simile of the beast, politicians are right to think that their study of what pleases the people is a study of what is good for society. If there isn't a distinction between what is good and what pleases people, Plato's arguments against democracy don't work.

See VARIATIONS ON HAPPINESS, p. 252.

There are two responses to this objection. First, it is only as strong as the claim that utilitarianism is right, and there are many objections to utilitarianism. Second, even if it is true that what is good is what makes people happy, this doesn't mean we should give people what *they think they want*. People often *don't know* what makes them happy, and they tend to care more about *short-term* happiness. If people get it wrong about what will make them happy in the long term, we shouldn't ask them about what is good for society. Democracy will still not produce a good society. We need rulers who know about true, long-term happiness – this is the knowledge of the Good that is necessary.

Assess Plato's claim that there can be knowledge of the Good, and this is distinct from knowledge of what people want.

Going further: is politics only about the common good?

Even if Plato is right about there being a distinction between what is good and what people want, we can argue that there are *other values* that (only) a democracy embodies, values that would be lost in Plato's ideal republic. In other words, there are some good things a democracy has that other types of society do not.

First, we may object to Plato saying that the only freedom in a democracy is getting what you want. There is also the freedom of 'self-rule'. While Plato might be right that it is valuable to choose what is good, John Stuart Mill argues that it is valuable simply to be able to live as you choose. Autonomy is essential, he argues, to human well-being, and a life in which someone else makes all the decisions for you is not a good life. In politics, this means that the people should have a say in the decisions about how to live. Being told how to live by those who know best – even if they do know best! – is not as good as being able to make the decisions oneself. Democracy is collective autonomy.

See INDIVIDUALITY, FREEDOM AND HAPPINESS, p. 125.

Second, Mill also argues that having this responsibility will make for better citizens, people's rational and moral senses are developed. Plato is interested in a just society, one in which everyone respects the law and fulfils their own role. But he doesn't say how the people should be educated so that they are happy to do this; he only talks about the education of the guardians. Mill argues that democracy is the best way to create citizens who understand and care about what is right.

See THE DEVELOPMENT OF THE INDIVIDUAL, p. 133.

Third, Mill argues that democracy expresses a sense of collective identity, of 'being in it together'. This is good in itself. Human beings are social animals, as Plato recognises. It is part of a good human life to be able to identify with the society in which one lives, it is bad if one feels alienated.

On Representative Government, Ch. 3.

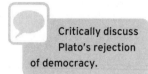

Critically discuss Plato's rejection of democracy.

Again, Plato implies that everyone will feel part of the just society, happy to play their role. Mill argues that this is much more likely if everyone has a say in how society is run. Otherwise, they won't feel that they, as individuals, are expressing themselves. Plato isn't concerned with self-expression, only with what is good. We can argue that identifying with society through self-expression is a good thing, and only a democracy can have it.

Key points • • •

- The simile of the beast illustrates Plato's claims that politicians in a democracy are ignorant of what is good, confusing it with what people want.
- Plato assumes that politics is just about realising the common good, and that there can be knowledge of what is good. He has argued that philosophers have this knowledge. All three assumptions can be challenged.
- Using his two similes, Plato argues that people in a democracy do not vote on the basis of what they think is good for society, and even if they did, they rarely have this knowledge. So they elect politicians who will give them what they want, not what is good for society. Plato's assumption that what is good is different from what people want is challenged by utilitarianism.
- John Stuart Mill argues that democracy realises many values that non-democratic states do not, including collective autonomy or self-rule, citizens who understand and care about what is right, and a sense of collective identity.

MILL *ON LIBERTY*

In this chapter, we examine Mill's text in the light of three key issues: his views on democracy; his defence of the freedom of the individual; and the importance of individual development. A fourth section examines the application of Mill's principles. Students should be able to explain Mill's views clearly and accurately and critically evaluate his arguments and objections to them. They should also be able to make connections between his theories and other views on the same topics discussed elsewhere in the syllabus.

All quotations and page references come from the AQA recommended edition from Penguin Classics (ISBN 0-14-043207-8).

SYLLABUS CHECKLIST ✔

The AQA A2 syllabus for this chapter is as follows.
Candidates should demonstrate an understanding of the following:

✔ the kind of liberty with which Mill is concerned
✔ liberty and the state
✔ the power of the state
✔ development of democracy and inherent dangers

- ✔ the role of civil convention and the pressure of public opinion; tyranny of the majority
- ✔ the Harm Principle; what is harm? harm and offence, negative freedom
- ✔ the arguments in support of freedom of thought and expression, and freedom of action
- ✔ exceptions and their justification
- ✔ the importance of truth, the importance of variety
- ✔ the development of the individual
- ✔ whether liberty is intrinsically or instrumentally valuable
- ✔ the applications of Mill's principles.

Essay questions will focus on the following problem areas:

- ✔ freedom of the individual
- ✔ individual development
- ✔ democracy.

I. DEMOCRACY

Development of democracy and inherent dangers

In the first few pages of *On Liberty*, Mill discusses how the nature of society and government has changed over time, and how these changes have altered people's understanding of liberty. We can pick out four stages in the development of society towards democracy.

Liberty and the state

The first stage follows a struggle between people (the ruled) and government (the rulers). When the rulers do not answer to the ruled, the danger is that they will rule in a way that suits their own interests, and not the interests of the ruled. Liberty is therefore understood as 'protection against the tyranny of the political rulers' (59). Liberty involves limiting the power of the government, by recognising certain political rights or, later on, by having a constitution that divides political power, for example, separating the legislature (which makes laws) and executive (which enforces them) or balancing power between a leader (emperor, monarch, president) and a group (senate, assembly, parliament). Liberty in this structure is not liberty of the *individual*, but of the ruled collectively.

In the second stage, democracy emerges. The ruled elect the rulers for a fixed period of time, and therefore can vote them *out* of power. The interests of the rulers are therefore, theoretically, identical to the interests of the ruled. This is a further step towards making sure that the rulers will not abuse their power. Liberty is equivalent to self-government – the people rule themselves (through voting).

In the third stage, first present in the United States, it is recognised that even in a democracy there is a division between rulers and ruled. Everyone is ruled, but the *majority* are the rulers. And the majority may well abuse the power they have over the minority. In a simple democracy, the government, expressing the will of the majority, can make whatever laws it wants, laws which may not be in the interests of a minority. The TYRANNY OF THE MAJORITY (p. 101) is an inherent danger of democracy. Liberty is now not only self-government, but also involves limiting the power of the government, for example, by rights that establish limits on what laws the government can pass.

However, Mill thinks that society has entered a fourth stage of development, one in which even these legal restrictions cannot ensure the liberty of the individual. The power of the *state* is restricted by the political rights recognised in stage three. However, the power of *society* can also be expressed through 'prevailing opinion and feeling' (63) in such a way as to impose on everyone the majority's views on how to live. With the development of mass communications, such as newspapers – and, after Mill's time, radio, TV and the internet – 'popular opinion' has acquired a power it didn't have previously. So just as we need restrictions of the power of the state, so 'There is a limit to the legitimate interference of collective opinion with individual independence' (63).

> Explain the meaning of 'liberty' in each of Mill's four stages of social development.

The power of the state

With each development of society, the power of the state changes. At first, rulers had an absolute power over the ruled, because there was no politically recognised means by which the ruled could resist. The power of the state protected them against external enemies and against being exploited or oppressed by other people within society (59). These two kinds of protection, then, are the first purpose of political power. But power enables the rulers also to exploit or oppress the ruled. So in the first stage of development, the power to protect remains, but the power to exploit is restricted.

In the second stage, democracy, the power of the rulers is no longer their own power, but is 'lent' to them by the people. The power of 'the people' is borrowed and used by the rulers, for as long as they are not elected out of power. Power can now have a different purpose, namely, to *express the will of the people*, to aim towards whatever social goals they want.

The third stage, like the first stage, doesn't change the nature of power, but seeks to restrict it. The majority are in the same absolute position as the rulers were before the first stage placed restrictions on them. So the third stage creates more restrictions on that power, to protect the minority from the majority.

The fourth stage, however, sees both a further development in power and calls for a further restriction. The nature of the power of 'popular opinion', and how the power of the state should be exercised to deal with the problem, are discussed in the next section.

While Mill is concerned with limiting the power of the state, he is not an anarchist, that is, he does not object to the state having power per se. 'All that makes existence valuable to anyone depends on the enforcement of restraints upon the actions of other people' (63–4). For this reason, and because 'everyone who receives the protection of society owes a return for the benefit' (141), the state may legitimately enforce laws.

See ANARCHISM: THE STATE AS OPPRESSOR, p. 78.

Explain how the nature of power changes as society develops.

Key points • • •

- Mill identifies four stages of development in society and corresponding notions of liberty and power:

  1. The rulers are restricted by political rights or the separation of powers. Liberty is liberty of the people, not the individual. Power protects people against enemies and other individuals in society.
  2. Democracy identifies the interests of rulers and ruled. Liberty is self-government. Power now expresses the will of the people.

3. The third stage recognises the majority have power over the minority and introduces rights that limits the laws the rulers can pass. Liberty is protection of the individual from the laws a majority would pass. The power of the majority is restricted.
4. The majority can exercise power through popular opinion. In the fourth stage, liberty restricts this power.

Tyranny of the majority

There are two ways that the majority can exercise its power over minorities. First, it can do so through democratic government, unless this is restricted. For example, a democratic government could pass a law forbidding people to criticise a particular form of religious belief, or, alternatively, a law forbidding them to practise it, if that is what the majority of people in society wanted. In Mill's day, public declarations of atheism were very controversial; in our day, discussion of Islam has taken centre stage.

Limitations on the power of democratic government are therefore very important. But Mill is particularly concerned about the second way the majority can exercise power:

> Society can and does execute its own mandates: and if it issues wrong mandates instead of right, or any mandates at all in things with which it ought not to meddle, it practises a social tyranny more formidable than many kinds of political oppression, since, though not usually upheld by such extreme penalties, it leaves fewer means of escape, penetrating much more deeply into the details of life, and enslaving the soul itself . . . there needs protection . . . against the tyranny of the prevailing opinion and feeling, against the tendency of society to impose . . . its own ideas and practices as rules of conduct on those who dissent from them . . . and compel all characters to fashion themselves upon the model of its own. (63)

Everyone thinks that their way of doing things, what they like and dislike, should be the standard for everyone else. Think of the disapproval of other religious practices, of other cultures' traditions, of homosexuality, of standards of music and taste; think how quick people are to 'take offence' and think 'something should be done about it', and how such attitudes are communicated in the tabloid press. This disapproval, when socially expressed and endorsed, affects how people think and what they do; they are not free to think, feel and experiment with life as they please.

People's liberty is interfered with by these social expressions of disapproval and calls for legal or social penalties, such as legally banning a distasteful activity or discriminating against people who practise it. Such 'public' feelings tend to reflect prejudice and the self-interest of particular groups.

The tyranny of the majority is also the effect of 'custom' (64). When a particular way of acting is customary, we lose the sense that there could be reasonable alternatives. Customary ways of acting are just 'what we do' – we don't feel we need to understand why or give reasons and fall back on preferences, prejudices and emotions in our responses to others.

As an example, Mill gives the relationship between men and women (65). In his day, it was simply 'understood' that women were not equal to men. Women's place was in the home, looking after the children. This made it very difficult for women who didn't want to live like this – if they seriously tried to live 'as men', they faced strong public censure. Much of this 'understanding' has now, fortunately, been left behind.

> Explain the 'tyranny of the majority'. Why is Mill so concerned by it?

Social opinion and morality

Mill argues that social opinion and feeling can legitimately seek to impose *certain* ways of behaving on others, namely, the rules of morality:

> The acts of an individual may be hurtful to others or wanting in due consideration for their welfare, without going to the length of violating any of their constituted rights. The offender may then be justly punished by opinion, though not by law. (141)

This legitimate use of the power of social opinion requires an understanding of what the rules of morality are. Mill argues that morality concerns *only* those actions that *affect other people adversely*. As we will see throughout this chapter, merely being offended by what someone does or what they think does not amount to being harmed by them. Public opinion should not be used to prevent people from living however they choose, however offensive their choices seem to the majority, as long as they don't actually harm anyone else.

> See especially THE HARM PRINCIPLE, p. 107, and HARM AND OFFENCE, p. 138.

But can we distinguish between disapproving of what someone does on grounds of distaste and on the grounds of morality? Mill responds:

It makes a vast difference both in our feelings and in our conduct towards [someone] whether he displeases us in things in which we think we have a right to control him or in things in which we know that we have not. (146)

If someone merely offends us, we may dislike him, but we won't get angry or resentful or try to make his life uncomfortable.

But many moral codes and societies have not accepted the distinction, at least in the way Mill suggests. Contemporary Western society seems to think that not being offended *is* something that we have a moral right to, as though being offended is a kind of harm.

Why does Mill allow public opinion to enforce morality but not offence?

Social opinion and the power of the state

The power of the state is limited by society's adopting and accepting certain rights. How is the power of public opinion to be limited? First, society can enforce these limits itself; it simply becomes 'accepted' that no one tries to create an oppressive public opinion or to use public opinion oppressively. Second, the power of the state could be used to punish abuses of public opinion. If individuals have rights to live however they like, and believe whatever they like, as long as they don't harm others, then those rights should be enforced by the state, if possible. If it could be demonstrated that some act violated those rights, for example, by attempting – through publications, demonstrations, campaigns and so on – to create a public atmosphere in which some group can no longer live as a normal part of the community, then those acts would be punishable by law. The difficulty with creating and enforcing such a law is that it could wrongly interfere with the freedom to express one's opinion.

Explain and discuss Mill's concern with the inherent dangers of democracy.

Key points • • •

- The majority can exercise power over the minority through law and/or public opinion. By public opinion, it can impose a model for how to live that alters people's characters.
- Such tyranny can be an effect of custom or of people imposing their preferences on others.
- Mill allows that public opinion can legitimately impose moral rules, but

argues that morality relates only to actions that harm others. Public opinion should therefore not penalise people who merely offend others.

- However, many moral codes do not recognise the distinction between immorality and offence.

II. FREEDOM OF THE INDIVIDUAL (I)

The kind of liberty with which Mill is concerned

> 'Liberty' and 'freedom' are used interchangeably.

In our discussion of the DEVELOPMENT OF DEMOCRACY (p. 98), we noted that what a society understands by liberty changes in different societies. At first, it is liberty of community from political oppression; then it is self-government and democracy; and then it involves recognising certain individual rights, preventing the oppression of the minority (whoever the minority are in any particular dispute). This is not enough to secure the full liberty of the individual, who can be enslaved by oppressive public opinion as much as by oppressive laws.

Mill opens Chapter 1 by saying that 'The subject of this essay is . . . the nature and limits of the power which can be legitimately exercised by society over the individual' (59). This illustrates that his concern is not with the conditions of a 'free society', but with the conditions of a society in which individuals can be free; and not just 'politically' free, but free to develop as individuals. And so he is concerned with *all* the ways in which society exercises power over individuals.

Negative freedom

See NEGATIVE AND POSITIVE FREEDOM, p. 83.

Mill understands the freedom of individuals in terms of the absence of power being exercised over them, free from interference or limitation by society. This interprets freedom in 'negative' terms – it is what someone is free from, what is absent, that makes them free.

Negative freedom is contrasted with 'positive' freedom. Positive freedom is understood in terms of having and exercising certain capacities or abilities. At the social level, this is usually understood in terms of self-rule; 'the people' are free if they rule themselves. Individual positive freedom involves the ability (and resources) to make choices and live as one thinks best.

It is possible for someone to be free from interference by society without having positive freedom. For instance, they may be very weak-willed, so never do what they think it is best to do. Or again, they may lack a sufficiently strong sense of morality, and so cannot form a proper conception of how they should live. Or again, they can lack their *own* conception of how to live because their ability to make judgements for themselves has never developed. Or again, they may have all these abilities, but so severely lack any resources, such as money, that their choice over how to live is significantly restricted.

Therefore, there is potentially a gap between what is required for individuals to be free in the negative sense and what is required if they are to be free in the positive sense. Furthermore, in the negative sense of freedom, everyone who lives in a society that does not interfere with their choices of how to live is equally free. In the positive sense, even in such a society, someone becomes *more free* as their ability to make choices according to their own conception of a 'good life' develops.

While Mill's concern is to establish negative freedom, his *aim* by doing this is to allow individuals to develop as individuals. He famously says that 'the only freedom which deserves the name is that of pursuing our own good in our own way' (72). Given that *pursuing* our own good in our own way is the exercise of a capacity, this sounds as though Mill endorses a theory of positive freedom. But the context shows that this is a misinterpretation. Mill is not discussing the development of capacities that enable an individual to form, choose and act in accordance with a conception of their own good. Both before and after the remark, Mill is concerned with the social exercise of power over the individual. There is no question of whether the individual can, if left alone, pursue their own good. The issue is that they should be left alone to do so. Mill maintains a distinction between (negative) freedom and individual development.

> Explain the difference between negative and positive freedom.

The liberties involved

Mill argues that a person should have freedom in 'that portion of a person's life and conduct which affects only himself or, if it also affects others, only with their free, voluntary, and undeceived consent and participation' (71). Of course, we can respond that nothing affects *only* oneself, but Mill clarifies his claim – the person should have freedom if his actions affect only himself 'directly and in the first instance'; it may affect others through him.

> This is discussed in SELF-REGARDING ACTIONS, p. 112.

Mill identifies three types of freedom that this covers. First, freedom of thought, 'absolute freedom of opinion and sentiment on all subjects' (71); and as a derivative of this, freedom of expression. Second, freedom of 'tastes and pursuits', to act however we choose as long as we don't harm others. Third, as a consequence of this, freedom to unite with others for whatever purpose we agree to, as long as we don't harm others and we haven't been deceived into agreement.

Mill is not concerned in *On Liberty* to give a comprehensive account of the liberties that should be respected in a democracy. For instance, there is no mention of freedom to vote or stand for political office; and in THE APPLICATIONS OF MILL'S PRINCIPLES (p. 144), we will see that economic 'freedoms' – the freedom to buy or sell whatever one wants – involve social acts that may legitimately be restricted according to Mill. He is concerned with a much narrower – but no less important – sphere of liberty, that area of life over which society should have *no* say at all.

> Explain Mill's concept of 'liberty'.

Key points • • •

- Mill is concerned with the freedom of the individual from constraints imposed by society, either through political means or public opinion.
- His conception of freedom is 'negative', that is, someone is free if they are not constrained.
- Negative freedom contrasts with positive freedom, which interprets freedom in terms of being able to exercise certain abilities, such as live as one thinks best. Someone can be free in the negative sense without being free in the positive sense.
- While Mill's concern is with individual development, he distinguishes between this and freedom, so he does not adopt a positive theory of freedom.
- He argues that we should be free in whatever does not affect others, or affects them only with their consent. He names freedom of thought (and expression), freedom of action and freedom to unite with others, as freedoms we should have as long we don't harm others.

The Harm Principle

The principle

Mill argues for 'one very simple principle, as entitled to govern absolutely the dealings of society with the individual in the way of compulsion and control' (68). That principle is that 'The only purpose for which power can be rightfully exercised over any member of a civilized community, against his will, is to prevent harm to others. His own good, either physical or moral, is not a sufficient warrant' (68). We may still argue, entreat and remonstrate with people who seem bent on doing themselves harm (as we judge it) or are simply acting in a way we don't like. But we should not use either the law or moral condemnation to alter their behaviour, unless they are causing harm to other people.

However, the Harm Principle does not apply universally, that is, there are circumstances in which society is justified in interfering with what someone is doing even when it doesn't harm others. First, it does not apply when the person is a child. Until someone 'comes of age' – whenever society agrees that is – they may need protection against their own actions. Second, it does not apply in 'backward' societies, for example, when society is barbaric. Both children and 'backward' societies have not yet developed to a point at which force can be replaced by 'free and equal discussion'. Once they have, however, the Harm Principle applies. At this point, to help them to realise what is good for them, we need only talk with them. If they disagree with us, it is not because they cannot understand or respond rationally to what we say, but simply because they disagree with us about what is good for them, and we should not override them with force.

> Explain why the Harm Principle doesn't apply to children.

Developing the details

There are several key points about the principle that we need to look at before looking at objections to it.

First, many defenders of freedom today would, at this point, appeal to rights. We have a *right* to freedom, and that is the last word on the matter. But Mill rejects this move, because he is a utilitarian. Instead, he argues that observing the Harm Principle will be better for a society and the people in it than not observing it. However, many philosophers have thought that his utilitarianism conflicts with his statement that the Harm Principle should govern the exercise of power *absolutely*.

See Act Utilitarianism, p. 248.

This conflict is discussed in TRUTH, LIBERTY AND UTILITARIANISM, p. 118, DO UTILITY AND FREEDOM CONFLICT?, p. 128, and WHETHER LIBERTY IS INTRINSICALLY OR INSTRUMENTALLY VALUABLE, p. 135.

See THE APPLICATIONS OF MILL'S PRINCIPLES, p. 146.

Mill recognises this potential conflict, so he says immediately that his appeal to utility is to 'utility in the largest sense, grounded on the permanent interests of man as a progressive being' (70). Precisely what Mill means by 'the permanent interests of man as a progressive being' we will leave for when we discuss the **arguments** he gives for thinking that the Harm Principle promotes them (pp. 115 and 124).

Second, the Harm Principle states a *necessary* but not a *sufficient* condition for interfering with people's actions, that is, an action *must* cause harm if it is to be prohibited, but this might not be a good enough reason on its own to prohibit it. And this is where the appeal to utility comes in a second time. Society should only interfere with the harmful action, for example, outlaw it or declare it immoral, if doing so is in the general interest. There are some actions which harm others, but which should nevertheless be allowed. For example, economic competition leads to some people losing money or going out of business. This is clearly a harm to them, and if someone caused someone else to lose money by fraud, we would rightly condemn their action. But allowing economic competition, Mill thought, contributes more to the general welfare of society than preventing it. So society should only interfere with someone's actions when they cause harm *and* when interfering with them is in the general interest.

Third, the Harm Principle applies to 'inactions' or 'omissions' as well as actions that harm others. Society can be justified in exercising power over people to get them to perform actions which, if they failed to do, would harm others. More simply, society can compel people to help others under certain circumstances, for example, in defending society against attack, in rescuing someone in danger of dying (e.g. saving someone from drowning), in giving evidence in court. Not doing these things can be declared illegal or immoral.

Of course, compelling people to act is only justified if their inaction will cause harm; and, once again, if compelling them will lead to better consequences than not compelling them. It may well be that compulsion is not the right response, because it would be better if people are left free to choose, or because compulsion will produce other bad consequences.

[?]   In what way does Mill connect the Harm Principle to utilitarianism?

Going further: harm and morality

In *Utilitarianism*, Mill argues that many of the rules of morality are based on the principle of utility. Actions that are not in the general interest we condemn as immoral, while those that are in the general interest are morally permissible. Yet, as in the case of economic competition, we allow some actions that harm other people. Our sense of what is moral has picked up on the distinction between harmful actions we should not allow (because allowing them is not in the general interest) and harmful actions we should allow (because allowing them is in the general interest).

And so morality can help us decide whether or not to allow a harmful action. If the action harms others but is not judged immoral, then we shouldn't interfere with it. It is only those actions that harm others and are also immoral that society should seek to exercise control over.

Now, of course, according to some moral views, there are actions that are immoral that do *not* harm others. Many traditional rules of sexual morality are like this, for example, rules against masturbation, consensual sex outside marriage and homosexuality. And there is a class of 'self-regarding vices' – traits of character that harm only the person themselves, such as being rash, conceited, self-indulgent, weak-willed, that some people think are moral vices for which people may be punished.

Because they do not harm others, Mill argues that such actions should not be thought of as immoral and publicly condemned. Individually, we may nevertheless think them foolish, offensive or degrading. But this is a different matter.

See ACT
UTILITARIANISM, p. 248.

> Discuss the relation between morality and the Harm Principle.

Five questions

Several issues about the Harm Principle have been debated ever since Mill first published *On Liberty*.

1. What does Mill mean by 'harm'?
2. Is it possible to draw a distinction between harm and other forms of adverse effect, such as offence?
3. Is it possible to draw a distinction between actions that affect others and ones that only affect the agent 'directly and in the first instance'?

4. Is Mill right to claim that the Harm Principle is supported by utility, or do they conflict in particular cases?
5. Is the Harm Principle right – should we never interfere with what someone does if it does not harm other people?

We will discuss the first three questions in turn over the next few sections, but a longer discussion of the second question will be deferred to HARM AND OFFENCE (p. 138). The fourth and fifth questions are discussed as objections in TRUTH, LIBERTY AND UTILITARIANISM (p. 118) and DO UTILITY AND FREEDOM CONFLICT? (p. 128) and we will return to them again in THE APPLICATIONS OF MILL'S PRINCIPLES (p. 144).

What is harm?

Unfortunately, Mill never explicitly defines what he means by harm, and he uses various different words at different times (hurt, damage, loss, injury). However, Chapter 4 (141–6) contains a discussion, which if we read very carefully, provides a sense of what harm includes and what it excludes.

The Harm Principle declares that the only purpose for which power can be legitimately exercised by society over individuals is to prevent harm. Society may use the law to regulate conduct that consists in 'injuring the interests of one another, or rather certain interests which, either by express legal provision or tacit understanding, ought to be considered as rights' (141). And society may use public opinion to regulate conduct that 'may be hurtful to others or wanting in due consideration for their welfare, without going to the length of violating any of their constituted rights' (141). In general, 'As soon as any part of a person's conduct affects prejudicially the interests of others, society has jurisdiction over it' (141).

So, in the first instance, harming someone means injuring their interests. Some of these interests are so important that they ought to be protected by law as rights. Utility dictates that it is the 'permanent interests of man as a progressive being' (70) that should be protected in this way. However, many actions that we recognise as immoral harm other interests, not protected as rights.

The nature of these interests is discussed in THE DEVELOPMENT OF THE INDIVIDUAL, p. 133.

Harm, rights and immorality

So is whatever violates other people's rights and whatever is immoral harmful? This *would* be right if society had the *correct* conception of rights and morality. However, society is often wrong about which rights individuals should have, and again, on many moral views, some actions are immoral because they are offensive or because they harm the agent, not other people. Mill wants to use his idea of 'harm' to *change* what society believes about rights and morality. Nevertheless, our usual ideas about rights and morality are a good start. 'Harm' to our interests clearly involves physical injury and death, being confined against our will, having our reputation hurt, financial loss, being coerced through deception or threat, having promises and contracts broken, being unfairly treated, and even, Mill adds, other people's selfish refusal to defend us from injury by a third party (145).

> Explain the relation between harm, interests and rights.

Harm and offence

Mill wants to distinguish between harm and having our *feelings* adversely affected (143f.). We may come to any number of negative opinions about what someone does or believes, even when their actions or beliefs don't affect our interests. In these cases, Mill argues, the person has not harmed us, even though we may feel that they are offensive, foolish or depraved.

But why don't these feelings, for example, feeling offended, count as harm? Surely there is such a thing as 'mental' harm, just as there is physical harm. Mill agrees that there is such a thing as mental harm, in the sense that an individual's development – and the mental capacities involved in development – can be injured. However, this is quite different from and much more serious than having our feelings hurt. Furthermore, being harmed usually involves being harmed against our will. By contrast, if we find someone offensive, *we can avoid them*, and then continue our lives with no damage done.

But what about being offended by the *mere existence* of people who do or believe something offensive to us? Isn't their doing or believing what they do a kind of harm to me, since I am offended, even if I never have to deal with them personally? Ultimately, Mill's response is that my 'interest' in not being offended is simply not the same as my interests in not being physically damaged, deceived, imprisoned and so on. His argument that offence should not count as a harm regulated by the Harm Principle is part of his argument in favour of freedom of thought, expression and action. We need to look at those arguments first, and return to this issue in Harm and offence (p. 138).

> Discuss the difference between being offended and having one's interests adversely affected.

Harm and the Harm Principle

What is harmful per se is broader than what should be interfered with, in two ways. First, according to the Harm Principle, we should not forcibly stop someone from harming themselves. This doesn't mean that we ignore them or don't care about them, just that we don't coerce them.

Second, as discussed above (p. 108), some conduct that does harm others should not be prevented, for example, economic competition, because interfering with such actions will do more damage than good. So 'actions that cause harm' is a much wider class of actions than 'actions that should be regulated by society'.

Again, this only applies to adults capable of listening to arguments, not children.

What does Mill mean by 'harm'?

Self-regarding actions v. harm to others

Self-regarding actions, which should not be interfered with in any way, are ones that affect only the agent 'directly and in the first instance' (71). They may still affect other people, but if they do so, they will affect other people 'through' the agent. Mill discusses the issue at length in Chapter 4 (146–50).

He first raises an objection: 'No person is an entirely isolated being' (146), so it is impossible that anything someone does that harms themselves will not also harm people close to them. For example, if they harm themselves financially, this will impact on people they support. Or if they harm their minds or bodies, they may become dependent on others. If nothing else, their behaviour will harm others 'by example'.

Mill accepts that harming oneself can cause harm to others and even, in a small way, society as a whole. But *he does not say that all self-harm should be allowed*.

Three restrictions

First, if by harming themselves, someone harms other people by violating their rights, then we can interfere with their actions on this ground. For example, if through being unable to control their spending, someone becomes unable to pay their debts or unable to support their children, then we can condemn and punish them. But it is important that we punish them for being unable to pay their debts or support their children; we do not punish them just for being unable to control what they spend.

Second, a person's specific duties can change self-regarding actions into ones regulated by the Harm Principle. If a doctor or policeman got drunk while on duty, they may be punished, because they have a duty to the public to be capable of doing their job during that time.

Third, if the harm that the person does to themselves 'causes grief to his family' (148), then we can reproach him for not taking their interests and feelings into proper consideration. But again, it is this, not the harm he does himself, that should be the focus of our condemnation. The harm is irrelevant; we can reprimand someone for behaving in *any* way, harmful or not, that would make his family very unhappy.

> ### Going further: family feelings
>
> Mill here allows that we *may* interfere with behaviour that hurts other people's feelings. But other people's feelings only count in the context of what we think *morality* requires of us in relation to our *families*. Family is different from everyone else, including friends, because no one else has to keep our company - if they don't like who we are, they can leave. That option is not as easily open to other family members. And family is different because we have special obligations to our family's happiness as a result of the nature of the family bond.
>
> However, while we should take their feelings into account, morality may condemn their taking offence rather than condemning our behaviour. If a man is offended that his wife has male friends who are not other members of the extended family, Mill would not say that the wife should give up her friendships. It is the husband's feelings that are at fault. Taking someone's feelings into 'proper consideration' does not mean letting them decide one's every choice, and morality does not require this of us. Families must cope with disagreements.

Explain and illustrate Mill's three restrictions on 'self-regarding' actions.

Is Mill inconsistent in allowing family feelings to restrict self-regarding actions?

FREEDOM TO HARM ONESELF

The three cases discussed are not the only ways in which actions that 'directly and in the first instance' affect only the agent may nevertheless harm other people. But, Mill says, if the person 'neither violates any *specific* duty to the public, nor occasions *perceptible* hurt to any *assignable individual* except himself, the inconvenience is one which society can afford to bear, for the sake of the greater good of human freedom' (149, my italics).

An example: should people be allowed to climb mountains? It is dangerous, and if they hurt themselves, then other people's interests may be affected in two ways: first, the person will need to be rescued, which involves risk to those who rescue them; second, their injuries will need medical attention, which – under a welfare state that provides at least emergency medical care for free – costs money that must be raised through taxes and could have been spent on something else. A similar example is whether people should be allowed to take 'recreational' drugs, which could lead to their needing medical care.

We may appeal to these effects to argue that society should prevent people from climbing mountains; or at least, refuse to rescue and treat people who injure themselves climbing mountains or taking drugs. But the question here is whether climbing mountains can be considered self-regarding, given that it can have these effects on other people.

Self-regarding actions are not actions that cause *no* harm to others. Instead, first, their effects harm others only 'through' the individual. A person's mountain-climbing risks harming themselves 'directly and in the first instance'; it is only through their injuries that their actions have any consequences for others. Second, their actions don't violate a specific duty or cause a perceptible harm to a particular other person.

Society, Mill says, has the whole of a person's childhood to influence the development of their character so that they know right from wrong, and choose to live in a way that does not harm themselves and involves concern for other people (149). Furthermore, people who harm themselves, or otherwise live in a way that others feel is depraved or foolish, will most likely be disliked and shunned for that reason. These two influences on self-regarding behaviour are enough; society does not need to act coercively in addition.

But what about harming others by example? The points just made apply here. If there is such harm, the actions are very likely to be self-regarding. It is through the effects on themselves that the agent is a 'bad example'. And their actions, if they only cause harm to others by example, are very unlikely to violate any specific duty or produce a perceptible harm to a particular, identifiable other person. But Mill also questions whether any harm *is* caused through being a 'bad example' (150). If the action has no harmful consequences for the agent, then in what way is the person's action 'bad'? If, on the other hand, the action has harmful consequences for the agent, surely the lesson that will be learned by others is that acting in this way will cause you harm. This is not a bad thing to learn.

Discuss Mill's claim that self-regarding actions that do not harm others should not be regulated by society.

Key points • • •

- The Harm Principle says that 'The only purpose for which power can be rightfully exercised over any member of a civilized community, against his will, is to prevent harm to others' (68). It applies only to adults capable of responding rationally to free discussion. It is a necessary condition for interfering, but not sufficient – some harms should be allowed, if allowing them is in the general interest. It applies to both actions and omissions.
- Mill defends the principle on the grounds of utility – it is in 'the permanent interests of man as a progressive being' (70).
- Morality recognises the distinction between harmful actions to be prohibited and those to be allowed. However, many moralities (wrongly, according to Mill) ban non-harmful actions.
- The Harm Principle raises five philosophical issues: the nature of harm, the distinction between harm and other adverse effects, the boundary of self-regarding action, the relation between the principle and utility, and whether the principle is correct.
- Harm is harm to interests. Some interests are protected in law as rights; others are protected by morality. What violates rights or is immoral would be what is harmful if we had the right theory of rights and morality.
- Not having our feelings hurt or offended is not an interest in this sense. We can also avoid people who avoid us, and suffer no harm.
- Mill argues that we may restrict actions that harm the agent 'directly and in the first instance' if they also violate others' rights, violate specific duties, or, in some cases, hurt family feelings. Otherwise, we should not restrict the action, as we can bear the inconvenience it causes for the sake of greater freedom.
- Harming others 'by bad example' does not fall under self-regarding actions we may restrict, and Mill questions whether it does, in fact, cause harm to others, or just educate them.

The arguments in support of freedom of thought and expression; the importance of truth

The first liberties that Mill identifies the Harm Principle as protecting is freedom of thought and freedom of expression. These freedoms are distinct, because while thought is without exception self-regarding, expression of one's thoughts clearly has consequences for other people. It is possible, therefore, that expression could cause harm to others, and, in such cases, could legitimately be regulated by society. However, freedom of expression, 'being almost of as much importance as the liberty of thought itself and resting in great part on the same reasons' (71), is practically inseparable from freedom of thought. And so in his discussion, Mill argues for both together.

See Freedom of expression: exceptions and their justification, p. 122.

The state may only interfere with people holding and expressing their views if those views cause harm to others (and even then, it should only interfere if doing so would be more beneficial than not doing so). So there should be 'absolute freedom of opinion and sentiment on all subjects, practical or speculative, scientific, moral, or theological' (71), however immoral the opinion or sentiment may seem.

In Chapter 2, Mill provides four arguments to support his position. He does not defend it by appealing to the Harm Principle, since he is using his arguments to show that the Harm Principle is correct. Instead, he argues that the freedom of thought and expression will contribute to 'the permanent interests of man as a progressive being'. Two arguments appeal to the value of truth – he takes it for granted that to discover and know what is true is in our interests. The other two arguments relate the manner in which we believe what is true. His arguments amount to this:

> the peculiar evil of silencing the expression of an opinion is that it is robbing the human race . . . If the opinion is right, they are deprived of the opportunity of exchanging error for truth; if wrong, they lose, what is almost as great a benefit, the clearer perception and livelier impression of truth produced by its collision with error. (76)

Truth and fallibility

Mill sums up his first argument (76–96) like this: 'if any opinion is compelled to silence, that opinion may, for aught we can certainly know, be true. To deny this is to assume our own infallibility' (115–16). Someone who is fallible is someone who fails or is mistaken sometimes. We are all fallible, not just individuals, but also governments and societies. This argument from fallibility claims that we do not always know the truth about morality and religion, even when we think we do.

We must make a distinction between certainty and the truth. Our confidence that some opinion is false cannot justify suppressing the expression of that view, as this implies not only that we are confident of being right, but that we are infallible. We may not *censor* points of view we think are in error.

A censor may make two objections. First, we may surely claim enough knowledge, and confidence in it, to justify censoring certain expressions of opinion. For example, can't we be completely confident that racism is wrong, and therefore that expressions of racism may be censored without any danger that we shall 'lose the truth'? Second, claiming this degree of confidence is not to assume infallibility. Every time we act we must act on what we believe to be true. It would be cowardice to allow false and unethical opinions expression just because we 'may' be wrong.

Mill's response is that there is nothing wrong with certainty. But if we have it, it must and *can only* rest on the freedom of expression itself (79). To develop and defend our points of view, to correct our opinions and weigh their value, we need free discussion. The only reason we have to think that our belief is true is that no one has shown it is false, although there is every opportunity to make the argument. We cannot be sure that our belief is true if we *prevent* opposing beliefs from being expressed and discussed.

But still, should we not censor those opinions that we think are, not false, but *dangerous* to society? Mill makes two responses (82). First, the belief that an opinion is dangerous can be disputed – as above, we cannot be certain that the view is in fact dangerous to society unless we allow free debate on the matter. But for this, we must allow the 'dangerous' view to be discussed, and cannot censor it. Second, if the view to be censored is true, then the view that opposes it must be false. Many people argue that no belief that is false can, in the end, be useful. So it is never in the best interests of society to defend a false belief against the 'dangerous' truth.

> This is not to endorse any kind of relativism; Mill still believes there is a *truth* to be discovered. And we are not required to give every point of view equal credence.

> Discuss Mill's argument that censorship assumes infallibility.

Truth, balance and opposition

Mill sums up his second argument (it appears third in the text, 108–15) thus:

> though the silenced opinion be an error, it may, and very commonly does, contain a portion of the truth; and since the general or prevailing opinion on any subject is rarely or never the whole truth, it is only by the collision

of adverse opinions that the remainder of the truth has any chance of being supplied. (116)

This is because 'Truth, in the great practical concerns of life, is so much a question of the reconciling and combining of opposites that very few have minds sufficiently capacious and impartial to make the adjustment with an approach to correctness' (110).

Most people's opinions, if true, are only part of the truth, often exaggerated, distorted or at least not connected with other relevant and balancing truths. For example, in politics, we usually find a party of 'reform' and a party of 'order or stability' – no one knows exactly what ought to be changed and what kept, but having the two parties in opposition to each other keeps each 'within the limits of reason and sanity' (110). Another example that Mill picks, deliberately controversially (in his society), is Christian ethics. He points out the many flaws and incompleteness: Christian ethics has been more concerned with 'thou shalt not' than with a positive image, it has a horror of bodily pleasures, it encourages passive obedience and does little to develop a sense of dignity. All these aspects need balancing and correcting by sources from outside Christianity.

Explain Mill's idea of truth as a balance between opposing opinions.

Truth, liberty and utilitarianism

In both these arguments against censorship, Mill assumes that opinions can be true or false. But is this always right? For example, many people believe that opinions in morality are not 'true' or 'false' because there is no fact about what is right or wrong. There are just people's opinions and feelings, nothing more.

Mill disagrees. Morality is ultimately about utility – to deny that there are moral truths is to claim that there are no facts about whether an action contributes to the general happiness or not. So, for instance, there is no fact about whether depriving people of liberty is bad for them or not. This is quite hard to believe. However, we shall not discuss this issue further here.

We turn instead to the question of whether utility could ever require us to censor a view. We may be able to think of cases in which it would be immediately useful to prevent certain views being expressed. But *long-term* utility is the *only sort that counts* for Mill. Appealing to the short-term interests of the government in power, for example, is completely illegitimate.

But we can ask whether free debate will ensure that the truth prevails. Mill assumes that freedom of speech will enable us to discover the truth better than

See THE DENIAL OF MORAL TRUTH, p. 233.

This discussion picks up a question raised on p. 109, namely, 'Does the Harm Principle conflict with utility?'

(selective) censorship. If people take turns at speaking and listen respectfully to each other, this might be true. But this is not how the exchange of ideas occurs in society at large, where the expression of an idea is often accompanied by a derogatory and emotive depiction of those who may disagree, and powerful vested interests can be at stake. Given the emotive appeal of ideas and the use of this in public debate, we may not always be able to adequately defend the truth, and so falsehood – perhaps pernicious falsehood – spreads.

Compare allowing racist speech to banning it. Which will lead to fewer people making the mistake of thinking racism is right? If we allow it, the emotional arguments appealing to vested interests ('they come over here, taking our jobs') may persuade some people. If we ban it, then they won't hear these arguments, and so will be less likely to form a false belief. We may argue Mill's faith in reason is overly optimistic, and that utility may provide us grounds for censorship after all.

Mill answers this by pointing again to the long view: given how often people, even great thinkers, get things wrong, how is it that humanity has achieved the large degree of rational opinions and conduct? It can only be because over time, false opinions give way to true ones (80).

Furthermore, if society censors the expression of 'heretical' opinions, people will become more cautious not only in expression, but also in their thoughts as well. Many good and true ideas begin by being 'heretical'. If there is public censure of people expressing such views, this will undermine intellectual courage, and so the discovery of new truths is slowed down (94). Finally, unless false 'heretical' opinions are shown publicly to be false, they won't die, but 'smoulder in narrow circles of thinking'.

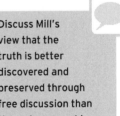

Discuss Mill's view that the truth is better discovered and preserved through free discussion than through censorship.

Going further: restriction and pornography

There is a middle ground between censorship and (complete) freedom of expression that we haven't considered: restriction. To protect the expression and exploration of points of view on the grounds of truth and rationality, perhaps we need only ensure that they have some opportunity to be aired. But, on the grounds of utility, perhaps the form and type of publication in which they are aired could be limited. For example, racist views might be permitted to be expressed in serious journals, and their truth and rational basis carefully discussed, but not in more public contexts where they would tend to be emotive and might cause offence.

Mill considers this at the end of Chapter 2 (116-18). Should we restrict not what people say but how they say it? He says that 'the manner of asserting an opinion . . . may be very objectionable and may justly incur severe censure' (116). However, he continues, the most serious threats to freedom of discussion and its usefulness do not arise from passionate or offensive attacks, but from deliberately suppressing facts or opinions in one's discussion of an issue, misstating the evidence and misrepresenting the opposition. Although they are more serious, we cannot identify these violations easily, and so in the end, it is not in the general interest to try to impose penalties related to them. We can identify when an attack is offensive, but again, it is not in the general interest to interfere, because those who disagree with prevailing opinion are more likely to be restrained than those who agree with it. It is those who most need to be heard - the opposition - that will most likely be suppressed if we start interfering on grounds of offensive or emotional expression. Instead, we should leave individuals to condemn all bigotry and intolerance, whoever expresses it.

Would Mill change his mind in contemporary society, for example, in the light of the prevalence of pornography? There is a question of whether pornography should count under 'freedom of expression' at all, since much of it does not express an opinion (e.g. the opinion that women are sexual objects whose purpose is to gratify the sexual desires of men), but visually displays a situation (in which women are gratifying the sexual desires of men). On this (controversial) interpretation of pornography, it is not an expression of a sexist view, it is a form of sexism.

Let us assume that pornography is covered by 'freedom of expression'. The question then is whether it may, nevertheless, be censored. One recent argument, that Mill did not consider, is that one person's freedom of expression might in fact undermine someone else's. If the views presented by a racist or sexist make it more difficult for their 'victim' *to be heard and understood* in society, then this is a more serious issue than mere offence. Some recent feminists have argued that the way women have been depicted in the culture generally, and more specifically in pornography, has made it more difficult for women's views to be understood and taken seriously.

Should this count as a 'harm' or should the sexist's freedom of expression be protected? We could argue that the freedom of expression does not entail a right to be understood. Every idea must be allowed to heard, even if other ideas are misunderstood as a result.

?

Does an argument from utility favour either restriction of freedom of expression or censorship?

How to hold a true belief

Mill provides two further grounds for freedom of thought and expression (96–108). These concern our relation to the truth. The first is this:

> even if the received opinion be not only true, but the whole truth; unless it is suffered to be, and actually is, vigorously and earnestly contested, it will, by most of those who receive it, be held in the manner of a prejudice, with little comprehension or feeling of its rational grounds. (116)

Not to be able to defend our (true) beliefs against objections is not to understand *why* they are true, what the evidence is in favour of them. Faced with an objection, our belief crumples or is shown to be a mere prejudice. This is no way for a rational creature to hold beliefs, nor will it help us develop the ability to think for ourselves.

To hold our beliefs rationally and be justified in holding them, we need to understand alternative viewpoints, and the challenges they raise for our own position. Many of the objections we must counter will be put most forcefully by those who really believe them, so we must allow others to express their points of view if we are to rationally believe our own.

Mill's second argument is this: if a true belief is not challenged,

?

Why must we allow our beliefs to be challenged if we are to hold them rationally?

> the meaning of the doctrine itself will be in danger of being lost or enfeebled, and deprived of its vital effect on the character and conduct; the dogma becoming a mere formal profession, inefficacious for good, but cumbering the ground and preventing the growth of any real and heartfelt conviction from reason or personal experience. (116)

The battle between ideas is necessary for us to fully *understand* our beliefs – what do they really imply, how do they require that we act? Mill's example is again

Christian morality. Many people say they believe in Jesus' teaching, but do they really understand what it means for one's life to 'turn the other cheek'? Second, without understanding the real meaning of our beliefs, we do not act on them. The beliefs are 'dead dogma, not living truth' (97), they do not motivate us. Third, when we hold beliefs in this dogmatic way, no alternatives can get through to us. We stop listening and thinking. So opposition is necessary for us to stay open-minded and thoughtful. Freedom of expression challenges hypocrisy, self-satisfaction and intellectual lethargy.

All this applies as much to our beliefs in liberty, in freedom of expression, in democracy, in equality, as to any others. So even *these* beliefs should be challenged. It is necessary in a democracy for people to criticise democracy and liberty – or people will start to forget what is really valuable about this form of society.

Are Mill's empirical assumptions in these arguments true? For example, there is plenty of evidence to suggest that views that are not challenged can be held passionately by a whole society. The ability of an idea to motivate has as much to do with its emotive appeal as with its rational grounds being laid out clearly and forcefully, because reason is by no means the strongest spring of action.

Mill's arguments give us a picture of what he thinks is in the 'permanent interests of man as a progressive being'. It is better for people to be able to think for themselves, to understand what they believe, to develop their rational and intellectual faculties. It is better for them to be open-minded and to hold beliefs that motivate them because they understand them, than because they are strongly held prejudices. An enquiring, open mind is better than a thoughtless, closed one.

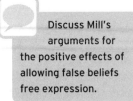

What beneficial effects come from allowing true beliefs to be challenged?

Discuss Mill's arguments for the positive effects of allowing false beliefs free expression.

Freedom of expression: exceptions and their justification

We said (p. 115) that while freedom of thought is absolute, there may be restrictions of freedom of expression, because expressions of opinion and feeling are actions that affect others, and, therefore, may also harm them.

There can be cases where the expression of an opinion causes harm directly, for example, by attacking someone's reputation. In such cases, the expression is directly regulated by the Harm Principle. But, as in other cases of harmful action, we should not immediately conclude that society should try to prevent every attack on someone's reputation. Is interference in the general interest? One criterion that the law currently uses is whether the attack constitutes slander (if spoken) or libel (if printed). If the expressed opinion is true, then even if it does harm someone else's reputation, it is allowed. If it is shown to be false, then there are legal penalties for the person who expressed it. A similar situation applies to expressing false opinions about someone that causes them financial harm. But expressions of offensive opinion that do not cause harm should not be restricted under any circumstances.

What about expressions that don't cause harm directly? Mill says 'opinions lose their immunity, when the circumstances are such as to constitute their expression a positive instigation to some mischievous act' (119). For example, if someone argues that Salman Rushdie should be assassinated for writing *The Satanic Verses*, and we can show that *their expression* of this view causes someone else to begin to plan the assassination, society may have cause to limit that expression.

However, limiting that expression of the opinion is not limiting every expression of it. The opinion can still be expressed in other ways on other occasions, for example, generally through the newspapers. There must be a fairly direct connection between the expression and the action taken. If there is not, then society should only seek to prevent the harmful action and not also the expression of opinion that such an action would be right.

> Discuss when it is justified to constrain freedom of expression.

Key points • • •

- Freedom of thought is always self-regarding, so should never be restricted. Freedom of expression may be restricted if it causes harm, directly or indirectly.
- Mill provides four arguments for thinking that allowing freedom of thought and expression will contribute most to utility, interpreted as 'the permanent interests of man as a progressive being'.

1. To censor an opinion may deprive us of the truth. Society is not infallible in its beliefs. Our confidence in our beliefs can only rest on allowing free discussion.
2. Censorship may deprive us of part of the truth, a part that balances what we already believe.
3. Without free debate, our true beliefs will become prejudices, as we won't understand why they are true.

4.   Without free debate, our true beliefs will become 'dead dogmas', as we fail to act on them or appreciate their value.

- Is Mill right to assume that there is a 'truth' about how to live? If not, then censoring opinions cannot deprive us of the truth.
- Is he right to think that free debate will lead to discovery of, and belief in, the truth better than selective censorship? He argues that, while it may not in the short term, it will *in the long run*. For instance, censorship will not prevent false beliefs, and will lead to greater caution in developing new ideas.
- Is he right to think that without debate, we will no longer understand or be moved by our beliefs? Must we understand our beliefs rationally to act on them?
- Mill's arguments do not necessarily prevent us from restricting how views are expressed, though he comments that people who hold minority views that need to be heard are more likely to be inoffensive than people who hold the majority view.
- Where the expression of an opinion directly causes harm (e.g. slander or libel), or where it causes harm indirectly (e.g. through inciting a harmful act), it may be constrained. But the connection to harm must be strong.

III. FREEDOM OF THE INDIVIDUAL (II) AND INDIVIDUAL DEVELOPMENT

The arguments in support of freedom of action; the importance of variety

In Chapter 3, Mill turns to freedom of action, and the importance of individuality and variety. There need to be different 'experiments of living' (120). Through trying out different lifestyles, people discover what works in life and what doesn't, what leads to their good and what detracts from it. In other words, there should be freedom for a variety of characters and for a variety of different modes of life – as long as these don't harm others, of course.

'Individuality' is the development and expression of one's own, particular character. People should act according to their own character, as opposed to going along with traditions and customs, because individuality is 'one of the principal ingredients of human happiness, and quite the chief ingredient of individual and social progress' (120). But for a person to develop their individuality, there needs to be freedom and a variety of possible ways of life.

So, in outline, Mill's argument for freedom of action follows this structure: Freedom is necessary for the development of individuality. Furthermore, '[t]he only freedom which deserves the name is that of pursuing our own good in our own way' (72). There is no genuine freedom without individuality. Individuality is central to happiness and both individual and social progress, and so, utility. If he is right, freedom is necessary to utility 'in the largest sense'. The Harm Principle defends freedom, so it promotes utility.

So Mill needs to establish three things: that freedom and individuality are linked as he says; that individuality is central to happiness (utility); and that individuality is necessary for individual and social progress. Correspondingly, objections to Mill's argument can challenge any or all of these claims.

Individuality, freedom and happiness

'Individuality' is an *ideal* of character for Mill. It will benefit both the person and others. Mill quotes the German thinker and politician Wilhelm von Humboldt approvingly: each person's end 'is the highest and most harmonious development of his powers to a complete and consistent whole' (121). Each person's 'powers' are different, as are the desires and emotions which need to be developed to be 'complete and consistent'. So each person's development is individual to them, not a copy of anyone else.

Will one person's individual development interfere with or undermine someone else's? Mill thinks that individuality should be developed within the limits imposed by the Harm Principle, by other people's rights and interests. Here the idea of 'complete and consistent' is important. Individuality (as a character ideal) involves a harmony between one's ability and willingness to obey social rules and not to harm others, and one's ability to think and choose on the basis of one's own character.

So, on the one hand, to develop our abilities to think and choose for ourselves, we must have the freedom to practise doing this: 'The mental and moral, like the muscular, powers are improved only by being used' (122). On the other hand, individual development is helped by the social restraints placed on people's inclinations to selfishness (128). It makes us kinder, more considerate, and just, and these are developments of our 'higher' powers. There is therefore no inconsistency between aiming at individuality and restraining people's actions if they harm others.

What are the parallels between Mill's arguments in support of freedom of action and his arguments in support of freedom of thought and expression?

Explain Mill's argument that individual development is compatible with restricting individual freedom according to the Harm Principle.

Is this too quick? Someone with individuality is not easily swayed by others, but has strong desires and emotions of their own, feelings that they identify with and seek to express. But people who do not have a strong will are more submissive, and will be more likely to obey moral rules.

Mill responds that it is a mistake to think that a strong will is dangerous. The problem is not strong desires but a *weak conscience* (124). And the development of conscience is part of the development of individuality. Of course, people can obey rules without individuality, without reasoning or thinking for themselves, without exercising their power of choice, 'But what will be his comparative worth as a human being?' (123).

These arguments rest on Mill's fundamental belief that 'Human nature is not a machine to be built after a model' (123). Each person is – potentially – different in what they need to develop as who they are, and this individual development is central to their happiness. Mill doesn't discuss his theory of happiness here, but in *Utilitarianism*, Chapter 2. He argues that the core of happiness is pleasures that involve thought, feeling and imagination; in other words, they depend upon people using their 'higher' faculties. But the pleasures of thought, feeling and imagination are only fully available to people who think, feel and imagine *for themselves*. People without individuality ask 'What do other people think or feel about this issue? What would other people choose?' (125). They do not ask what suits them, as individuals. And so they miss out on a good part of human happiness.

See VARIATIONS ON
HAPPINESS, p. 252.

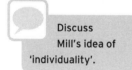

Discuss
Mill's idea of
'individuality'.

Individuality, society and utility

If Mill can show that society as a whole benefits from the existence of individuality, or at least the existence of the freedom in which individuality will flourish, his case for the Harm Principle is strengthened. Mill presents five arguments for this conclusion (128–40).

First, just as we need freedom of expression to discover new truths (see p. 116), so we need freedom of action to discover new, better ways of living (129). But it takes a special sort of originality, a kind of genius, to introduce new practices into society. And geniuses have highly developed individuality. For such people to exist, we need freedom of action (within the limits of the Harm Principle).

Second, genius is needed for good government as well as good society, because there is a general tendency for mediocrity to dominate, so that 'public opinion' comes to rule society:

No government by a democracy or a numerous aristocracy, either in its political acts or in the opinions, qualities, and tone of mind which it fosters, ever did or could rise above mediocrity except in so far as the sovereign many have let themselves be guided . . . by the counsels and influence of a more highly gifted and instructed *one* or *few* . . . (131).

(This is not an argument for a benevolent *dictatorship* by genius, only for the freedom necessary for genius to 'point out the way' (132). If this is done, Mill trusts everyone to be able to see the wisdom of the advice, and willingly accept it.)

Third, everybody will benefit from not having particular ways of life imposed on them. 'If a person possesses any tolerable amount of common sense and experience, his own mode of laying out his existence is the best' (132–3), that is the best for him. People have different tastes and require different conditions in order to develop.

Fourth, people with highly developed individuality will have strong characters. Society needs strong people who are vigorous in their pursuit of making life better. If everyone in society is submissive, weak-willed, without strong opinions, then society itself will be weak. It will not progress towards better ways of doing things for lack of will and energy (135).

Fifth, societies that prevent originality stagnate. When custom is the final appeal for how to live, society ceases to progress (136). Mill cites the example of the 'whole East', and later specifies China. It was, in the past, a great country, in which many advances in arts and sciences occurred. But then it ground to a halt, inhibited by custom. It only did as well as it did because it had an unusually good set of customs.

In these arguments for freedom of action, Mill has defended the Harm Principle in terms of utility – happiness and progress. The freedom the Harm Principle guarantees is necessary for the development of individuality. This is not only the highest end an individual can aim at – a principal ingredient in individual happiness – it is also a quality that greatly contributes to the general utility in society.

> Why does Mill believe that individuality contributes to social utility?

Freedom of action: exceptions and their justification

According to Mill, there are no exceptions to applying the Harm Principle to actions. If an action is self-regarding, then it is not to be restricted. If it harms others, then it may be restricted if restricting it is in the general interest.

However, it is not always easy to know whether an action should be restricted or not. Whether it is self-regarding and then whether it is in the general interest to restrict it are difficult questions. So it may *appear* that there are exceptions to the Harm Principle. We will discuss such cases in THE APPLICATIONS OF MILL'S PRINCIPLES (p. 144) and HARM AND OFFENCE (p. 138). It will emerge that, in some cases of offence, it seems that Mill *does* make an exception to the Harm Principle, and it is very unclear as to why he does.

Do utility and freedom conflict?

The main objection that Mill's arguments face is whether there are situations in which coercion may lead to greater happiness than freedom.

That utility and freedom *can* conflict is illustrated by the potential drug addict. If we prevent someone from trying a powerfully addictive drug, for example, heroin, we contribute more to their utility (and likely the utility of others) than if we allow them to try it. But this is no objection, because Mill does not say that utility and freedom never conflict. First, some freedom is ruled out by the Harm Principle for this very reason. Second, Mill recognises that even freedom protected by the Harm Principle can conflict with utility in some situations. His answer to it is to once again point us towards the bigger picture:

> The spirit of improvement is not always a spirit of liberty, for it may aim at forcing improvements on an unwilling people; and the spirit of liberty, in so far as it resists such attempts, may ally itself locally and temporarily with the opponents of improvement; but the only unfailing and permanent source of improvement is liberty, since by it there are as many possible independent centres of improvement as there are individuals. (136)

As long as we think that Mill's appeal to utility is about what is best in this or that individual situation, we misunderstand him. It is what *permanently* contributes to utility that interests him. Preventing someone from taking an addictive drug is one example of preventing people from engaging in activities that can endanger their health; do we always want to do this? Furthermore, utility, for Mill, relates to our interests as *progressive* beings. This involves our learning – and an excellent source of learning is mistakes.

But is Mill right that liberty is, in general, a 'source of improvement'? For instance, is he right to think that allowing diversity will help people find *better*

Explain Mill's response to the objection that utility and freedom conflict in some cases.

ways of living, ones that will make them happy? Mill assumes that people learn from their and others' mistakes, so that diversity will lead to knowledge of what is truly good. But in the time since Mill wrote, we can argue that there has been greater diversity – the development of pluralistic societies – but no great increase in happiness or good living. Is individuality in the sense of pursuing our own good in our own way such a good thing? Or would people be happier with strong social guidance on how to live? We discuss this below, in LORD DEVLIN'S ARGUMENT (p. 131).

We can agree with Mill that thinking and choosing for oneself is a key component of happiness. But do we really require *as much freedom* as Mill argues for in order to gain these benefits? If not, he has not defended the Harm Principle successfully.

If freedom and utility conflict, we are faced with a choice between them. If we continue to appeal to utility and limit freedom, Mill will challenge us to say on what basis can we claim to know what contributes most to utility 'in the largest sense' (see p. 116). Or we defend freedom even when it conflicts with utility, for example, arguing that we have certain rights to freedom that are more important than utility. Mill's reply is that if we think this, we are probably not understanding utility 'in the largest sense'.

We can challenge the assumption made here that individuality *has* increased. See TOLERANCE, CRITICAL FACULTIES AND FALSE NEEDS, p. 267.

See RESOLVING CONFLICTS BETWEEN RIGHTS AND UTILITY, p. 101.

See WHETHER LIBERTY IS INTRINSICALLY OR INSTRUMENTALLY VALUABLE, p. 135.

See THE DEVELOPMENT OF THE INDIVIDUAL, p. 133, for a further objection.

Going further: objections regarding individuality

Mill argues that freedom enables individuality, and this contributes to utility. Both these claims are empirical, and we can ask whether the facts support them.

Freedom and individuality

Is Mill right to think that if we limit freedom, we will necessarily limit the development of individuality and 'genius'? For instance, 'genius' has flourished under some dictatorships, not just in liberal democracies. But Mill agrees: 'Even despotism does not produce its worst effects so long as individuality exists under it' (128). Despotism is not inconsistent with the freedom necessary for the development of individuality (although, of course, it can harm utility in other ways).

In Chapter 2 (96), Mill points to eras in which genius and new ideas have flourished, namely, the time immediately following the Reformation, the late eighteenth century in Europe, Germany in late eighteenth and early nineteenth centuries. In each case, a 'mental despotism' had been thrown off and no new consensus had begun to dominate society. But none of these societies was a liberal democracy. Mill's argument from individuality defends the freedom protected by the Harm Principle, not *political* freedoms.

To challenge Mill's claim about the connection between freedom and individuality, we need to find, if we can, an example of individuality flourishing in conditions of social suppression of new ideas and ways of behaviour. This does not mean finding an example of *one individual* who develops a new way of living under such conditions, but of individuality being a more widespread characteristic.

Individuality and utility

Does the general utility require individuality? Mill claims that individuality contributes new ways of living and good government, and its energy and originality drive progress. But could ideas about new ways of living come from a few, privileged individuals who are granted the freedoms necessary for individuality, while the government does not extend these freedoms to society generally? I.e. the aristocracy is free, but the majority, the 'common' people, are required to obey a strict code. If such societies have progressed, then we don't need freedom for progress.

But the example actually supports Mill's position. If the development of individuality among the aristocrats drives progress, then won't extending their freedoms to everyone drive progress faster? For example, there may be a genius among the common people whose ideas revolutionise society for the better. If freedom to express such new ideas or experiment with new ways of life is limited to the aristocracy, society loses the benefit of those geniuses who exist among the common people.

This doesn't necessarily follow. There may be *other* benefits to utility that come from imposing a strict moral code on (most) people that outweigh the chance that some individual genius will be restricted as a result. We shall look at an example of the potential benefits of coercion next.

 Does Mill succeed in showing that freedom contributes to utility via individuality?

Lord Devlin's argument

The Law Lord, Lord Devlin, argued against the Harm Principle in the 1950s. If the government failed to preserve and enforce common moral values, he argued, society would begin to disintegrate.

> [A]n established morality is as necessary as good government to the welfare of society. Societies disintegrate from within more frequently than they are broken up by external pressures. There is disintegration when no common morality is observed and history shows that the loosening of moral bonds is often the first stage of disintegration, so that society is justified in taking the same steps to preserve its moral code as it does to preserve its government and other essential institutions.
>
> The suppression of vice is as much the law's business as the suppression of subversive activities; it is no more possible to define a sphere of private morality than it is to define one of private subversive activity. It is wrong to talk of private morality . . . You may argue that if a man's sins affect only himself it cannot be the concern of society. If he chooses to get drunk every night in the privacy of his own home, is anyone except himself the worse for it? But suppose a quarter or a half of the population got drunk every night, what sort of society would it be? You cannot set a theoretical limit to the number of people who can get drunk before society is entitled to legislate against drunkenness.

'Morals and Criminal Law'

In summary, Devlin argues that:

1. Morality is essential to the welfare of society.
2. Morality is social, not private.
3. It is the business of government to look after the welfare of society.
4. So it is legitimate for government to pass laws on the basis of preserving moral values.

This means that society should not tolerate practices that conflict with these common moral values. Now, if these common moral values were aimed just at preventing harm to others, Mill would agree. But Devlin includes moral disapproval of self-actions, for example, drunkenness and homosexual activity (his article argued against the legalisation of homosexuality). He appeals to utility, and points to the importance of social cohesion for the general welfare of society. Mill's 'experiments of living' threaten to undermine this social cohesion. Therefore freedom and utility conflict.

Mill would respond that in Devlin's society, we will not get at the truth about morality and correct our mistakes. Social morality may well *need to change*, as it might be inhibiting individual and social welfare. For example, homosexuality has been legalised. Has this led to the disintegration of social morality or society itself? Or is social morality better because it no longer condemns homosexuals?

But Devlin's argument returns us to a question we raised earlier (p. 129). Mill assumes that people are reasonable and will learn both from their own mistakes and from the good, original ideas of geniuses. If he is wrong, then Devlin may be right that people need strong moral guidance. They need to be told the difference between right and wrong, or they will not be happy.

These thoughts lead to the question of whether Mill is right to think that humanity *progresses*. Mill's reply to the objection that freedom and utility conflict depends *entirely* on his claim that freedom doesn't conflict with utility in the sense of 'the permanent interests of man as a progressive being'. But if we are not progressive beings, if history does not show that the human race is moving towards happiness, reasonableness and virtue, then Mill's theory of human nature is questionable. As societies have allowed more freedom of expression and action over the last 150 years, what 'progress' has been made? On the one hand, we could argue that there is greater recognition of human rights and the development of individuality; on the other, we can argue that any such recognition is more theoretical than practical, that all the wars of the twentieth century demonstrate that we are no more reasonable or virtuous than we used to be, and that the dominance of global capitalism is undermining individuality and variety.

> **?** Is Lord Devlin
> right that a social
> moral code, beyond the
> Harm Principle, needs
> to be enforced?

Key points • • •

- Individuality is the development and expression of one's own character, which requires the possibility of 'experiments of living'.
- In defending freedom of action, Mill argues that freedom is necessary for the development of individuality, which is 'one of the principal ingredients of human happiness, and quite the chief ingredient of individual and social progress'.
- Individuality does not need unlimited freedom, but is best developed within the moral and legal constraints of the Harm Principle. Strong-willed

individuals are not necessarily more likely to act immorally than weak-willed ones.

- Mill gives five arguments for thinking that society as a whole will benefit from the freedom for experiments of living.

1. Genius, which needs this freedom, can introduce new and better ways of living.
2. Genius can guide good government.
3. Everyone has different tastes and needs different conditions to develop.
4. Strong individuals have the energy to drive progress.
5. Societies that prevent originality stagnate.

- The freedom necessary for individuality is primarily a social freedom, which can exist under benevolent despots as well as in liberal democracies.
- Mill accepts that there are situations in which utility and freedom can conflict. However, freedom is necessary for utility *in the long term*. It is a 'permanent source of improvement'.
- This assumes that people learn from mistakes, but is Mill right to think human beings progress?
- Is Mill right that individuality contributes to happiness? Even if we need some freedom to be most happy, do we need as much as the Harm Principle gives us?
- Lord Devlin argues that without enforcing a moral code, society will disintegrate. Self-regarding actions may therefore be regulated by the law.
- Mill can respond that a social morality that disapproves of self-regarding actions may itself be wrong, and need to change.

The development of the individual

In The arguments in support of freedom of action (p. 124), we noted Mill's claim that the development of individuality is a main ingredient in individual happiness. In the development of one's powers into a 'complete and consistent whole', the powers of one's 'higher' faculties – thought, feeling and imagination – are most important. So Mill is concerned with individuals' abilities to think for themselves, to feel emotions that are truly one's own rather than a copy of other people's, to have an element of originality, a good knowledge of their own character, a keen sense of morality combined with a healthy self-esteem, and the strength of will to act as they choose. Mill accepts that the greatest development of these powers occurs only in exceptional people. But that does not make his ideal of individuality elitist. There is no one who will not benefit from these abilities.

Individual development is encouraged not just by certain freedoms, but also through education. Mill argues (176–8) that education (as it is now should be compulsory, though not directed by the government (in case that limited variety). He also argues that when people undertake certain activities for themselves, for example, participation in local government and trial by jury, it contributes to their development. This is part of the 'training of a citizen' (181).

Philosophers have objected that Mill's theory of individual development conflicts with the social nature of culture and tradition. Mill appears to oppose individuality and tradition: 'Where not the person's own character but the traditions or customs of other people are the rule of conduct, there is wanting one of the principal ingredients of human happiness' (120).

This suggests that people should stand back from and evaluate the culture around them. Yet we are *naturally cultural*, born and raised with customs and traditions. Being part of our culture and society makes us who we are. It is an inescapable part of our identity. If Mill thinks that a person's culture is, in some way, 'incidental' to them and their development as an individual, he has an objectionable theory of human nature.

But Mill never denies that custom and tradition can be part of someone's identity nor does he say that the development of individuality must involve breaking with custom and tradition. His defence of thinking and choosing on the basis of one's own character is compatible with character being formed by their culture. However, we should not think that being 'embedded' in a particular culture is something identical for all members of that culture. There are still many individual differences.

Mill wants to balance two influences on thought and action. On the one hand, 'it would be absurd to pretend that people ought to live as if nothing whatever had been known in the world before they came into it' (122). There is a great deal that we can learn from other people. On the other hand, 'to conform to custom merely *as* custom does not educate or develop [the individual]' (122). So he wants people to reflect critically on customs and traditions. After such reflection, we may freely choose to live in a traditional and customary way, because it suits us best. Our reflections in making this choice will, of course, be informed by our culture; Mill never emphasises this fact – and we can criticise him for this – but we need not interpret him as denying it.

These ideas are discussed in National community and positive liberty, **p. 128.**

Mill also gives us a theory of the development of thought that emphasises the originality of the individual genius. Yet even the most original thinkers and artists develop the ideas of others within an inherited tradition. We should balance Mill's frequent remarks that suggest originality comes entirely from within against his explanation of why, given how fallible we are, humanity is nevertheless guided mainly by rational and moral ideas: 'it is owing to a quality of the human mind, the source of everything respectable in man either as an intellectual or as a moral being, namely, that his errors are corrigible' (79–80). Progress is made by people working with and improving upon the ideas of others.

Critically discuss Mill's theory of individual development.

Key points • • •

- The development of individuality is, in particular, the development of the abilities of thought, feeling and imagination, including self-knowledge, moral sense and strength of will.
- Individuality is encouraged through freedom and education.
- Does Mill's theory conflict with the view that individuals are formed within cultures? He certainly emphasises the need to critically assess one's customs and traditions, but he recognises that they contain much wisdom and he does not claim that individuality requires us to break with them.

Going further: whether liberty is intrinsically or instrumentally valuable

Whether liberty is intrinsically or instrumentally valuable is a question about the relation between liberty and utility. If liberty is valuable only because it contributes to utility, then it is instrumentally valuable, i.e., it is valuable as a means to an end. But if liberty is valuable in itself, not just because it contributes to utility, then it is intrinsically valuable. We have discussed Mill's argument that liberty is always instrumentally valuable for utility, i.e., it never conflicts with utility in the largest sense (pp. 118 and 128). The question now is whether liberty has any further value of its own.

Because Mill is a utilitarian, we can expect him to say that liberty is instrumentally valuable. The only thing that is intrinsically valuable is utility. It is the final appeal on all ethical questions (70). In his arguments for the value of liberty, he defends liberty as a means to individual development and for social progress.

And yet the tone of *On Liberty* seems to be a celebration of liberty in its own right. For example, Mill talks about an individual's freedom in self-regarding actions as being 'absolute' (69). Is this only because it is always the case that such freedom contributes to utility or is the absolute nature of the freedom a reflection of freedom's intrinsic value?

We cannot find the answer to whether liberty is intrinsically or instrumentally valuable in *On Liberty*. The reason is this: if we say that liberty is instrumentally valuable to utility, we are assuming that liberty (means) and utility (end) are *distinct*. Mill only clarifies this issue in *Utilitarianism*, Chapter 4.

We have already noted (p. 108) that by 'utility', Mill means the permanent interests we have as progressive beings. In large part, these interests are those involved in our development of individuality, particularly the powers of thought, feeling and imagination. In *Utilitarianism* Chapter 2, Mill argues that the pleasure we derive from the development and use of these powers is much more *valuable* to us than, say, bodily pleasures.

In Chapter 4 of *Utilitarianism*, Mill argues that we should not think of utility (happiness) as something distinct from what contributes to it. 'The principle of utility does not mean that any given pleasure . . . is to be looked upon as means to a collective something termed happiness.' Instead, 'besides being means they [the pleasures] are a part of the end'. In other words, instead of thinking that the development and use of thought, feeling and imagination bring us happiness (or contribute to utility) as something distinct, happiness and utility *consist in* the development of these powers. They 'are desirable in and for themselves', just as utility is, because they are the 'ingredients of happiness'. They are intrinsically valuable as *part* of utility.

Can we say something similar for liberty? To be free (in expression and one's self-regarding actions) is not just a means to being happy; it is part of what happiness is. Liberty is not just a means to our permanent interests as progressive beings, it is one of these interests in its own right. Liberty is both instrumentally and intrinsically valuable.

This may well be the best reading of Mill, but there are several objections to it as a theory. First, Mill stretches the concept of 'utility' until it breaks. If freedom is part of utility, they *could* not conflict. But clearly freedom and utility *can* conflict. Whether they do, in fact, conflict is a real question, and one that Mill recognises.

Second, the idea that freedom is part of utility does not sit well with Mill's arguments that freedom is a necessary means to utility. Can freedom be both necessary for the development of individuality and part of individuality? Can anything be a means to itself?

In reply, Mill can say that 'to be free' is part of the essence of being human. This involves both becoming and being free. Realising my individuality includes becoming free in the sense of being able to think and act for myself. But for this, I must be free in the sense of given the opportunity to think and act for myself. 'The mental and moral . . . powers are improved only by being used' (122). So there is no contradiction here.

Does Mill believe that liberty is intrinsically valuable?

Compare this reply with the debate between NEGATIVE AND POSITIVE FREEDOM, p. 83.

Key points • • •

- Liberty is only instrumentally valuable if its only value lies in its contribution to utility. Mill repeatedly defends liberty as a means to utility.
- However, in *Utilitarianism* Chapter 4, Mill argues that utility – happiness – is not a distinct 'thing', but comprised of many pleasures, especially the pleasures of exercising those powers we identified as central to individuality.
- Liberty could therefore be seen as not merely a means to realising our permanent interests as progressive beings, but one of those interests. It would then be part of utility, and so intrinsically valuable.
- But is it coherent to make liberty part of utility? This stretches the concept of utility too far, and it is unclear how liberty could be both a means to individuality and a part of it.
- One reply is that we need the opportunity (freedom) to think and choose for ourselves to develop the ability to do so (individuality), and thus be free as individuals.

IV. APPLICATIONS

Harm and offence

In our discussion of WHAT IS HARM? (p. 110), we noted that Mill contrasts harm and offence. Harm is harm to our interests, in particular, our permanent interests as progressive beings. Now that we have discussed Mill's theory of individuality, we can see that being offended is not a harm to our interests, it does not in any way prevent us from developing as individuals or living out our own lives as we see fit. However, attempting to coerce someone into not acting in a way that offends us does harm their interests, as it limits the freedom they need to develop as individuals. So to allow offensive practices causes no harm, but to ban them causes harm.

Going further: customary morality and offence

This is the core of Mill's view on offence. However, matters are not so simple. Mill uses customary morality as a yardstick for judging when society may interfere with harmful actions. If a harmful action violates someone's rights, then it may be punished by law. When a harmful action violates moral rules, it may be punished by public moral disapproval (141). Customary morality is a good guide to utility, because over time people have automatically, through trial and error, worked out which actions tend to produce happiness. This is what our inherited moral rules actually are: 'tell the truth', 'don't steal' and 'keep your promises' are embodiments of the wisdom of humanity that lying, theft and false promising tend to lead to unhappiness.

However, many people morally disapprove not just of harmful actions, but also of offensive ones. Does this mean that what is offensive is detrimental to utility? We know Mill's response is that it is better for people's self-development, and for society, for them to learn to cope with being offended and allow other people freedom. But if offence is not harmful, yet customary morality disapproves of offence, then customary morality can't be a good guide to utility.

It is not often noted by commentators, but Mill distinguishes between public and private morality precisely on this issue of offence:

See WHAT IS HARM?, p. 110.

Utilitarianism, Ch. 2

On questions of social morality, of duty to others, the opinion of the public . . . though often wrong, is likely to be still oftener right, because on such questions they are only required to judge of their own interests . . . But the opinion of a similar majority . . . on questions of self-regarding conduct is quite as likely to be wrong as right. (151)

Customary morality is only a good guide to restricting actions that harm others; it is not such a good guide to 'how to live' more generally that it can be imposed on people's self-regarding actions as well.

Explain Mill's view of the relationship between offence and customary morality.

But is Mill right that we should not ban offensive behaviour? Mill mentions four causes of offence. There is what someone simply doesn't like (e.g. 151). But, Mill replies, 'there is no parity between the feeling of a person for his own opinion and the feeling of another who is offended at his holding it, no more than between the desire of a thief to take a purse and the desire of the right owner to keep it' (151). This cause is too insignificant for us to discuss it further. Second, there is what someone judges to be harmful to the individual, though not to others, or foolish or depraved (142f.). Third, there is what goes against someone's religious beliefs, including their religious morality (e.g. 152f.). Finally, there are cases which are not offensive in private, but are offensive when done in public (168). We shall look at each in turn.

Offence and folly

In arguing that we should not constrain self-regarding actions, Mill does not claim that our feelings should not be affected by them. Of course they are:

There is a degree of folly, and a degree of what may be called (though the phrase is not unobjectionable) lowness or depravation of taste, which, though it cannot justify doing harm to the person who manifests it, renders him necessarily and properly a subject of distaste, or, in extreme cases, even of contempt. (143)

Mill cites rashness, obstinacy, self-conceit, hurtful self-indulgence and pursuit of animal pleasures. To people with these character traits, we can express our opinions and try to persuade them to change. But if they do not listen, then we can express our opinions in our actions, by avoiding their company and even cautioning other people against them.

But – and this is the crucial point – all of this is a natural extension of our feelings of offence. None of it is intended as constraint, coercion or punishment. We cannot go that far because a person's interest in their own well-being is much stronger than anyone else's, so they have say over it. They should suffer from no more than our bad opinion, and the actions we freely take on the basis of that opinion.

By contrast, we are not merely offended by, but morally disapprove of cruelty, malice, envy, insincerity, disproportionate anger or resentment, greed, pride based on denigrating others, and egotism. Actions that demonstrate these qualities we seek to punish.

But won't someone who suffers from others' bad opinion be just as harmed as someone who is punished? Mill responds that there is a considerable difference between the responses of offence and of seeking punishment. In the latter, we try to make the person's life difficult for them and prevent them from doing as they choose; in the former, we leave them alone. To them, this makes a good deal of difference. Second, society does not get involved in questions of offence. You can only be shunned by people who know you, your circle of acquaintances. *Public* opinion cannot legitimately be brought into play with questions of offence, only with questions of harm.

We may still worry that the reactions to offensive behaviour that Mill endorses can act as a tyranny of the majority just as much as the moral dis-approval he wants to curb. With busybodies going around making remarks to everyone they are offended by (143–4), will society be the place of freedom and toleration Mill advocates? On the one hand, Mill wants to protect individualism from the tyranny of social opinion; on the other, he thinks that certain self-regarding actions or ways of life are, on utilitarian grounds, nevertheless simply wrong, and it would be better if the person was informed of this. Perhaps he was wrong to think that it would be good if we felt free to tell people who offend us what we think of them.

> **Discuss the differences between being offended and seeking to punish.**

Offence and religion

Cases of offence on religious grounds can be difficult to separate from cases in which the person morally disapproves on religious grounds, as many religious moralities do not draw the distinction between harm and offence. Nevertheless, it is clear that some violations of religious codes provoke disgust (and disapproval), while others are disapproved of without disgust. Here are three cases that Mill looks at.

Islam prohibits the eating of pork, some Muslims are disgusted by the practice, and some societies with a Muslim majority have prohibited the eating of pork. In a society with a Muslim minority, the ban on pork certainly wouldn't be accepted. But how can we protest against it? For example, it is not religious intolerance, in that no one's religion *requires* them to eat pork. So no one is prevented from practising their religion. If we resist the ban, it must be because we do not accept Muslims' disgust as a legitimate reason for preventing other people from eating pork. But this applies just as much in societies with a Muslim majority.

In the sixteenth and seventeenth centuries, a Christian movement known as Puritanism gained political power in Britain and some parts of the United States. Puritans – like the Taliban in Afghanistan recently – banned many forms of amusement and entertainment, including music, dancing, public games and the theatre. We can object that the moral and religious sentiments of such people should not be the basis for restricting other people's leisure.

In the nineteenth century, a religious sect emerged called Mormonism. They were persecuted largely because their religion permits polygamy (for men only). In the face of such persecution, they moved to uninhabited Utah. Despite the fact that they were no longer part of the same society, people called for them to be prevented from practising polygamy. But Mill argues that as long as people living in Mormon society are allowed to leave if they choose (which has, in fact, *not* always been the case) and no one within Mormon society calls for help from other societies, there is no justification for forcibly interfering with their way of life. If we want to show them the error of their ways, we can send missionaries.

(This example can be extended to any case in which one society seeks to change the practices of another when those practices are not enforced on people against their will. It does not extend to cases in which members of society are harmed or coerced by social customs, e.g. female circumcision and sati.)

So far, Mill consistently rejects offence as grounds for restricting what people do. This obviously has implications in contemporary society, in which offence is not infrequently invoked as a reason to ban some activity or censor a book or play.

These examples are intended to demonstrate the appeal of the Harm Principle. Anyone who believes that offence *is* a good reason for society to constrain what people do must answer these examples.

Is religious offence ever a good reason to stop or prevent an action?

Public indecency

There are certain offensive acts, for example, public indecency, that Mill is willing to prohibit:

> there are many acts which, being directly injurious only to the agents themselves, ought not to be legally interdicted, but which, if done publicly, are a violation of good manners and, coming thus within the category of offences against others, may rightly be prohibited. Of this kind are offences against decency . . . the objection to publicity being equally strong in the case of many actions not in themselves condemnable. (168)

We will use sexual intercourse as an example of 'offence against decency' and 'violation of good manners' when performed in public. Is sex in public harmful? Does it violate someone's rights or the rules of morality? The ground Mill cites is 'good manners'. Does being offended by a violation of good manners count as a harm?

If Mill is *not* appealing to the Harm Principle, then this kind of 'offence against decency' would be a genuine exception to the Harm Principle. Since he is willing to prohibit them, offences against decency are just wrong, on utilitarian grounds. Here the law should follow utility, not the Harm Principle, it seems.

Apart from the inconsistency in Mill's thought, we can object that banning public sex is *not* in our permanent interests as progressive beings. More generally, we can object that there is no defensible account of what is decent and what is indecent. For instance, can anyone give us a good criterion for when a sense of decency is 'correct' (in accordance with utility 'in the largest sense') and when it is not?

If Mill is appealing to the Harm Principle, then he must think that violations of good manners is a form of harm. The text certainly indicates that Mill makes use of the self-regarding/other-regarding distinction – *any* public act is no longer self-regarding. But he seems to move from the act being other-regarding to it being one that may be regulated. But, on the Harm Principle, it is only *harmful* acts to others that may be regulated. Therefore, we must conclude that violations of good manners are a form of harm.

But Mill never defends this premise, and it is hard to see how he could do so, except by using the same argument as above, namely, that 1) customary morality is a good guide to harm, 2) it disapproves of indecency, therefore 3) indecency damages the general interest.

Philosophers have defended a distinction between offence caused by some public display and offence caused by the belief that people are engaged in private in an activity that offends you. The general interest is not served by taking the second kind of offence into account, but it is served by taking the first kind of offence into account, and restricting certain permissible activities from taking place in public. But there is no evidence that this view is Mill's.

Mill says the issue of acts that offend against decency when performed publicly is 'only indirectly connected with our subject' (168), which is why he doesn't discuss it at length. Why is it only indirectly connected? Perhaps because restrictions on publicity are not attempts to restrict the activity in general. They do not seek to prevent or punish the activity within society, only its public display; nor do they express disapproval or condemnation for the activity, only its public display. Because there is no attempt to prohibit the activity in general, we do not need to invoke the Harm Principle to protect it. Mill's arguments are concerned with the individual's freedom to engage in certain activities, not to engage in them publicly. This makes the issue of publicity 'only indirectly connected' with his core concerns.

We can object that to ban public sex is to ban a type of activity that may be some part of some people's 'experiments of living'. But we then have to say that public sex is not simply sex, done in public; it is a different activity. Mill doesn't grant this. The quotes above show that he considers the act – whether done in public or private – as the same act.

Is there a coherent argument in support of banning public indecency?

Key points • • •

- Mill argues that offence causes no harm to our permanent interests as progressive beings, and therefore offensive actions should not be prohibited.
- However, he also says that customary morality is a good guide to utility – but it obviously disapproves of many offensive actions that are not harmful. Mill's response is that morality is only a good guide when it comes to harmful actions, not when it comes to self-regarding actions.
- Some actions and character traits we are offended by because they are foolish or contemptible. But we should do no more than express our feelings and ignore the person. This is distinct from seeking to punish them.
- We can object that freely expressing our offence to people may inhibit freedom and toleration.
- Mill discusses three cases of religious intolerance – banning eating pork,

banning leisure activities and banning polygamy. In the first two, he argues that to accept offence as a good reason for limiting freedom would require us to give up these practices; in the last, he argues that we should not seek to forcibly change the practices of another society that does not harm or coerce its members.

- Mill allows us to ban the public performance of acts that are offensive when performed in public. His reasoning is unclear. Is the violation of good manners a harm or not? If not, Mill violates the Harm Principle; if so, how does Mill show this?

- One possibility is that Mill feels the Harm Principle does not apply in these cases, because it is not the act, but its public performance, which is banned.

The applications of Mill's principles

Mill turns to the question of applications once he feels he has established his *two* principles that regulate when society is justified in restricting individual conduct. The first principle is the Harm Principle, which he rephrases as: 'the individual is not accountable to society for his actions in so far as these concern the interests of no person but himself'. The second principle is the application of his utilitarianism:

> for such actions as are prejudicial to the interests of others, the individual is accountable and may be subjected either to social or to legal punishment if society is of opinion that the one or the other is requisite for its protection. (163)

There are, once again, cases of 'legitimate harm', where an action harms others, but society should not seek to prevent it, because to do so would cause greater harm. For instance, two people may compete for a job – the one who does not get it is harmed by the other's success. But it is good for society that there is competition like this.

His discussion of cases, Mill says, is not intended as further argument for the principles, but an illustration of the kinds of decisions that they support. For reasons of space, we will not cover all Mill's examples, but just five which continue to be highly relevant in today's society.

Religion

We have looked at three cases of religious morality being invoked against activities not harmful to others (p. 140). In each case, Mill argues that the interference by society is not justifiable. In the first two cases – an Islamic prohibition on eating pork and a Puritan (or Taliban) prohibition on many forms of entertainment – he expects his readers to resist the prohibition. In the third – the persecution of polygamous Mormons – he expects his readers to approve of the prohibition. Part of Mill's argument from the very beginning has been that *there is no consistency* in what society is willing or unwilling to ban. People want to ban what they disapprove of, but will not to tolerate a ban on their own activities that offend others.

Two more examples: at the time Mill was writing, Catholicism was the only religion you could practise legally in Spain. His Protestant readers would want to resist the ban. But then they cannot consistently use their own religion as the basis of laws. If anyone replies, 'but we are right to ban other religions, because our religion is right', they should recognise that when the *other* religion says exactly the same thing, they resent it. There are no grounds they can appeal to which the other religion can't also appeal to.

Second, Christianity says that one day of the week should be kept for rest and worship. Until the 1950s, people were not allowed to work on Sundays. And until 1994, the exception was made only for sports, entertainment and Sunday markets. The first day shops were allowed to open on Sundays was 6 July 1994. Mill argued that society had no justification in preventing everyone working, when allowing some to work would enable others to enjoy themselves.

Again, no one can legitimately appeal to divine law, because 'It remains to be proved that society . . . holds a commission from on high to avenge any supposed offence to Omnipotence which is not also a wrong to our fellow creatures' (159). To suppose otherwise would legitimate complete religious persecution. Mill's point applies against any appeal to divine law. So, for instance, he would be completely against the imposition of those aspects of sharia law that do not relate to harm to others.

Can law be legitimately based on religious doctrine?

Alcohol

Mill opposed the Temperance movement, which attempted to restrict the consumption of alcohol. Restrictions on alcohol involve a prohibition on much that is perfectly innocent in an attempt to prevent what is considered bad (156). One opposer to alcohol argued that drinking undermined his 'social rights' – it creates social disorder, but he has a right to security; it weakens and demoralises society, but he has a right to intellectual development. But this is equivalent to saying that we have a right that everyone behaves just as they ought to! We have no such right, and drunkenness, where it does not cause harm to others, should not be prohibited.

We can, however, ban drunken behaviour that causes harm, and someone who has harmed others while drunk may be legitimately banned from drinking – as this increases the *risk* of harm to others (167). We can also place restrictions on the sale of alcohol (171). Wherever it is sold will need policing, and so society can regulate who can sell it and at what times. But the purpose of this should not be to make alcohol *more difficult* to obtain; that would be a violation of people's liberty.

What about taxing alcohol? If the purpose of the tax is to discourage people from drinking (which is the argument often used by governments today – it is a 'sin' tax), then this is illegitimate. However, governments have to raise taxes, and however this is done, it will adversely affect someone. So the state can consider what people don't need – which obviously includes things that harm them – and tax those.

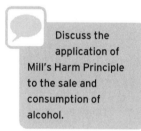

Discuss the application of Mill's Harm Principle to the sale and consumption of alcohol.

Trade

There is no general argument in Mill against taxation in general. All trade, he says, is a social act; *selling* is not primarily self-regarding, but affects the interests of others. (He must mean that trade affects third parties, people not immediately involved in the exchange of goods and money. The buyer consents to trade with the seller, and consenting acts count as self-regarding.) Because it affects others, and clearly can harm them, there can be legislation governing how trade is conducted.

Mill argues that 'the principle of individual liberty is not involved in the doctrine of free trade [trade with minimal restrictions], so neither is it in most of the questions which arise respecting the limits of that doctrine' (164). Other political philosophers have disagreed, and argued that the freedom to trade is a fundamental right.

On trade, see THE RELATIONSHIP BETWEEN DISTRIBUTIVE JUSTICE, LIBERTY AND RIGHTS, p. 116.

Prostitution

What about restrictions on *what* we can trade? The issue of prostitution is interesting and complex. We cannot ban people from having sex; and it would be impossible to regulate people having sex for money. But should someone be allowed to be a pimp? If someone is free to sell their body, should someone else be free to encourage and enable them to do so?

Mill says that people must be free to receive advice about what to do, so they must also be free to give advice. But the issue is more complicated when the advisor receives personal gain, as in the case of the pimp who makes his living by enabling people to sell sex. On the one hand, surely if you are allowed to do something (advising people to sell their bodies), just making money from it shouldn't make it illegal. On the other hand, for activities that are quite possibly harmful to the individual (the prostitute), society should protect people from advice that is not disinterested, helping them to make up their minds on their own.

Mill does not discuss a more pressing question about prostitution. If we allow pimping, will we be able to prevent many of the *clear* harms that pimps inflict on prostitutes, including violence and extortion? Of course, these are illegal anyway, but more such actions will occur if pimping is allowed than if it is not. In other words, can we ban pimping because it is associated with harm, even if we think that, in itself, it should not be banned?

We could invoke Mill's view that, although we cannot ban drinking, we can ban someone who has harmed others while drunk from drinking. But in the case of pimping, we are not talking about banning people who have harmed prostitutes from pimping again; we are talking about banning the whole profession.

All trade involves the interests of others, so restrictions on trade do not necessarily violate the Harm Principle. All we need, then, is a good utilitarian argument against pimping. Mill's discussion illustrates the complexities involved when weighing individual liberties against social harms.

What implications does Mill's theory of liberty have for prostitution and pimping?

Social benefits

Mill's final discussion is not, he says, an application of the Harm Principle. Instead of looking at when government may interfere to prevent harm, it looks at when government may interfere to benefit its citizens. It is worth briefly noting some of Mill's remarks, as they are illustrative of his view of the relation between government and citizens.

The government should *not* intervene to help its citizens in three sorts of case:

1. When individuals will do it better themselves, that is, being given freedom will produce a better result than compliance with government directives, for example, free trade and (interestingly, in these days of a 'national curriculum') the provision of education.
2. When doing it themselves will benefit people's development as individuals, for example, trial by jury and local government.
3. Whenever it is unnecessary, because any addition to the state's power is problematic. The more people that are employed by the government, the less real freedom there will be. No reform that went against the interests of the government would be possible if many people were dependent on the government for their livelihoods.

Instead of intervening to benefit its citizens, it is better if the government provides opportunities for them to benefit themselves: 'A government cannot have too much of the kind of activity which does not impede, but aids and stimulates, individual exertion and development. The mischief begins when . . . it substitutes its own activity for theirs' (187).

> **?** On what grounds does Mill seek to limit the aid the state gives to citizens?

Key points • • •

-   Mill's two principles regulating individual conduct are the Harm Principle (which protects individual freedom) and the principle of utility (which allows punishment of harmful actions).
-   Not all actions that cause harm should be punished, namely, those cases in which greater harm would be done by preventing the actions by allowing them.
-   Mill argues that religious believers are very inconsistent in allowing offence or religious doctrine as a grounds for making law. Apart from the question of which religion is correct, we cannot show that society is charged with the duty for punishing religious offences.
-   Alcohol should not be banned, but harmful drunken behaviour may be punished and restrictions placed on when and where alcohol is sold.

- Trade does not fall under the protection of the Harm Principle, as all trade affects people's interests generally.
- There may be restrictions on what we trade, for example, sex. We cannot prevent people selling sex, but whether we should prevent people from making a living enabling others to sell sex (pimping) is contentious.
- Mill argues that the state should not intervene to benefit its citizens when citizens will achieve the benefit better on their own, or it will benefit their development as individuals to leave them alone, or when it is unnecessary (as the fewer people employed by the state, the better for freedom).

4

UNIT 4 SECTION 4

DESCARTES *MEDITATIONS*

I–III, V and VI

In this chapter, we examine Descartes' text in the light of three key issues: his quest for certainty; his theory of the mind and its relationship to the body, including his proof of the existence of the material world; and Descartes' views on the existence of God. Students should be able to explain Descartes' views clearly and accurately and critically evaluate his arguments and objections to them. They should also be able to make connections between his theories and other views on the same topics discussed elsewhere in the syllabus.

All quotations and page references are from the AQA recommended edition of Sutcliffe's translation (Penguin Classics, ISBN 0-140-44206-5).

SYLLABUS CHECKLIST ✔

The AQA A2 syllabus for this chapter is as follows.
Candidates should demonstrate an understanding of the following:

✔ the method of doubt and its purpose
✔ total deception. Absolute certainty of the *cogito* and its implications

✔ arguments for distinguishing mind and body: knowledge argument, appeal to God's omnipotence and indivisibility

✔ essential natures of mind and body; Descartes' rationalism, the wax example and its purposes

✔ clear and distinct ideas. Intellect and imagination and their respective roles

✔ the 'proof' of material things. The role of God and the ontological proof

✔ mind-body independence and the intermingling thesis (pilot and ship).

Essay questions will focus on the following problem areas:

✔ certainty
✔ God
✔ mind and body.

I. CERTAINTY

The method of doubt and its purpose; total deception

Descartes begins *Meditation* I by declaring that he has known for a long time that in order to establish anything 'firm and constant in the sciences' (95), he would have to start from the very foundations of all knowledge. He does not need to reject as *false* everything he thinks he knows, but he needs to 'avoid believing things that are not entirely certain and indubitable' (95). Descartes is adopting **scepticism**. He is only aiming to doubt, not to reject, his beliefs.

So Descartes begins by understanding knowledge in terms of certainty. To establish certainty, he tests his beliefs by doubt. Doubt, then, is the opposite of certainty. If we can doubt a belief, then it is not certain, and so it is not knowledge.

Descartes' understanding of knowledge, certainty and the need for doubt has been strongly criticised. Many philosophers have argued that Descartes sets the standard for knowledge too high. It seems that Descartes thinks that

Certainty is discussed on p. 37.

See THE NATURE OF THE SCEPTIC'S CHALLENGE, p. 143.

See INFALLIBILISM, p. 172.

See CLEAR AND DISTINCT IDEAS, p. 157.

Explain the relation between certainty and knowledge, according to Descartes.

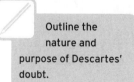

Outline the nature and purpose of Descartes' doubt.

knowledge must be *indubitable*; we must be *unable* to doubt it. If that is true, then the belief must be, in some way, infallible. However, this only seems to be true at the beginning of the *Meditations*. By *Meditation* III, Descartes argues that he can know whatever is 'clear and distinct'. This is not indubitable or infallible, because we can make mistakes, but what is clear and distinct is certain *if we are careful*.

But philosophers have also criticised Descartes' idea of certainty. It appears to be psychological: he is after beliefs that *he* is certain of. And this is not the same thing as a belief *being certain*. After all, we can make mistakes, and think something is certain (we can be certain of it), when it is not certain. But, Descartes responds, this is where the Method of doubt comes in. Because we have the habit of jumping to conclusions, only the prudent can distinguish what is genuinely certain from that which merely seems so.

Certainty, as Descartes understands it, is not a feeling; it involves a type of rational insight. He later argues that only claims that are 'clear and distinct' can be certain, and these properties are established by what is immediately apparent to the mind. In *Meditation* III, he says 'things which I see clearly cannot be other than as I conceive them' (115). So certainty is tested by reason; things *cannot* be otherwise. Descartes thinks that certainty will establish truth, because what cannot be otherwise must be true. To show that something is certain in this way is to prove it must be true, so it is true.

We will see **arguments** below that suggest that Descartes doesn't achieve this standard for many ideas, and so his method of doubting everything leaves us with scepticism, rather than the foundations of knowledge.

It is important to notice that Descartes only doubts his beliefs in order to find what is certain. Because certainty is the opposite of doubt, finding out what he can and can't doubt will establish what he can be certain of. Descartes' doubt, as we will see, is very 'methodical'. He could, he says, consider each belief of his in turn; but this would take forever. So instead he considers whether the principles on which his beliefs are grounded, principles like 'believe what you perceive', are certain or not. Descartes' doubt is *universal* – he attacks his beliefs all at once by attacking their foundations; and it is *hyperbolic*, extreme to the point of being ridiculous, for example, the possibility of an evil demon whose whole aim is to deceive me. But this is how it needs to be. One false or uncertain first principle can lead us completely astray, so he must attack these. And it is not easy, he remarks, to really withhold assent from beliefs we have held since we were children. We can't doubt just by an act of will – that's why he gives arguments, and hyperbolic doubt helps make the point and support the arguments.

Arguments from perception

Descartes begins his method of doubt by considering that he has, in the past, been deceived by his senses – things have looked a way that they are not. Things in the distance look small; sticks half-submerged in water look bent; and so on. But, Descartes remarks, such examples from unusual perceptual conditions give us no reason to doubt all perceptions, such as that you are looking at a piece of paper with writing on it. More generally, we might say that perceptual illusions are *special cases* (and ones we can frequently explain). Otherwise we wouldn't be able to talk about them as illusions. So they don't undermine perception generally.

However, a stronger scepticism can arise from thinking about perception: perception only ever informs us what the world looks like *to us*. How do we know anything about what it is 'really' like? Descartes' argument from perceptual illusions notes a difference between appearance and reality. Maybe this distinction applies to all 'appearances', all perceptions, and the world is nothing like how it appears. Descartes suggests this possibility, but for different reasons, with his argument from dreaming.

> Why is the distinction between appearance and reality philosophically important?

An argument from dreaming

Descartes extends his doubt by appealing to dreaming: he is 'a man, and consequently . . . in the habit of sleeping' (96). Sometimes when we dream, we represent to ourselves all sorts of crazy things. But sometimes we dream the most mundane things. Yet 'there are no conclusive signs by means of which one can distinguish clearly between being awake and being asleep' (97). So how can we know that what we experience we perceive rather than dream?

This argument attacks all sense-perception, even the most mundane and most certain. You cannot know that you see a piece of paper because you cannot know that you are not dreaming of seeing a piece of paper.

Some philosophers have responded to Descartes by claiming that there are, in fact, certain indications by which we can distinguish perception from dreaming, such as the far greater coherence of perception. But Descartes could respond: we could be dreaming a perfect replica of reality. Do we really *know* that all dreams have less coherence than perception? We cannot know that what is apparently perception is not really a particularly coherent dream.

Other philosophers argue that this response makes no sense. The concept

> Explain and illustrate *two* differences between the argument from dreaming and the argument from perception.

of a dream *depends* upon a concept of reality that it contrasts with. If everything were a dream, we wouldn't be able to have the concepts of dreaming and reality. So it literally doesn't make sense to suppose that everything is a dream.

While the objection makes a good point about our concepts of dreaming and reality, it isn't conclusive. First, we might argue that even in a dream, we can dream that we wake up, but we are still asleep. Perhaps the development of our concepts of 'dream' and 'reality' are analogous: they refer to a difference within our experience, but this doesn't mean that the *whole* of our experience is disconnected from reality in the way that we think dreams are. It is not obvious that this supposition makes no sense. Second, and perhaps more importantly, the objection *misunderstands* scepticism. Descartes does not *need* to say 'perhaps everything *is* a dream'; he only needs to argue that we *cannot know when* we are dreaming and when we are awake. This would allow us to develop concepts of dreaming and reality on the basis of our different experiences; but the correct application of those concepts isn't secure.

However, Descartes presents a different argument. At the very end of the *Meditations*, Descartes agrees that we can distinguish between dreaming and waking experience, by the greater coherence of perception (168). But this answer, he claims, is not available to him at the beginning of the *Meditations*, because of the possibility of the evil demon.

Before introducing that possibility, Descartes presses the argument from dreaming further. It may *seem* that 'whether I am awake or sleeping, two and three added together always make five' (98). But people do make mistakes about matters they believe they know certainly. And so even truths of logic and of mathematics come under attack. Descartes says, 'it is possible . . . that I should be deceived every time I add two and three' (98). Are not just his perceptual experiences, but also his thoughts, open to doubt?

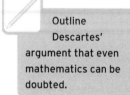

Assess Descartes' argument from dreaming.

Outline Descartes' argument that even mathematics can be doubted.

The demon

In order to take his scepticism to heart, Descartes introduces the suggestion that God does not exist and that all our experiences are produced in us by an evil demon who wants to deceive us. The possibility of the demon means that it is possible that even if I could tell the difference between being awake and dreaming, my experiences when I am awake are no more real than when I am dreaming. All beliefs about the external world and events in time are thrown into doubt, as they are based on my experience, which the evil demon controls. And all knowledge, such as mathematics, I believed that I had on the basis of thought alone is undercut, because the demon can control my thoughts, too.

Total deception

Descartes has reached a point of total deception. If he has no mental *agency*, no control over his mind at all, over what he experiences or what he thinks, then the very idea of knowing anything seems to be undermined.

In *Meditation* II, however, Descartes reconsiders this idea, and argues that, even if the evil demon exists, there is one thing he can be sure of. And in *Meditation* VI, Descartes goes on to resolve the issues that led him into doubt in the first place. To do this, he needs to establish, in reverse order, that there could be no evil demon deceiving him; that he is not dreaming, and that a physical world, including his body, really does exist; and that he can trust his senses. The answers to all these doubts, it turns out, is that God exists and is not a deceiver (see THE ROLE OF GOD, p. 187).

For further discussion of scepticism and how to resolve it, see THE REFUTATION OF SCEPTICISM, p. 143.

Assess Descartes' use of doubt in search of certainty.

Key points • • •

- Descartes adopts scepticism, bringing his beliefs into doubt, but not rejecting them as false. He does this in order to find out, in the end, what (we can know) is true.
- He understands doubt as the opposite of certainty. What we can know needs to be certain if we are careful. We can be certain of what is clear and distinct.
- His doubt is methodical, universal and hyperbolic. Descartes uses his method of doubt to undermine his beliefs systematically.
- His argument from perception throws doubt on believing everything our senses tell us.
- His argument from dreaming throws doubt on all sense perception, and on truths of logic and mathematics. Some philosophers have objected that it does not work, because we can tell the difference between dreaming and being awake. Others argue that the idea that we are always dreaming makes no sense, because the concept of dreaming logically requires a concept of reality to contrast it with.
- Descartes' argument from the evil demon makes the previous doubts more

vivid, and throws doubt on all beliefs, because the demon is able to control my experiences and my thoughts.

Absolute certainty of the cogito *and its implications* (Meditation *II*)

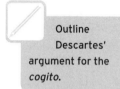

Outline Descartes' argument for the *cogito*.

See DESCARTES' RATIONALISM, p. 179.

Descartes argues there is one thing he can be completely sure of, even if the evil demon exists: that he thinks, and from this, that he exists. He cannot doubt that he thinks, because doubting is a kind of thinking. If the demon were to make him doubt that he is thinking, that would only show that he is. Equally, he cannot doubt that he exists: if he were to doubt that he exists, that would prove he does exist – as something that thinks. The *cogito*, 'I think', is Descartes' first certainty, the first stepping stone to knowledge.

In this argument, Descartes lays the foundations for his **rationalism**. When he reflects on why he is certain of the *cogito*, he says 'In this first knowledge, there is nothing except a clear and distinct perception of what I affirm' (113). He goes on to argue for the general principle that *at the time he considers it*, a thought which is clear and distinct he must believe to be true, he cannot doubt it.

The status of the *cogito* as the first certainty, and how he has arrived at it, also lays the foundations for Descartes' **dualism**, which we will look at in the next section.

Going further: do 'I' exist?

What does it mean to say 'I exist' or 'I think'? We will see below that Descartes claims that 'I' am a thinking *thing*, a substance. Many philosophers have thought he means to show that I am the *same* thing from one moment in time to the next. The same 'I' persists from one thought to another. But how can Descartes be certain of this? Philosophers have objected that, with the hypothesis of the evil demon, Descartes cannot know that there is anything that persists in time which is a unity. There is *only a succession of thoughts*. When this objection was presented to him, Descartes' response, in the appendix to the *Meditations* called 'Objections and Replies', is to say that thoughts logically require a thinker. This claim, he thinks, is clear and distinct, so we can be certain of it.

That depends what he means by a 'thinker'. If he means a subject that persists over time, then this is not obvious. It doesn't seem to be contradictory to deny it. Perhaps the evil demon is simply creating a series of false thoughts, among which is the thought that a thinker, a substance, an 'I', exists. How could Descartes know otherwise?

But by 'thinker', Descartes may only mean a *momentary* subject of a thought: there can't be a thought unless something thinks it. Descartes is not arguing here that this thinker persists in time. But then there is a question whether this is enough for Descartes' later arguments. If I don't exist over time, only at a moment, it is difficult to see how I could ever know more than the thoughts 'I exist' and 'I think'. As soon as Descartes says that to be a thinker is to doubt, will, imagine and so on, he assumes we can say these activities belong to the *same* subject, that he (the same thinker) does all this. But that means he is taking it for granted that thinkers persist in time. But we have argued that Descartes can't know this.

> See THE ESSENTIAL NATURES OF MIND AND BODY, p. 160.

> Assess whether Descartes successfully proves the *cogito*.

Key points • • •

- 'I think', the *cogito*, is Descartes' first certainty.
- He cannot doubt that he thinks because doubting is a kind of thinking.
- His argument for the *cogito* inspires his rationalism and his theory of clear and distinct ideas.
- His argument rests on the claim that thoughts logically require a thinker.

Clear and distinct ideas (Meditation III)

To be clear, an idea must be 'open and present to the attending mind'; to be distinct, it must not only be clear, but precise and separated from other ideas, so that it 'plainly contains in itself nothing other than what is clear'. We saw that the *cogito* is the first clear and distinct idea. When Descartes reflects on why he is certain of it, he says 'In this first knowledge, there is nothing except a clear

> *Principles*, I.45

Explain and illustrate what Descartes means by a clear and distinct idea.

and distinct perception of what I affirm' (113). He goes on to argue that *at the time we consider it*, a thought which is clear and distinct we must believe to be true, we cannot doubt it.

At this point, Descartes has only argued that we can know a clear and distinct idea to be true at the time we hold it in mind. However, he goes on, we cannot think of that one thing all the time so as to keep perceiving it clearly. When our attention is turned away from it, we can no longer be certain of it, even though we remember that we were certain of it. This is because we can go wrong, we can *think* we clearly and distinctly perceived some idea when we did not. In order to be certain that what we once thought was clear and distinct really is certain, we need to know that we are not being deceived by an evil demon. Descartes sets out to show that we can know this, because we can know that God exists, and would not allow an evil demon to deceive us, nor would God deceive us.

See THE ROLE OF GOD, p. 187.

The Cartesian circle

In trying to prove the existence of God, Descartes will, of course, have to rely on what he can clearly and distinctly perceive, because this is the only way he can know anything. But Descartes also needs to prove that God exists for us to know what we clearly and distinctly perceived. This leads to a famous objection: that he uses the existence of God to establish his doctrine of clear and distinct ideas, and that he uses his doctrine of clear and distinct ideas to establish the existence of God. It seems that he says

We consider another objection in DESCARTES' RATIONALISM, p. 179.

1. I am certain that God exists only because *I am certain of whatever I clearly and distinctly perceive*; and yet
2. *I am certain of whatever I clearly and distinctly perceive* only because I am certain that God exists.

Explain and illustrate the difference between an idea being clear and distinct at the time we consider it, and being clear and distinct in general.

But Descartes, in his replies to objections, rejects this reading. I can be certain of what I clearly and distinctly perceive without knowing that God exists, but *only at the time* that I perceive it. God's existence adds a *general* certainty that what I clearly and distinctly perceive is true: 'When I said that we can know nothing for certain until we are aware that God exists, I expressly declared that I was speaking of knowledge of those conclusions that can be recalled when we are no longer attending to the arguments by which we deduced them.'

In other words, there are two interpretations of the phrase in italics, and one interpretation is used in (1) and the second in (2). According to the first interpretation, while I am clearly and distinctly perceiving some *particular* **proposition**, then I am certain of that proposition. But because of the possibility of the evil demon, I lose this certainty as soon as I turn my attention away from it, as I may be deceived that I did perceive it clearly and distinctly. So I don't yet know that proposition is true unless I'm actually attending to it.

In his proofs of the existence of God, Descartes uses our clear and distinct understanding of the idea of God, held in our mind throughout each proof. Having proved God's existence, he can now claim (the second interpretation, in 2 above) he is certain that *whatever* he has clearly and distinctly perceived, he can be certain of. And he is certain of this *general principle*, linking clearness and distinctness to truth, because God exists, and is no deceiver.

The difficulty facing Descartes is whether he is entitled to claim that he can be certain of what he clearly and distinctly perceives, even at the time he perceives it, while it is still possible that he is being deceived by a demon. His response is that it is simply our nature to assent to such clear and distinct thoughts – we cannot but believe them, because 'things which I see clearly cannot be other than as I conceive them' (115).

> **Discuss** Descartes' claim that God's existence is necessary for him to be certain of clear and distinct ideas in general.

> **Assess** Descartes' principle that we can know that whatever can be clearly and distinctly perceived is true.

Key points • • •

- Clear and distinct ideas are the foundation of knowledge. A clear idea is 'open and present to the attending mind'; a distinct idea is precise, separated from other ideas.
- We can know that an idea that is clear and distinct is true while we consider it. We can only know that all ideas that are clear and distinct are true once God's existence is proven.

II. MIND AND BODY

The essential natures of mind and body, the wax example and its purposes (Meditations II and V)

The nature of mind

In *Meditation* II, after his argument that he is a thinking thing, Descartes lists the type of activities that a 'thinking thing' engages in, providing us with a more detailed description of the nature of the mind: 'a thing that doubts, perceives, affirms, denies, wills, does not will, that imagines also, and which feels' (107) (Descartes adds love and hate in *Meditation* III).

But doesn't this connect mind and body? Surely sense perception requires a body, and I cannot doubt that I *have* sensory experiences, whether or not they are **veridical**. But, Descartes notes, I have sensory experiences in my dreams as well, when I am not in fact seeing or hearing at all. So all I can be certain of is the experience, not that the experience is caused by sensing. Understood like this, independent of their cause, these experiences are nothing other than a form of thinking (107), and so don't depend on having a body. So he puts forward a type of **sense-data** theory – what is immediately available to the mind is perceptual experience, irrespective of whatever lies 'beyond' that experience in the external world: 'it is very certain that it seems to me that I see light, hear a noise and feel heat; and this is properly what in me is called perceiving, and this, taken in this precise sense, is nothing other than thinking' (107).

Further knowledge of the mind comes from realising that every thought we have about physical objects illustrates something about the mind. In Descartes' famous example of the wax, he talks a little about the nature of body, but he is also exploring what we can know about the body, and how this knowledge can show us more about the nature of mind.

The wax example

Descartes' discussion goes like this:

1. When I melt a piece of wax, it loses all of its original sensory qualities (the particular taste, smell, feel and shape it has); yet I believe it is the same wax. So what I think of as the wax is not its sensory qualities.

> Outline and illustrate Descartes' claim that we have different 'modes of consciousness'.

Sense-data theories of perception – representative realism and idealism – are discussed in KNOWLEDGE OF THE EXTERNAL WORLD, p. 199.

2. So when I think of the wax, I am thinking of something that is extended, i.e. takes up space, and is changeable, i.e. its sensory and spatial properties can change.

3. I also think that the possible changes it can go through outstrip what I can imagine; I can't imagine all the changes I know the wax can undergo. So it's not through my imagination that I have my conception of the wax. Rather, and somewhat surprisingly, I 'perceive' (comprehend) the wax through my understanding.

4. The wax I think of this way and the wax I detect through my senses is the same wax.

5. Although we say we 'see' the wax (through vision), in fact we judge (through understanding) that it is present from what we see.

The argument is about *our knowledge* of physical objects, rather than the real nature or existence of physical objects. The title of the meditation is 'Of the nature of the human mind; and that it is easier to know than the body'. Descartes' claims about the nature of body actually come in *Meditation* V, and his proof that they exist in *Meditation* VI.

See THE PROOF OF MATERIAL THINGS, p. 176.

Descartes' question is not 'What is the wax?' but 'What is our idea of the wax?'. So in (1), Descartes is not attempting to assert the identity conditions of the piece of wax, he is noticing that our conception of 'the wax' doesn't appear to depend on its particular sensory qualities. So what is our conception? That the wax is something that endures through such changes (it is changeable), but also that it is extended (takes up space). If this is our conception of the wax, then it is not a conception derived from our senses or imagination, but an intellectual conception of it, and as such, given by our understanding.

This is discussed further in INTELLECT AND IMAGINATION, p. 171.

So, Descartes argues, at first, our idea of the wax is of something defined by its sensory properties. But this idea is muddled. When we realise that we comprehend the wax through understanding, as something extended and changeable, our comprehension of the wax has become clear and distinct. To find out what can be known, Descartes pursues his method of forming a clear and distinct idea of the object of knowledge. The best idea we can form of physical objects is that they are extended and changeable. We also realise that talk of 'seeing the wax' is misleading. We judge or infer the presence of physical objects from our sensory experiences.

Descartes puts these conclusions to use in two ways as described in the next two sections.

Outline and explain Descartes' wax argument.

The nature of body

In *Meditation* V, Descartes does ask the question 'What is the nature of physical bodies?' Although Descartes has shown what our *idea* of physical objects is in the wax argument, we may have got an entirely wrong-headed conception of them, for we don't know that our clear and distinct conception of them corresponds to anything real or even possible. But in *Meditation* V, he claims that we can know that CLEAR AND DISTINCT IDEAS (p. 157) are true. He has argued, in the wax example, that we can clearly and distinctly conceive of physical objects as extended and changeable, but not as having particular sensory properties. He therefore concludes that physical objects, if they exist, are essentially extended and changeable.

Explain and illustrate Descartes' argument that physical objects are extended.

More on the nature of mind

Descartes argues that the example of the wax helps us understand the mind in three ways. First, every thought about the wax confirms the existence of the mind. Second, thinking about how we know the wax helps separate the different faculties of sensory perceptual experience, imagination and the understanding. So we gain a clearer and more distinct idea of what happens in the mind, we understand the different 'modes of thought' (113). Finally, because we comprehend the wax through understanding, rather than by sensory perception, although it seemed that bodies were known better than the mind, in fact they are not. Nothing could seem more obvious and certain than the beliefs we have about what we experience through our senses. But it turns out that we use the understanding to comprehend bodies. We use the understanding to comprehend our minds as well, but this is much clearer and more easy than in the case of comprehending bodies. So we know the mind better than the body.

Modes of thought should not be thought of as 'parts' of the mind; see INDIVISBILITY, p. 166.

See DESCARTES' RATIONALISM, p. 179.

On the basis of introspection alone, Descartes feels able to confirm the different modes of consciousness that the mind is capable of. He doesn't consider the possibility that I might be mistaken about my mode of thought – I can't mistakenly think that I'm imagining when I'm conceiving, can't think I'm doubting when I'm willing and so on, at least when what I am thinking about is immediately available to consciousness.

Critically discuss the purposes to which Descartes puts the wax argument.

Going further: Hume on extension

As an empiricist, Hume challenges Descartes' argument that our knowledge of physical objects as extended comes from understanding, not the senses. He argues that our only chance of forming an idea of extension is *by abstraction* from particular sensory experiences. We have no conception of extension that is neither visible, and therefore derived from sight, nor tangible, and therefore derived from touch.

Descartes explicitly rejects this claim. In the wax example, he argues that his conception of the wax as extended is not given by the imagination, because he can understand that the possibilities of extension outstrip my imagination. The idea of extension outstrips what the senses can provide. But his claim that our concept of extension therefore derives from the understanding instead does not mean extension is neither visible nor tangible: the wax conceived by the understanding is the *same* wax that is perceived through the senses. However, it is certainly debatable whether Descartes is right that our concept of extension is not derived from the senses, formed through abstraction.

> Assess Descartes' claim that we know physical objects are extended through the intellect, not the senses.

Going further: the different natures of mind and body

Descartes' insight into how minds and bodies are different still poses questions for philosophers today. Thoughts, in all of Descartes' varieties, are always 'about' or refer to something. For example, if I believe Paris is the capital of France, my belief is about Paris. Every desire is a desire for something, for example, chocolate. Every decision is a decision to do something. The 'something' in each case is *represented* in the thought, and this representation is essential to the thought. But the states of physical things, such as chairs or trees, are never 'about' anything, they never represent something (unless we use them in this way). Physical states, such as an arrangement of certain molecules, just exist without reference to anything else. The states of your brain are just chemical states, like the states of a

See INTENTIONALITY AND ARTIFICIAL INTELLIGENCE, p. 30, and The 'HARD PROBLEM OF CONSCIOUSNESS', p. 43.

Explain the challenge of representation and consciousness to the view that the mind is just the body.

chair. How could they ever be about anything? So how could beliefs, desires, and so on be states of your brain?

Consciousness poses a similar problem. Visual perceptions look a certain way, you experience colour and shape; emotions feel a certain way, as do bodily sensations. There's nothing in what we know about the chemistry of the brain that would indicate these properties exist.

Key points • • •

- Descartes argues that the nature of the mind is thinking, that is, doubting, perceiving, affirming and denying, willing, imagining and feeling. These are different 'modes of consciousness'.
- In the wax example, Descartes discusses what our idea of physical objects is. It is not until *Meditation* V that he claims our idea is correct.
- Our idea of a physical object, for example, the wax, cannot be the idea of its sensory properties, because these can change while we think the object is the same object. Our idea of a physical object is therefore of something extended and changeable.
- This is not an idea that comes from the imagination, but from the understanding, because we understand that the object can go through more changes than we can imagine.
- We know the mind better than the body. We use the understanding in both cases, but the mind is easier to know and our ideas of it are clearer.

Arguments for distinguishing mind and body (Meditations II and VI)

The knowledge argument

As we saw in THE ESSENTIAL NATURES OF MIND AND BODY (p. 160), in *Meditation* II, having argued that he knows he thinks, Descartes then asks what kind of thing he is. Discussions of identity seek to establish the essential properties of something, what makes it the thing that it is. The question 'What am I?' can be answered by considering the question of what it is for me to exist. Descartes is trying to identify his essence, those properties which, if he lost them, would mean he was no longer what he is. (An island, for instance, must be surrounded by water. If the water dried up, joining it to the mainland, it would cease to be an island.)

He remarks that he can continue to doubt whether he has a body; after all, he only believes he has a body as a result of his perceptual experiences, and so the demon could be deceiving him about this. But he cannot doubt that he has a mind, that is, that he thinks. So he knows he exists even though he doesn't know whether or not he has a body. From this Descartes concludes that it is possible for him to exist without a body. He is essentially a mind, not a body. He would not necessarily cease to be himself if he ceased to have a body, but he would necessarily cease to be himself if he didn't have a mind.

Appeal to God's omnipotence

Descartes' argument so far is that minds can exist without bodies. However, on its own, it doesn't establish dualism. For this, we need to know that bodies exist and that their nature is quite different from that of the mind. Descartes argues in *Meditation* II that the nature of body (as extended) is different from mind (as thinking thing). He doesn't present arguments for the existence of bodies until *Meditation* VI, when he also argues explicitly for substance dualism, the claim that there are two distinct types of thing which can exist independently of each other.

In *Meditation* V, Descartes argues that he can know that clear and distinct ideas are true; and in *Meditation* VI, he expresses this as 'I know that all the things I conceive clearly and distinctly can be produced by God precisely as I conceive them' (156). He then reasserts that our ideas of mind and of body are clear and distinct. Furthermore, there is nothing further to the mind than thought; and nothing further to the body than extension. So the ideas of mind and body show that minds and bodies are completely distinct. So in creating minds, God would not need to create bodies; and in creating bodies, God would not need to create minds. This shows that they can exist separately, that is, that mind and body are two distinct substances.

In this argument, Descartes doesn't mean that God can *miraculously* create minds and bodies existing independently. He means that it is of the *nature* of minds and bodies to exist independently. That is, that they are separate substances is not miraculous, but natural. In fact, Descartes' argument doesn't

---

Explain and illustrate the difference between properties that are essential and those that are not.

Outline Descartes' argument that mind and body are different because he knows he has a mind, but does not (yet) know he has a body.

See THE ESSENTIAL NATURES OF MIND AND BODY, p. 160.

See THE PROOF OF MATERIAL THINGS, p. 176.

Explain Descartes' argument for dualism from the distinct concepts of mind and body.

really need the appeal to God's omnipotence at all. Given that he can know that his clear and distinct ideas are true, and he clearly and distinctly perceives that the essence of mind and the essence of body are fundamentally different, he can conclude that minds and bodies – if they exist at all – exist as separate substances.

Indivisibility

Mind and body are distinct things, because they have different properties. Descartes develops this further when he argues that, unlike the body, the mind does not have any parts and cannot be divided. He argues: 'when I consider my mind, that is to say myself insofar as I am only a thinking thing, I can distinguish no parts' (164). It is with the *whole* mind that one thinks, wills, doubts and so on. These are just different ways of thinking, not parts of the mind. By contrast, the body does have parts. You can literally lose part of your body, for example, a hand. So mind and body are entirely distinct types of thing. Since he has also argued that both exist, he concludes that substance dualism is true.

In the seventeenth century, the issue of the relationship between mind and body was much discussed, and the view that man is part angel, part beast was advocated by so many philosophers and theologians, it was almost deemed an orthodoxy. But unlike many of his contemporaries, Descartes defended dualism not (in the first instance) on the basis of theology, but by these arguments from **epistemology** and **metaphysics**.

Explain Descartes' argument that the body can be divided, but the mind cannot.

Why does Descartes' think that his mind can exist independently of his body?

Objections to Descartes' argument

Going further: knowledge and reality

Most philosophers believe Descartes' argument that the mind can exist without the body, as it is given above, doesn't work. Just because Descartes can *think* of his mind existing without his body, this doesn't mean that his mind *really can* exist without his body. Perhaps there is some metaphysical connection between his mind and body that would make this impossible that Descartes doesn't know about.

There are two difficulties facing Descartes' argument. The first relates to claims about whether one thing (e.g. mind) is the same thing as another (e.g. body), or whether they are different. We can illustrate this idea with a different example. Suppose I believe (rightly) that the Masked Man has robbed the bank. I also believe that my father has not robbed the bank. I conclude that my father is not the Masked Man. Is the conclusion justified?

No, and here's why. It is true that if two things (in this case, people) have different properties, then they cannot be identical. If the Masked Man robbed the bank and my father didn't, then my father is not the Masked Man. But it is not true that if I *believe* that two things have different properties, then they cannot be identical. I could be mistaken about the properties things have. Suppose my father is the Masked Man. Then my father did rob the bank, and my belief that he didn't is wrong.

Descartes argues that the mind is independent of the body (and so not the body), because he can conceive of it existing without the body. Now if the mind can exist without the body, then it cannot be the same thing as the body. But from just Descartes' thought, we cannot infer this. If the mind is the body, then obviously it cannot exist independently of the body. In this case, Descartes' conception is wrong.

A second difficulty follows this one. Descartes is using his thought to infer what is possible. If the mind is the body, then it is impossible for the mind to exist without the body. So to know what is possible here, we first need some independent reason to think that the mind is something distinct from the body, such as the argument from indivisibility.

Even then, we need to be very cautious using what we can conceive of as a test of possibility. For example, if my father is the Masked Man, then it is impossible that the Masked Man robbed the bank, but my father didn't. Yet it is easy to imagine precisely this, that the Masked Man robbed the bank, but my father didn't. What I am imagining, though, is that the man who is the Masked Man is not my father; and it is questionable how coherent that is.

> Identical things must have exactly the same properties. This is known as Leibniz's Law of the Indiscernibility of Identicals.

> **?**
> Does Descartes' argument from knowledge support the conclusion that the mind can exist independently of the body?

APPEAL TO GOD'S OMNIPOTENCE

Descartes can use his argument from God's omnipotence (really from the truth of clear and distinct ideas) to reply to this objection. Our clear and distinct ideas of mind and body are *complete* and *exclusive*. The mind is *nothing but* thought;

the body is *nothing but* extension. We know this to be true, because the ideas are clear and distinct. It is therefore impossible that the mind is, or depends on, the body. If it were, then the mind would be extension as well as thought. But we know that it is not.

Descartes is no longer resting his argument on knowledge and doubt. He is resting it on the doctrine of clear and distinct ideas, and the claim that whatever can be clearly and distinctly conceived shows us how the world really is.

Is Descartes' appeal to God's omnipotence an improvement on his argument from knowledge?

INDIVISIBILITY

What about Descartes' argument that the mind doesn't have parts? It does seem right to say that we will, think, imagine, with the whole of our minds, not a literal part. However, cases of mental illness, for example, multiple personality syndrome, might be used to suggest that the mind can be divided. In such cases, it seems that some aspects of the person's mind are unable to communicate with other aspects. Freudian ideas of consciousness and the unconscious suggest something similar: people may desire one thing consciously and the opposite thing unconsciously. While this doesn't make the mind *spatially* divisible, it makes sense of talking about 'parts' of the mind. However, Descartes could respond that the *way* in which the mind is divisible is entirely different from the way in which the body is. So his argument that mind and body are different because they have different properties is still valid.

We can respond, though, that the argument assumes that *minds exist*. If minds do not exist as things at all, then we cannot talk about 'their' properties. A materialist will claim that there are no 'minds', only mental properties, which are properties of persons or brains.

Assess Descartes' arguments from the distinct ideas of mind and body to the separate existence of mind and body.

ON THE SELF

Another objection is this. When discussing the *cogito* (p. 156), we noticed a problem with Descartes' assumption that for there to be thoughts, there must be a mind which has these thoughts, if we suppose that a mind is something that persists in time, which is the same 'I' for all the different thoughts it thinks. Descartes has not shown that such a thing exists for more than a moment. So he has not shown that he is '*a* thing that thinks', that is, that the same thing thinks in many different ways, rather than a sequence of such things.

To illustrate this further, consider that Descartes allows that 'it might perhaps happen, if I ceased to think, that I would at the same time cease to be or to exist' (105). In dreamless sleep, we certainly cease to think (at least consciously). If Descartes wishes to establish that he is the same person from one day to the next, he will again need the idea of the mind as a substance that persists even through those times when there is no thought. For example, when he comes to say he can distinguish dreaming from waking, he is presupposing that he – the same mind – has experienced both. But that means he must persist between dreaming and waking, and during some of that time, he will have no thoughts at all. However, Descartes can reply that at this point, he knows God exists, and God guarantees that Descartes' clear and distinct memories are true. And memory logically requires being the same person from one moment to the next.

Arguments about dualism

Quite independently of these arguments, we may ask whether Descartes' dualism is a good philosophical theory. It is most often rejected because it cannot give an adequate account of mental causation. The mind and the body have very different natures: the mind is essentially thinking, the body is essentially extended, that is, it exists in and takes up space. The mind is not extended, it does not have parts. So how is it that something mental, which is not in space and has no physical force, can affect something physical, which is in space and moved by physical forces? Descartes admitted that this was a problem he never solved.

Substance dualism famously faces a number of other objections as well. Here are two. First, substance dualism seems to make me, a person with both mind and body, essentially *two* things, connected together. This doesn't do justice to our experience of being just *one* thing, which we might call an 'embodied mind'. It 'splits' our experience, which fundamentally seems unified. Descartes agreed that our experience was of the unity of mind and body, and we'll discuss this further in the next section.

Second, Descartes' claim is that the mind is not dependent on the body. That is why he can say the mind is a separate substance (substances, by definition, are not dependent on anything else to exist). But modern work on the brain suggests that the mind is very dependent on the brain to function, and in the end, to exist at all. Most importantly for Descartes' claim that the mind's essential property is thinking, damage to certain parts of the brain can make someone unable to think. So alterations in the body can affect the essential property of the mind; so the mind does not have even its essential property independently

'Descartes fails to establish that the mind is a substance.' Discuss.

SUBSTANCE DUALISM is discussed at length on p. 7.

See ACCOUNTS OF MENTAL CAUSATION, p. 58.

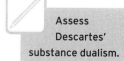

Assess Descartes' substance dualism.

of the body. Since this property of thinking defines the mind, we can say that our minds are not independent of our bodies.

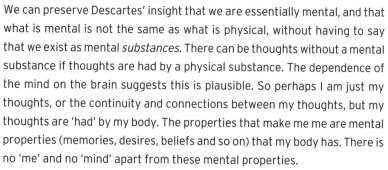

> ### Going further: minds without substance dualism
>
> We can preserve Descartes' insight that we are essentially mental, and that what is mental is not the same as what is physical, without having to say that we exist as mental *substances*. There can be thoughts without a mental substance if thoughts are had by a physical substance. The dependence of the mind on the brain suggests this is plausible. So perhaps I am just my thoughts, or the continuity and connections between my thoughts, but my thoughts are 'had' by my body. The properties that make me me are mental properties (memories, desires, beliefs and so on) that my body has. There is no 'me' and no 'mind' apart from these mental properties.
>
> An objection from Locke suggests this is the right way to answer the question 'What am I?' He argued that even if substance dualism were true, personal identity is comprised by psychological continuity, not by the continued existence of a mental substance. If all my thoughts, desires, beliefs, emotions, memories and so on were swapped with those of another thinking thing, 'I' would go with my thoughts and so on rather than remain the same thinking thing, but now with a completely different set of mental properties.

The question of what I am, the question of PERSONAL IDENTITY is discussed on pp. 174 and 187.

Key points • • •

- Descartes asks 'What am I?', a question about his essence, those properties which, if he lost them, would mean he was no longer what he is.
- He argues that he is a mind, but does not know if he has a body. This means, he thinks, that having a body is not essential to being what he is, a mind, and so minds can exist without bodies.
- Philosophers object that Descartes' conclusion doesn't follow: what he knows is not a good test of what is *really* possible.
- Descartes argues that we have clear and distinct ideas of mind and body as essentially different, and that God can create whatever Descartes can clearly and distinctly conceive. So mind and body can exist separately.

- Again, minds and bodies have different properties – minds are indivisible; bodies have parts – so they aren't the same kinds of thing. Considerations from mental illness and psychoanalysis suggest that minds might be divisible, but in a very different way from bodies.
- If I am my mind, independent of my body, and the mind only exists when it is thinking, I cease to exist in a dreamless sleep. Descartes can reply that once he has proved the existence of God, he can know that he is the same mind from moment to moment, and overnight, because he has clear and distinct memories.
- Three objections to substance dualism are:

  - Because it claims mind and body are so different, it cannot account for mental causation.
  - Because it claims mind and body are different substances, it cannot account for our experience of being a unified, 'embodied mind'.
  - The mind is very dependent on the brain to function. So it is not an independent substance.

Intellect and imagination and their respective roles (Meditations *II* and *VI*)

The distinction between intellect and imagination

In both THE WAX EXAMPLE (p. 160) and at the beginning of *Meditation* VI, Descartes distinguishes imagination from the intellect.

First, imagination works with images that are derived from sensing. By 'imagining', Descartes means creating images before one's 'mind's eye' (or if you imagine a sound, your 'mind's ear' and so on). The wax example is meant to show that the intellect does not work in the same way – I *understand* the wax can have indefinitely many shapes, but I cannot run through all these shapes in my imagination (109). So my understanding of the wax, my idea of what the wax is, isn't derived from my imagination. The intellect grasps what something is without depending on images. For instance, I can have ideas of very complex objects, like a chiliagon – a mathematical figure with 1,000 sides – without being able to form images of them. And I can understand that this figure is different from a figure with 10,000 sides (a myriagon).

Second, this also brings to our attention that imagining requires effort (try imagining a figure with just 20 sides, let alone 1,000!).

Finally, Descartes argues that while the intellect is essential to what I am, imagination is not. In *Meditation* VI, he says we may say that when I turn my attention to my intellect, my mind turns towards itself and its ideas; when I think about my imagination, my mind turns towards my body and ideas derived from the senses.

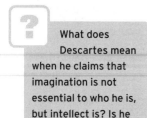

Outline Descartes' distinction between the intellect and the imagination.

Imagination and dualism

Because imagination uses images derived from the senses, in *Meditation* II Descartes considers imagination along with sense perception as a possible objection to his argument that the mind can exist without the body. But, as we saw in THE ESSENTIAL NATURES OF MIND AND BODY (p. 160), he concludes that just having these images is a form of thought, and doesn't depend on the body. In *Meditation* VI, he goes further and says that he can conceive of himself as existing 'whole and entire' (157) without imagination or sense perception.

This is not to say that imagination and sense perception are not parts of the mind. They are; it is just that, unlike the intellect, they are not *essential* to the mind. Instead, Descartes argues that they result from the fusion of mind and body (discussed in the next section). The fact that the imagination, unlike the intellect, uses images that it has apparently derived from the senses, and the fact it requires effort, could both be explained if we have bodies, and the imagination is in some way dependent on the body.

What does Descartes mean when he claims that imagination is not essential to who he is, but intellect is? Is he right?

Key points • • •

- Descartes distinguishes the imagination from the intellect in three ways:

  - The imagination uses images derived from the senses.
  - It requires effort.
  - It is not essential to the mind.

- Descartes argues that imagination (and sense perception) result from the fusion of mind and body. They are mental faculties, though the mind can exist without them.

Mind-body independence and the intermingling thesis (Meditation *VI*)

How is the mind related to the body? While Descartes has argued that the mind as intellect is distinct from the body, we have just seen that the existence of the imagination complicates the picture. In *Meditation* VI, Descartes says 'nature . . . teaches me by these feelings of pain, hunger, thirst, etc., that I am not only lodged in my body, like a pilot in his ship, but, besides, that I am joined to it very closely and indeed so compounded and intermingled with my body, that I form, as it were, a single whole with it' (159). Because 'one single whole' doesn't sound like 'two substances', this claim and its implications for Descartes' dualism are puzzling.

The argument from bodily sensations and emotions

Reflecting on perception, sensation and feeling, we notice that we perceive we have bodies, and that our bodies – this particular physical object that we have a close and unique relationship with – can be affected in many beneficial and harmful ways. This is brought to our attention through our bodily appetites, such as hunger and thirst, through emotions, such as anger, sadness, love, and through sensations, such as pain, pleasure, colours, sound and so on. All these experiences have their origins in the body.

This doesn't mean that mind and body aren't distinct; in *Meditation* VI, before giving his ARGUMENTS FOR DISTINGUISHING MIND AND BODY (p. 164), Descartes carefully considers what the idea of the mind really involves. He argues that we can still conceive of ourselves existing complete without imagination or feeling. Nevertheless, our experiences of our bodies through bodily sensations and emotions show that the connection between the mind and body is very close: 'these feelings of hunger, thirst, pain, etc., are nothing other than certain confused ways of thinking, which arise from and depend on the union and, as it were, the mingling of the mind and the body' (159). ('Confused' here is not being opposed to 'clear and distinct', but means 'as a result of the fusion of the mind and body'.) Descartes argues that if mind and body were not intermingled, then 'when my body is hurt, I would not on that account feel pain, I who am only a thinking thing, but I should perceive the wound by my understanding alone' (159). I wouldn't *feel pain*, I would merely observe damage.

> Explain what Descartes' example of the pilot and the ship shows about the relation of mind and body.

Furthermore, this union of mind and body is a union between the mind and the *whole* body. We feel pain in the various parts of our body. The soul does have privileged connection to the brain (a point of causal connection in the pineal gland), but the soul does not feel all pains to be in the brain! So Descartes argues that it is joined to all parts of the body, although it 'exercises its functions' at the pineal gland 'more particularly than elsewhere'. This is really just a physiological observation.

This 'intermingling' doesn't mean that the mind is divisible like the body. The mind is indivisible, and when I lose part of my body, I don't lose part of my mind with it! This again shows, 'if I did not already know it', that the mind and body are distinct.

The point of 'union'

Descartes himself found it difficult to understand how it is that the mind and body are distinct substances, yet form a 'union':

Letter to Princess Elizabeth, 28 June 1643

> It does not seem to me that the human mind is capable of forming a very distinct conception both of the distinction between the soul and the body and of their union; for to do this it is necessary to conceive of them as a single thing and, at the same time, to conceive of them as two things; and the two conceptions are mutually opposed.

However, he spells out what he takes to be the *point* of the theory. The 'union' theory enables us to understand the nature and meaning of sensations and emotions: they inform us of what is beneficial or harmful. In the production and experience of these, mind and body are working together to secure the good of the *whole*. Our emotions, if well-directed, remarks Descartes, allow us 'to taste the greatest sweetness in this life'. If we abandon the idea of union, then the significance of bodily sensations and emotions, working for the good of the whole, is lost. An angel connected to a body, having no sensations, would not necessarily understand that certain alterations in the body were good or bad for it. If it did make such judgements, they would have to be inferred rather than immediate.

Passions of the Soul, article 212

> **Explain and illustrate** why, according to Descartes, we have the experience of being 'united' with our bodies.

Going further: the metaphysics of union

It is hard to know what to infer metaphysically – about the mind and body as substances – from Descartes' appeal to what it is like to be a mind-body unity, experiencing bodily sensations and emotions. Descartes offers a suggestion as puzzling as it is illuminating in the same letter to Elizabeth: that the idea of the union between mind and body is a 'third primitive notion' – it is basic and unanalysable. Union is not *essential* to either mind or body, since either can exist without the other; but it is not accidental: 'since the body has all the dispositions necessary to receive the soul, and without which it is not strictly a human body, it could not come about without a miracle, that a soul should not be joined to it'. The comment that, unless united to a soul, a body is not a *human body*, suggests (but not conclusively) that the 'human body', body and soul together, can be considered as a unity, a thing, a *substance*, in its own right, a substance created from the union of body and soul. However, philosophers don't agree on whether this is the implication we should draw from his union theory or not.

Letter to Regius, December 1641

To the question, 'What am I?', Descartes' first answer is 'a thing that thinks' (105), and he repeats in *Meditation* VI that we can imagine ourselves existing 'whole' without feeling or imagination. But we might want to question this. Is it any less true to say 'I am a human being, a union of mind and body, an *embodied* mind' than 'I am a mind'? The mind takes on the body's experiences as its own, that is, we refer our sensations, emotions and so on to our *selves*. We 'own' these states just as much as we 'own' our thoughts. Our experience is as of one thing. So we experience ourselves as persons – embodied minds – not just minds. Descartes accepts all this, but his argument that minds can exist without bodies lead him to say that to lose the experiences that depend on the body would not be to lose our identities.

'Descartes' argument for intermingling undermines his arguments for dualism.' Discuss.

Key points • • •

- Descartes claims that we (our minds) are intermingled with our bodies, forming one whole with it. We are not 'lodged' in our bodies like a pilot in a ship.
- His reason for this claim is our experience of perceptions, bodily sensations

and emotions. These are not purely intellectual states, but direct experiences of our bodies, in particular what is harmful or beneficial for us as a whole.

- This doesn't mean mind and body aren't distinct: we can exist as ourselves (minds) without sensory perception, imagination or feeling.
- However, Descartes also suggests that perhaps the union of mind and body creates something new, that can't be analysed into mind + body.

The proof of material (physical) things (Meditation VI)

Having thrown doubt on the existence of an external, physical world in *Meditation* I, Descartes must work to once again secure our knowledge of it. The argument spans the whole of the *Meditations*, and takes in arguments about the understanding and the senses, the existence of God, the doctrine of clear and distinct ideas, and human nature.

Knowing the external world exists

We saw that Descartes' wax example doesn't show that physical objects really are extended (p. 160). But in *Meditation* V, Descartes asserts the principle that we can know that what we can clearly and distinctly conceive is true (p. 162). So physical objects really are extended, if they exist at all. In *Meditation* VI, Descartes argues that they do exist, and he seeks to establish that we can and do have knowledge of the physical world, including of course, our own bodies.

He first considers whether we can know bodies exist from our imagination. Unlike operations of the intellect, imagination uses images that it has apparently derived from the senses or created for itself, and it requires effort. Both of these features could be explained if we have bodies. So we 'probably' have bodies, but this is hardly a proof.

He turns, then, to consider perception. We have experiences which appear, very forcefully, to be experiences of a world external to our minds, whether they are experiences of our own body or of other bodies. These experiences produce ideas without our 'contribution', that is, they are involuntary. Among our perceptual experiences are sensations and feelings. We notice that we perceive we have bodies, and that our bodies can be affected in many beneficial and harmful ways, which we experience through our bodily appetites, feelings and emotions. Our faculties of feeling and sensation would seem to be dependent on our having bodies. But, again, this is not a proof.

?
Why does Descartes reject his first two arguments for the existence of physical objects?

So Descartes considers the matter from another angle. These experiences are involuntary, and if they were caused by our own minds, they would be voluntary. Because we know our own minds, we would know if they were voluntary. So they are not caused by ourselves. They must therefore have some cause which is sufficient to cause them. The options are: a real external world or God. If the cause was God, this would mean that God was a deceiver because He would have created us with a very strong tendency to believe something false. But we know that God is not a deceiver. So there must really be an external world.

So what can we know about the external world, having demonstrated that it exists? Descartes argues that God has set us up to learn from nature. Nature teaches us through sensation that we have bodies, and through perception that there are other bodies. This can't *simply* be the abstract truth that a physical world exists. It must be the stronger claim that, in many of our experiences, we are actually confronted with physical objects. Our senses, then, will not be set up so that, with careful employment and the search for clarity and distinctness, they would systematically lead to error. This doesn't mean that any particular belief based on our senses is certain – we can still make mistakes. But unless perceptual experience was generally reliable, when we do what we can to avoid error, it would be difficult for Descartes to defend that we can trust what we learn from nature.

See The Trademark argument, p. 190.

See The role of God, p. 187.

Does Descartes succeed in establishing the existence of physical objects?

Explain and illustrate what nature teaches us, according to Descartes.

Going further: knowing about the external world

This does not, however, mean that that world is just as perception represents it. First, Descartes does not claim that the external world is as we commonly think it is. His argument has established that the physical world exists and is an extended world. But the wax argument established that extension and changeability is *all* that is of the essence of the physical world. Descartes' representative realist theory of perception argues that all other properties, of colour, smell, heat and so on, aren't actually properties of physical objects at all, at least not considered on their own. Rather, 'all I have reason to believe is that there is something in [the external body] which excites in me these feelings' (161). We shouldn't think that the 'something' is itself colour, smell

See The secondary quality thesis, pp. 204 and 219.

and so on. The external world is a world of geometry, as physical objects only have spatial properties (e.g. size, shape, motion).

It is on the basis of its spatial properties that we judge, as in the wax example, that some physical object is in fact present. But we must accept that our particular perceptions of the world are often confused. God's assurance doesn't mean we are always able to avoid error: 'because the necessities of action often oblige us to make a decision before we have had the leisure to examine things carefully, it must be admitted that the life of man is very often subject to error in particular cases' (168-9). Furthermore, even with caution and recourse to clear and distinct ideas, we can still make mistakes since our nature is fallible. Poor conditions of perception, such as bad light, confused thinking, prejudice and other factors means that we can make mistakes; this does not make God a deceiver, because these are mistakes we must take responsibility for.

Outline and illustrate Descartes' claim that many of our particular perceptions are mistaken.

Key points • • •

- In *Meditation* II, Descartes argues that we have a clear and distinct idea of physical objects as extended. In *Meditation* V, he argues that clear and distinct ideas are true. In *Meditation* VI, he argues that physical objects actually exist.
- Imagination uses images deriving from the senses and requires effort. These are reasons to think bodies exist, but not a proof.
- We have sensory experiences of bodies, as well, which are involuntary. But this is also not enough to show that bodies exist.
- We have forceful experiences of our bodies and other physical objects. We do not cause these experiences, because they are involuntary. If God caused them, He would be a deceiver, since we are strongly inclined to believe physical objects exist. Therefore, physical objects must be the cause of our experiences of them. Therefore, they exist.
- The physical world only has, in itself, properties of extension (shape, size, location, motion), which can change. It does not have many of the properties, such as colour and smell, that we tend to think it has.
- So we can know about the physical world, but we must remember to stick to clear and distinct ideas to avoid error.

Descartes' rationalism

Rationalists claim that we have **a priori** knowledge of **synthetic** propositions, that is, knowledge of matters of fact that does not depend upon sense experience. They argue that there are two key ways in which we gain such knowledge:

1. we know certain truths **innately**, for example, as part of our rational nature; and/or
2. we have a form of rational 'intuition' or 'insight' which enables us to grasp certain truths intellectually.

Rationalism is discussed at length in Unit 1.1, REASON AND EXPERIENCE.

Descartes is a rationalist in both these ways. Many rationalists add that the synthetic a priori knowledge we gain through reason or have innately cannot be arrived at in any other way. They may also argue that it is superior, for example by being more certain, to the knowledge or beliefs we gain through the senses. Descartes agrees with this, too.

Rational intuition

Descartes' theory of CLEAR AND DISTINCT IDEAS (p. 157) is his account of rational 'intuition'. At the heart of the idea of rational intuition is the view that you can discover the truth of a claim just by thinking about it. The first claim Descartes defends this way is the *cogito*. He arrives at the *cogito* by pure reasoning, and we are supposed to recognise that it is true just by considering it.

As we have seen (p. 164), Descartes then goes on to argue that he, as a mind, can exist without having a body. It is therefore possible for minds to exist without bodies. This is a second claim Descartes believes he can establish by a priori reasoning.

How do we know about bodies, physical objects? First, how do we know what physical objects are, that is, what are we talking about? We might say we discover their nature through sense experience. But in the wax argument, Descartes argues that sense experience gives us only a confused idea of physical objects. In fact, we discover what physical objects are by analysing our concept of a physical object. In this way, and not through the senses, we discover that the essential nature of a physical object is to be 'extended', that is, to exist in space, with a size, shape and location.

Discuss the role played by Descartes' rationalism in his argument for minds being separate substances.

See THE ESSENTIAL NATURES OF MIND AND BODY, p. 160.

Second, how do we know whether bodies – physical objects – exist? They cause our experiences, we reply. But using THE METHOD OF DOUBT (p. 151), Descartes first argues that we don't know what causes our experiences – it could be a demon. Later, in THE PROOF OF MATERIAL THINGS (p. 176), he argues that there are only three options for what might cause these experiences: a real external world of physical objects, a demon or God. If the cause were God, this would mean that God was a deceiver because He would have created us with a very strong tendency to believe something false (namely, that a physical world exists). And if it were a demon, then if God exists, God is as good as a deceiver, since God is allowing the demon to deceive us. However, Descartes argues, God is perfect by definition. Because we know that God is perfect, we know that God is not a deceiver. So if God exists, then there must really be an external world.

Descartes offers two arguments, both a priori, for the existence of God – one is the TRADEMARK ARGUMENT (p. 190) and the other is the ONTOLOGICAL ARGUMENT (p. 182). Since he believes he has demonstrated that God exists, he concludes that we know the external world of physical objects exists. Not because sense experience shows us that it does, but through a priori intuition and reasoning.

> Outline and illustrate Descartes' rationalism in relation to his claims about our knowledge of physical objects.

Innate ideas

> When referring to a concept, I put the word in capital letters.

In the arguments regarding physical objects and God, Descartes takes the concepts, or ideas, of PHYSICAL OBJECT and GOD for granted. Where do these concepts come from? In his Trademark argument for the existence of God, he says there are three possible sources for a concept: that we have invented it (it is 'fictitious'), that it derives from something outside the mind (it is 'adventitious') or that it is innate. By 'innate', he doesn't mean we have it from the birth in the sense that a baby can think using this concept. It would be very strange if babies could think about God but didn't yet have a concept of power or reality or love! Innate ideas are *ideas that the mind has certain capacities to use, and which can't be explained by our experience.*

> Outline and illustrate the three types of ideas Descartes says there are.

To defend his claim that these ideas (of GOD and PHYSICAL OBJECT) are innate, Descartes needs to show that they cannot be explained by sense experience. And this is what his arguments try to do. Sense experience cannot tell us the essential nature of physical objects; it is an idea that we must use the intellect to analyse. How did it come to be part of the intellect? It is innate. Likewise with GOD.

Assessing Descartes' rationalism

As we have seen, there are many objections to Descartes' arguments. But what do such objections show about Descartes' *rationalism*? Is his *method* of doing philosophy wrong? Descartes has done his best to find what he thinks, using reasoning, is certain. His arguments are supposed to be **deductive**, and his premises established by rational intuition. But philosophers have still been able to point out unjustified assumptions and inferences. If intuition and deductive reasoning do not give us knowledge, then his rationalism is in trouble.

Before we become sceptical about intuition and reasoning, we should ask this: *how* have philosophers come up with objections to Descartes? It certainly isn't by using sense experience! So the objections themselves use the same *kind* of reasoning as Descartes. Only better reasoning, we hope. The objections cannot be objections to the *way* Descartes reasoned, only objections to the conclusions he drew.

But this is too generous, we can argue. Certainly, there is nothing wrong with using deductive reasoning; and we can use it to show that Descartes' arguments are faulty. But that doesn't mean we should also accept that there is such a thing as rational intuition or that Descartes' theory of clear and distinct ideas is correct. Someone like Hume would argue that we can only perceive the truth of a claim just by thinking about it when that claim is **analytic**. Our ability to tell that it is truth is not about insight; it is simply because the claim is made true by the meanings of the words it contains.

On this view, one reason Descartes' arguments fail is because many of his 'clear and distinct' ideas are not analytic, but contain some hidden assumption, and so can be challenged (e.g. the objection to the *cogito* (p. 156)). The certainty Descartes is after can only be found in analytic truths, not through rational intuition.

This can all be debated. Do Descartes' arguments fail or can he meet the objections? Is he wrong about rational insight? Can we not use a priori reason to discover the truth of (some) synthetic propositions, or is a priori reason limited to analytic truths? Are there any innate ideas? These were questions discussed at length in *Philosophy for AS*, REASON AND EXPERIENCE, so we won't take them further here.

> Hume's theory of knowledge is discussed in THE DISTINCTION BETWEEN RELATIONS OF IDEAS AND MATTERS OF FACT and THE SCOPE OF MATTERS OF FACT, p. 22.

> Critically discuss Descartes' rationalism.

Key points • • •

- Rationalists claim that we have synthetic a priori knowledge, which is either innate or discovered through rational intuition. Descartes argues for both forms of knowledge.
- Descartes' theory of clear and distinct ideas is his account of rational intuition. We can know the truth of a clear and distinct idea just by considering it.
- Descartes' rationalism appears throughout the argument of the *Meditations*:

  - The *cogito* and the independence of the mind from the body are argued for a priori.
  - We know through our understanding, not our senses, that physical objects are extended.
  - We know that physical objects exist not (only) because we sense them, but because God is not a deceiver.
  - The ideas of GOD and PHYSICAL OBJECT are innate. An innate idea is an idea that the mind has certain capacities to use, and which can't be explained by our experience.
  - The proof of God's existence depends on reason alone.

- We can object to Descartes' a priori arguments. But in doing so, we use a priori reasoning. Does this show that his conclusions are problematic, but his rationalism is not? This depends on whether we think rational intuition is possible at all.

III. GOD

The ontological argument (Meditation *V*)

St Anselm's version of the ontological argument is discussed on p. 129.

It is certain that I . . . find the idea of God in me, that is to say, the idea of a supremely perfect being . . . And I know no less clearly and distinctly that an actual and eternal existence belongs to his nature . . . existence can no more be separated from the essence of God . . . than the idea of a mountain can be separated from the idea of a valley; so that there is no less contradiction in conceiving a God, that is to say, a supremely perfect being, who lacks some particular perfection, than in conceiving a mountain without a valley. (144–5)

Descartes' argument is very simple. There are two ways we may phrase it:

a)   the idea of God contains the idea of existence;
b)   therefore God must exist (the conclusion is not just that God does exist, but that God cannot not exist, i.e. God's existence is necessary).

Or, with a little more unpacking,

a)   God is a supremely perfect being;
b)   existence is a perfection;
c)   therefore, God must exist.

The quotation makes it clear that the argument is grounded on two central claims of Descartes' philosophy – the theory of innate ideas and the doctrine of CLEAR AND DISTINCT IDEAS (p. 157). The first theory supports the first premise, the definition of God as supremely perfect. This is the idea of God we find that we have. The second theory supports the validity of the argument. Descartes claims that it is clear and distinct that the idea of existence cannot be excluded from the idea of God, a supremely perfect being.

Descartes is aware that we might misunderstand him as claiming that 'thinking makes it so'. He objects to himself: 'just as it does not follow that merely because I conceive a mountain with a valley, there is any mountain in the world, so similarly, although I conceive God as having existence, it does not follow from that, that there is a God who actually exists' (145). But, he responds, the analogy is not between mountains and existence and God and existence; but between mountains and *valleys* and God and existence. The idea of existence is no part of the idea of a mountain. But just as the idea of a valley is implied by the idea of a mountain, so the idea of existence is part of the idea of God. And so, as he says, 'I cannot conceive God without existence' (145).

But what does this show? Just because I can't think of God not existing, does that have any relevance to whether or not God exists? Absolutely. The bounds of our thought are, at least on some occasions, indications of what is possible. This isn't because our thought creates or influences reality, but because thought reveals reality. And so, Descartes argues, the necessary connection between God and existence isn't something I've come up with, it is something I discover:

> **Explain the disanalogy** Descartes identifies between thinking of a mountain and thinking of God.

the necessity which lies in the thing itself, that is, the necessity of the existence of God, determines me to think in this way: for it is not in my power to conceive a God without existence. (145)

It is not that my thought brings about God's existence (all my thinking can bring about is ideas!); rather the fact that God's existence is necessary makes me think of God in this way, namely, as existing. How things are determines what I am able to think, rather than vice-versa. There is a conceptual connection between the concept of God and God's existence, and this entails that God must exist.

This again rests on the doctrine of clear and distinct ideas. Descartes has argued that whatever one clearly and distinctly perceives is true. That we can clearly and distinctly perceive that existence is part of the idea of God, that is, that there is a conceptual connection between the concept of God and God's existence, entails that God must exist. Without this additional premise, Descartes admits elsewhere, the gap between thought and reality is not bridged.

Objections and replies

CONCEPT AND REALITY

We may doubt, with the philosopher Gassendi, whether Descartes is *right* to claim that existence is part of the idea of God as a supremely perfect being. Can't I form the idea of a God who does not exist?

Descartes replies by drawing our attention to the claim that the attributes of God all entail each other. Because our minds are finite, we normally think of the divine perfections – omnipotence, omniscience and so on – separately and so we might not see immediately that they entail each other. But if we attend carefully to whether existence belongs to a supremely perfect being, and what sort of existence it is, we shall discover that we cannot conceive any one of the other attributes while excluding existence from it. For example, in order for God to be omnipotent, God must not depend on anything else, and so must not depend on anything else to exist. God cannot, then, go in and out of existence – so there can be no concept of a God that does not exist but might.

The conclusion of the ontological argument is not simply that God exists, but that God *must* exist. This is quite a different type of existence from our existence. We can go in and out of existence – our existence is **contingent**. But God's existence is **necessary**.

Outline Descartes' ontological argument for the existence of God.

THE DIVINE ATTRIBUTES are discussed on p. 125.

The existence of a being is contingent if it could be true or false that that being exists,

At best, this is an argument for the claim that *if* God exists, God exists necessarily. But Descartes' argument is still open to the objection, made famous by Aquinas and cited by Johannes Caterus in response to Descartes, that this doesn't demonstrate that God actually exists. It only shows that the *concept* of existence is inseparable from the *concept* of God.

Descartes responds that this overlooks two things: first, his claim that clear and distinct ideas are true; and second, that necessary existence as part of the concept of God entails God's actual existence. If it is part of the concept of God that God must exist, then God must exist. However, this sounds like Descartes is begging the question, for Caterus' objection is precisely that the connection in the concept does not prove a connection in reality.

HUME'S OBJECTION

The ontological argument doesn't rely on sense experience, but on pure reasoning. So the argument, and its conclusion that God exists, are a priori. But, Hume argues, the only claims that can be known a priori are 'relations of ideas', or what we would now call analytic truths. These are 'demonstrable', that is, they can be proven using reason. Take the claim 'all vixens are female'. What is a vixen? By definition, it is a female fox. So 'all vixens are female' means 'all female foxes are female'. To deny this is to contradict oneself.

If 'God exists' is a priori, then we shouldn't be able to deny it without contradicting ourselves: 'Nothing is demonstrable, unless the contrary is a contradiction', Hume says. But, he goes on, 'Whatever we conceive as existent, we can also conceive as non-existent. There is no being, therefore, whose non-existence implies a contradiction. Consequently there is no Being whose existence is demonstrable.'

So Hume argues that God does not possess existence essentially – it is possible to conceive of God not existing (and still be thinking of God). And so the ontological argument fails.

However, Descartes denies that 'whatever we conceive as existent, we can also conceive as non-existent'. God is precisely a counter-example. Second, it may not be a contradiction *in terms* to say that 'God does not exist'. But it is not a coherent thought. A priori reason, for Descartes, does not use *only* contradiction as a test. His theory of clear and distinct ideas is richer than this, an account of rational intuition. Hume assumes that all 'demonstrable' truths must be analytic. Rationalists would argue that there are synthetic a priori truths, and the claim that 'God exists' – if it is not analytic – could be one of these.

for example, it could now exist, but later cease to exist. The existence of a being is necessary if it cannot come into or go out of existence; it is necessarily true that it exists (or doesn't).

Does Descartes bridge the gap between the concept of God and God's existence?

Dialogues on Natural Religion, § IX

Explain Hume's claim that 'Whatever we conceive as existent, we can also conceive as non-existent'.

EXISTENCE IS NOT A PROPERTY

Critique of Pure Reason, Book II, Ch. 3, § 4

According to Immanuel Kant, the ontological argument wrongly assumes that existence is a *property* (a perfection). But things don't 'have' existence in the same way that they 'have' other properties. To say that the concept GOD contains the idea EXISTENCE (necessary existence belongs to God's essence), Kant claims, is a mistake. Existence does not add anything to, or define, a concept itself; to say something exists is to say that some object corresponds to the concept. (To say something exists is always a synthetic judgement, not an analytic one, so it can't be arrived at by analysing concepts.)

When we list the essential properties of something, we describe our concept of that thing. For instance, a dog is a mammal. But now if I tell you that the dog asleep in the corner is a mammal and it exists, I seem to have said two very different sorts of things. To say that it exists is only to say that there is something real that corresponds to the concept 'dog'. It is not to say anything *about* the dog as a dog.

Existence, Kant argues, is not part of any concept, even in the case of God. To say that 'God exists' is quite different from saying that 'God is omnipotent'. So it is not true to say that 'God exists' must be true.

Assess Descartes' ontological argument.

Going further: necessary existence

If existence isn't a property that something 'has', then it can't be a property that God has necessarily! And yet it seems plausible to think that *if* God exists, God exists necessarily. God cannot be a contingent being. If God's existence were not necessary, God would depend on something else that could cause God to come into or go out of existence. If Kant were right, then not only can existence not be a property, necessary existence – as a type of existence – can't be a property. So God can't exist necessarily, even if God exists.

In fact, this doesn't follow. There is still a sense in which God can exist necessarily, if God exists. Rather than saying 'God has necessary existence', which suggests existence is a property, we should say that 'it is necessarily true that God exists'. The 'necessity' applies to the claim: 'God exists' must be true. Of course, we need an argument to support the claim, but at least it makes sense.

The ontological argument seems to say that because, according to the concept of God, God exists 'necessarily', that is not contingently, without dependence on anything else, then 'God exists' must be true. But this doesn't follow; it confuses two meanings of 'necessarily'.

Explain the difference between God having necessary existence and it being necessarily true that God exists.

Key points • • •

- Descartes argues that the idea that God exists is part of the idea of God. Existence is a perfection, and the idea of God is the idea of a being that has all perfections.
- Descartes' argument rests on his theory of innate ideas (this is the idea of God we find in ourselves) and his doctrine of clear and distinct ideas. If the idea of God having existence wasn't clear and distinct, we couldn't know that God really exists.
- The conclusion of the ontological argument is that God necessarily exists. Everything else only exists contingently.
- Gassendi objects that existence is not part of the idea of God. Descartes replies that it is entailed by God's other perfections.
- Caterus objects that Descartes at best demonstrates a necessary connection between the concept of God and the concept of existence, but this has no implications for whether God really exists.
- Hume objects that it is not a contradiction to deny that God exists, so God does not exist necessarily, and the ontological argument fails.
- Kant's objection claims that the argument is wrong to think that existence is a property of something. To say something exists is only to say that something corresponds to a concept we have; it is not to say anything further about that concept. So existence can't be an 'essential property'.

The role of God (Meditations III, V and VI)

The *Meditations* begin with, and take as their theme, the search for truth and what we can know. And so in *Meditation* VI, Descartes seeks to resolve the issues that led him into doubt about what was true in the first place. To do this, he needs to establish, in reverse order, that there could be no evil demon deceiving me; that I am not dreaming, and a physical world, including my body, really does exist; and that I can trust my senses.

God is not a deceiver

The answer to all these doubts is that God is not a deceiver. Descartes' claim to know this rests on his idea of God. First, he uses the idea of God to prove that God exists in both the TRADEMARK (p. 190) and ONTOLOGICAL (p. 182) arguments. Second, in those proofs, it is an essential part of the idea of God that God is perfect. God, therefore, would not deceive us, as this would be an imperfection.

What does Descartes mean by this? It is important to note that Descartes explicitly denies that his invocation of God means we must be infallible. Rather, Descartes' claim is that God 'has permitted no falsity in my opinion which he has not also given me some faculty capable of correcting' (158). The Method of doubt, and the central importance of clear and distinct ideas, is the best we can do in correcting our tendency to have false beliefs. By God's not being a deceiver, then, we are only assured that once we have done all we can to avoid error, and are judging on the basis of clear and distinct ideas, then we will not go wrong.

> Explain Descartes' claim that God is not a deceiver.

Going further: the connection to nature

Because God is not a deceiver, we can attain the truth. Descartes links this to the idea of nature (p. 177) in two ways. First, 'there is no doubt that every-thing nature teaches me contains some truth. For by nature, considered in general, I now mean nothing other than God himself, or the order and dispo-sition that God has established in created things' (158–9). So, again if we are careful, we can learn truth from nature, because God has created nature.

We might object that God's purposes are inscrutable, so we don't know if He has set up nature in such a way that we come to know the truth. We cannot know whether God might have arranged it so that we believe in an external world when there wasn't one.

Although Descartes allows that we cannot know God's purposes, he argues that the objection fails. And this is the second link to nature, this time human nature. Given that we would have no way of correcting our error, such a mistake would constitute a frustration of our essential nature as rational minds. We cannot help but assent to what we clearly and distinctly understand. And it is difficult to reconcile ourselves to the idea that God would create beings and then thwart the exercise of their very essence. We don't need to know what God's purposes are in order to judge that this would amount to God being a deceiver.

> Outline Descartes' argument that we can learn from nature.

How this solves scepticism

So how does the existence of God help solve Descartes' scepticism? First, because God exists and is not a deceiver, God would not allow us to be deceived by some demon. This would just be God being a deceiver by proxy.

What about the problem of dreaming? Descartes' answer is that we *can* tell the difference between dreaming and being awake, because 'our memory can never connect our dreams with one another and with the general course of our lives, as it is in the habit of connecting the things which happen to us when we are awake' (168). When we perceive, rather than dream, we know the object of perception and can connect the experience with others that we have. Again, as long as we judge only by clear and distinct ideas, God would not allow us to be deceived in this.

Finally, we saw, in THE PROOF OF MATERIAL THINGS (p. 176), that God is essential to establishing the existence of my body and physical objects in general. But can we trust our senses to deliver the truth about physical objects? Descartes recommends caution here. These judgements – about what properties physical objects have, and about particular perceptions – 'are very obscure and confused' (158). We can and do make mistakes about what we are perceiving. But, again, we can know that God has given us the means to correct mistakes and avoid error. If, therefore, we take care and only assent to clear and distinct ideas, 'I may conclude with assurance that I have within me the means of knowing these things with certainty' (158).

> Assess Descartes' argument that the existence of God solves the doubts he developed in *Meditation* I.

Key points • • •

- Descartes argues that we know that God is not a deceiver, because we know that God is perfect.
- This does not mean that God guarantees every belief we have. It means that we have the means to correct any mistakes we make. If we only believe what we can clearly and distinctly perceive to be true, we will not go wrong.
- Because God is not a deceiver, and God is omnipotent, God would not let an evil demon deceive us.
- We can now also tell dreaming from being awake by the way our memory connects up our waking experiences.
- Because God is not a deceiver, a physical world is the cause of our experiences of physical objects. However, individual perceptual judgements may still be wrong, unless we stick to clear and distinct ideas.

Appendix: the Trademark argument (Meditation III)

The syllabus does not mention Descartes' famous 'Trademark argument'. It is very unlikely, therefore, that any exam question will deal with it explicitly. However, for the sake of completeness, I have included a discussion of the argument here.

In the 'Trademark argument', Descartes tries to prove that God exists just from the fact that we have an idea of God. This idea is like the 'trademark' our creator has stamped on our minds.

Descartes says that every idea must have a cause, and argues that ideas can have any of three sources: they can be 'adventitious' (caused by something external to the mind), fictitious (caused by the mind) or innate. Innate ideas are not ones we think from birth, but ones that the mind has certain capacities to use, and which can't be explained by our experience. But what is the cause of innate ideas?

We cannot in general be certain which of the three types of cause an idea has. However, Descartes argues that a cause must have at least as much 'reality' as its effect. The philosopher Bernard Williams gives a common-sense example: if we discover a picture of a sophisticated machine, we automatically think it must have been the product of an advanced society or a highly fertile imagination, even though it's just a picture. If we actually found the machine, working

> **Explain and illustrate what Descartes means by 'innate idea'.**
>
> *Descartes*, pp. 138–9

as it should, this would be even more impressive – the machine has 'more reality' as a working machine than as a drawing.

Going further: degrees of reality

The idea of 'degrees of reality' is foreign to us, but was a standard part of medieval metaphysics. A 'substance' is defined as something that can exist independently. An 'accident' is a property of a substance. And a 'mode' is a particular determination of a property, for example, the substance is a book, the accident is 'colour' and 'red' is the mode. A substance has more reality than an accident, because a property cannot exist without a substance, and so is dependent on it. A mode has less reality than an accident. Furthermore, a substance that is in some way dependent on another substance has less reality than it, for example, an incomplete substance such as a hand has less reality than a whole human body.

Different types of thought are modes of the property 'thought', itself an accident of 'minds', which are thinking substances. Particular ideas are instances of these modes. As *ideas*, they all have the same degree of reality (the same 'formal' reality). But the *objects* of the ideas, what the idea is about, have varying degrees of reality. I can have ideas about a physical thing (a substance) or about the colour red (a mode). Whatever my idea is about, the idea is still an idea, and so an instance of a mode. But because they are about different things, ideas have different 'objective' realities. The objective reality of an idea is not the same as the formal reality the object would have if it actually existed; but it is correlated with it.

Descartes claims that the cause of an idea must have as much reality as the *object of the idea*, what that idea is about.

> Give two examples describing objects in terms of substance, accident and mode.

> Explain Descartes' view that the cause of an idea must have 'as much reality' as the object of the idea.

As thinking substances, we have considerable reality, and hence many ideas could be the products of our minds. But the idea of God is different, Descartes argues. The object of the idea of God is God, which has the greatest degree of reality, more reality than minds do, for the idea of God is the idea of a substance that depends on nothing else to exist. Our minds could not, therefore, have created it. This is a puzzling claim – the idea of God is still simply an idea, which is a mode, whereas I am a substance. But the special features of the idea of God,

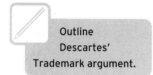

Outline
Descartes'
Trademark argument.

namely, the idea of something perfect and infinite, Descartes argues, place the reality of its cause far in excess of me, for I am imperfect and finite (this is clear, because I am in a state of doubt). Indeed, the only possible cause is God, because only God has enough reality to create the idea of God. So God must exist.

A variation

Descartes also presents a variation of the argument, which claims not just that God caused the idea of God, but God caused me. I, who have this idea of God, can't exist unless God does, because if I created myself, I could give myself every perfection. This is because to create substance requires more power than creating properties – hence causing myself (a substance) involves more power than creating perfections (which would be properties). But I can't give myself every perfection, so I could not have caused myself. Again, if I created myself, I could also have given myself the idea of God, but, as argued above, I can't do this either.

Of course, we might think, I was created by my parents. But if *only* my parents were involved in explaining my creation, then they must have sufficient power to cause the idea of God in my mind. But they have no more power than I do. We could continue back to their parents, and so on. Descartes allows that there could be an infinite series of creatures, each causing the other. But, he objects, this won't be able to cause the idea of God. So since I have the idea of God, God created me.

Why, according
to Descartes,
can't I have derived the
idea of God from other
people?

Objections

One objection Descartes responds to immediately. As imperfect and finite, I could be the cause of an idea of something that is '*not finite*' and '*not imperfect*'. Could I not come up with the idea of God by simply thinking away all limitations? But this *negative* conception of infinity and perfection is not the idea of God, Descartes claims, which requires a *positive* conception of these properties – not the absence of limits, but something for which there could be no limits.

What is the
difference
between a negative
and a positive
conception of
perfection?

Because of this insistence that our ideas of the infinity and perfection of God are not negative ideas, Descartes is claiming that we have a very powerful – clear and distinct – idea of God, and not some hazy notion of something indefinitely great. But this requirement conflicts with Descartes' *own claim* that as finite minds, we cannot form a *clear* idea of God's infinity. So he wants to say the idea of God is not clear, but it is clearly and distinctly positive rather than negative? This sounds like a contradiction, since an idea is not distinct unless it is clearly separated from other ideas, and it contains nothing other than what is clear. Yet Descartes must insist that the idea of God is positive; if we do only have a negative idea of God, because we are finite, then it becomes possible that we are the cause of that idea.

Second, the argument relies on the notion of 'degrees of reality', and the claim that a cause must have more reality than its effect. This is all outmoded. Indeed, we owe its rejection to Descartes' development of the mechanical view of nature.

Third, Descartes supposes that every idea must have a cause. Hume argued that we don't know this. It is not an analytic truth; so it is logically possible that some ideas have no causes. If the idea of God has no cause, Descartes' argument collapses.

> Discuss
> Descartes'
> Trademark argument.

Key points • • •

- Descartes claims that all ideas have a cause. There are three types of idea: innate, adventitious and fictitious.
- All causes must have at least as much reality as their effects. The cause of an idea must have as much reality as what the idea represents.
- Descartes argues that the idea of God is innate, and could only have been caused by God, because only God is a sufficient cause of the idea of God. The objective reality of the idea of God is greater than any finite substance.
- Likewise, because I have the idea of God, God must have caused (created) me.
- We can object that we invented our idea of God, by negating ideas of imperfection and finitude. Descartes replies that our idea of God is positive, not negative – but we can dispute this.
- We can also object to the claim that the cause of an idea must have 'as much reality' as its object.

5

NIETZSCHE *BEYOND GOOD AND EVIL*

Sections I-III, V, VI (209-13) and IX (257-70)

In this chapter, we examine Nietzsche's text in the light of three key issues: his views on philosophy and philosophers; his critique and theory of morality; and his account of religious belief, including the use of religion by philosophers in the future. Students should be able to explain Nietzsche's views clearly and accurately and critically evaluate his arguments and objections to them. They should also be able to make connections between his theories and other views on the same topics discussed elsewhere in the syllabus.

All quotations come from the AQA recommended edition from Oxford World Classics (ISBN 0-19-283263-8).

SYLLABUS CHECKLIST

The AQA A2 syllabus for this chapter is as follows.
Candidates should demonstrate an understanding of the following:

✔ critique of past philosophers; motivational analysis, e.g. philosophy as expression of self-interest or prejudice
✔ the bewitchment of language; truth and interpretation

✔ the 'correct' philosophical questions
✔ the new philosopher and his socio-intellectual status
✔ the notion of 'superiority'
✔ the will to power
✔ the different morality. Master slave morality. The three stages of morality
✔ Nietzsche's account of religion; self-denial and sacrifice
✔ advantages and disadvantages of religion, the future use of religion
✔ Nietzsche's 'history' of morality – particularity of moral systems
✔ morality and human nature; herd morality
✔ critique of 'modern ideas'
✔ the sceptic and the critic
✔ nobility: description of value systems
✔ social implications of Nietzsche's concept of noble values.

Essay questions will focus on the following problem areas:

✔ scope of philosophy
✔ nature of morality
✔ religious belief.

Reading Nietzsche

This chapter is, by design, considerably longer than any other in this book. There are two reasons for this. The first is that, in contrast to the other four texts, there are not many commentaries on Nietzsche's text which are accessible to teachers and students. I therefore wanted to spend additional time explaining and evaluating the **arguments**. Second, Nietzsche's text doesn't easily lend itself to the same kind of commentary and evaluation that other texts do, for several reasons which it is worth saying more about.

Nietzsche does not write as other philosophers write. This poses a challenge to interpreting and criticising his philosophy. Nietzsche is not a source of philosophical *theories*. The way the text is written demonstrates his resistance to systematic thought, and, as we will see, it is almost impossible to give a systematic exegesis of it that could amount to a 'theory'. Unlike other chapters in this book, which are able to move methodically from one part of a text to another, this chapter jumps around the text, trying to bring together the places in which Nietzsche returns to this or that theme.

Nietzsche said that he wanted to express in a page what it would take someone else a book to express (and even then, they wouldn't succeed). But for this very reason, reading Nietzsche can be tiring. The diet is too rich for the digestion. A good approach is to read through quickly, noting sections that make a particular impact and returning to these.

Nietzsche often says that his books are not for everyone; his insights should sound foolish, or even criminal, to those for whom they are not intended, to people who are not 'constituted' to hear them (§ 30). He was absolutely serious about this, and it is a key implication of his views. But it impacts on his style. On the one hand, he wants his readers to be able to respond to mere hints; on the other, he knows – from the response his works received – that we are deaf to his message and that he has to spell things out. The result can be a compromise, or subtle comments alternating with loud declamations.

Nietzsche's underlying position is that the last 2,000 years have been marked by fundamentally mistaken ideas, both philosophical and religious, and we are living in the last throws of these ideas. Unless we, the human race, radically change direction and make a fresh start, we are doomed to mediocrity, never to achieve greatness. The challenge human beings face is *suffering* – if we truly understand our existence, how can we make it bearable? Religion and philosophy have tried to give a *meaning* to suffering, especially a *moral* meaning, for example, that our suffering in this world prepares us for an afterlife. This kind of solution, says Nietzsche, denigrates this life and this world, not redeeming it from within but by relating it to something beyond it. He asks us to consider a different response to the misery of existence, one affirms *this* life and seeks nothing beyond it.

Furthermore, Nietzsche does not try to be compelling, at least through rational argument. As Bernard Williams expresses it, it is better to see him as appealing to an experienced, honest, subtle and unoptimistic observer of human beings. It is better to see his 'claims' as urging us to *ask* something, and in a deeper way than we are used to. He aims to transform his reader's consciousness, to show that our usual concepts and ways of thinking are *inadequate* to becoming all that we may be capable of.

For all these reasons, assessing Nietzsche requires great care, and quite a different approach from the one taken elsewhere in this book.

See THE PROBLEM OF EVIL, p. 320.

'Nietzsche's minimalist moral psychology'

In addition, many of his claims are *historical* and *psychological*, so if we know little of human beings and their history, we will not know how to assess these claims, and may be convinced by his rhetoric too soon. To complicate matters further, when interpreting such historical and psychological claims, we should note that Nietzsche is more concerned with movements, ways of living, *types* of psychology, than he is with individuals or specific historical events.

Finally, when interpreting and assessing Nietzsche, we must also note the subtlety of his response to other positions. He often agrees with some aspect of another philosophy, that of Plato or Kant, say, while disagreeing with another; he often disapproves strongly of some idea or event, for example, the beginning of Christianity, and yet simultaneously praises it. This, again, is part of his philosophy, his attempt to go *beyond* our usual ways of thinking.

In responding to Nietzsche as philosophers, what can we *do* with his ideas? Perhaps the main thing we can do, as we shall see, is to press philosophy, especially moral philosophy, on whether it begs its most basic questions, that is, whether the philosophical endeavour assumes the very things it needs to prove at the very start. This is where we shall begin.

Three final points on this chapter. First, because Nietzsche does not often discuss an idea in just one place, I have included many more references to the text, so you can identify the sections that support the argument. It is therefore worth having a copy of *Beyond Good and Evil* to hand as you read, to follow up the references. Second, while I have tried to contain the discussion using the three 'philosophical issues' identified by the syllabus – the scope of philosophy, the nature of morality and religious belief – this has not proved entirely possible. I have tried to indicate where discussion is continued by cross-references, but an understanding of the ideas discussed under each issue will not be complete without an understanding of the other issues. Finally, this chapter misses out a great deal in Nietzsche's text; it is not intended as a commentary on the passages set, but an exploration of the issues identified by the syllabus.

I. SCOPE OF PHILOSOPHY

Critique of past philosophers

Nietzsche identifies his two major grounds for criticising past philosophers in his Preface: that their theories are founded on 'some play on words perhaps, some seductive aspect of grammar, or a daring generalization from very limited, very personal, very human, all-too-human facts'. These are discussed later, under THE BEWITCHMENT OF LANGUAGE (p. 205) and MOTIVATIONAL ANALYSIS (p. 200). The worst errors of philosophy have been: first, a **metaphysics** of transcendence – the idea of a 'true' or 'real' world, which transcends this world of the senses, the world as we experience it; and, second, the denial of what Nietzsche calls 'perspectivity', discussed in TRUTH AND INTERPRETATION (p. 207). Both errors can be found in Plato's philosophy, in particular his theory of the Forms, which involves the ideas of spirit and goodness as independent and transcendent of this world. Plato left a legacy of error for Western philosophical and religious views; the idea of a 'real' world that is transcendent of this world can be found in Christian thought, and so in all Christian philosophers, including Augustine, Aquinas, Descartes, Locke and Leibniz. It also appears in Spinoza, Kant and the post-Kantian tradition in which Nietzsche is writing, including Hegel and Schopenhauer.

See Ch. 2, esp. THE THEORY OF THE FORMS, p. 58, EPISTEMOLOGICAL IMPLICATIONS OF THE THEORY OF THE FORMS, p. 66, THE FORM OF THE GOOD, p. 69, and ETHICAL IMPLICATIONS OF THE THEORY OF THE FORMS, p. 72.

Origins and opposites

Nietzsche argues that the origin of this false belief in a transcendent world is a moral belief, namely, that what is of value – truth, goodness, altruism, wisdom – cannot have its origins in its opposite, that is, in this 'lowly, deceptive world' of the senses and desire. These values must therefore come from, and refer to, something imperishable, not things as they appear to us, but Reality itself. 'The metaphysicians' fundamental belief is *the belief in the opposition of values*' (§ 2). So before we accept their theories and arguments, we should ask a series of questions, each developing the last:

1. Do opposites exist, that is, is truth the opposite of falsehood, is goodness the opposite of badness?
2. Why does it *appear* that opposites exist? Perhaps this is a shallow or misleading perspective.
3. Whatever the value of truth and goodness, could it be that deception, selfishness, lust are more valuable? Valuable to whom and for what, we have yet to see.
4. Can we explain the values of truth and goodness by their relation to their supposed opposites, so that the value of truth and goodness lie not in their transcendence but in their being necessary illusions and expressions of egoistic desire?

Throughout his philosophy, Nietzsche is concerned with origins, both psychological and historical. Much of philosophy is usually thought of as an **a priori** investigation. But if Nietzsche can show, as he thinks he can, that philosophical theories and arguments have a specific historical basis, then they are not, in fact, a priori. What is known a priori should not change from one historical era to the next, nor should it depend on someone's psychology.

Plato's aim, the aim that defines much of philosophy, is to be able to give complete definitions of ideas – 'What is justice?' 'What is knowledge?' For Plato, we understand an idea when we have direct knowledge of the Form, which is unchanging and has no history. If our ideas have a history, then the philosophical project of trying to give definitions of our concepts, rather than histories, is radically mistaken.

For example, in § 186, Nietzsche argues that philosophers have consulted their 'intuitions' to try to justify this or that moral principle. But they have only been aware of their *own* morality, of which their 'justifications' are in fact only expressions. Morality and moral intuitions have a history, and are not a priori. There is no *one* definition of justice or good, and the 'intuitions' that we use to defend this or that theory are themselves as historical and contentious as the theories we give – so they offer no real support. The usual ways philosophers discuss morality misunderstands morality from the very outset. The *real* issues of understanding morality only emerge when we look at the relation between this particular morality and that. There is no world of unchanging ideas, no truths beyond the truths of the world we experience, nothing that stands outside or beyond nature and history.

GENEALOGY AND PHILOSOPHY

Nietzsche develops a new way of philosophising, which he calls a 'morphology and evolutionary theory' (§ 23), and later calls 'genealogy'. He aims to locate the historical origin of philosophical and religious ideas and show how they have changed over time to the present day. His investigation brings together history, psychology, the interpretation of concepts, and a keen sense of what it is like to live with particular ideas and values. In order to best understand which of our ideas and values are particular to us, not a priori or universal, we need to look at real alternatives. In order to understand these alternatives, we need to understand the psychology of the people who lived with them.

And so Nietzsche argues that traditional ways of doing philosophy fail – our intuitions are not a reliable guide to the 'truth', to the 'real' nature of this or that idea or value. And not just our intuitions, but the arguments, and style of arguing,

Nietzsche is questioning the very foundations of philosophy. To accept his claims means being a new kind of philosopher, one whose 'taste and inclination', whose values, are quite different.

Explain why an a priori truth cannot have a history.

'Morphology' means the study of the forms something, for example, morality, can take; 'genealogy' means the historical line of descent traced from an ancestor.

Explain why
Nietzsche adopts
genealogy as a way of
philosophising.

that philosophers have used are unreliable. Philosophy needs to become, or be informed by, genealogy. A lack of any historical sense, says Nietzsche, is the 'hereditary defect' of all philosophers.

Key points • • •

- Nietzsche argues that the two worst errors of philosophers has been a belief in a transcendent world and the denial of perspectivity.
- The origin of the belief in a transcendent world is a belief that what is of positive value cannot come from its negative opposite.
- He asks us to challenge this belief, which challenges the foundations of philosophy.
- Nietzsche argues that philosophical theories have historical and psychological origins, and therefore cannot be a priori.
- He therefore develops the method of 'genealogy' to investigate the history of our philosophical ideas.

Motivational analysis

Having long kept a strict eye on the philosophers, and having looked between their lines, I say to myself . . . most of a philosopher's conscious thinking is secretly guided and channelled into particular tracks by his instincts. Behind all logic, too, and its apparent tyranny of movement there are value judgements, or to speak more clearly, physiological demands for the preservation of a particular kind of life. (§ 3)

A person's theoretical beliefs are best explained, Nietzsche thinks, by evaluative beliefs, particular interpretations of certain values, for example, that goodness is *this* and the opposite of badness. These values are best explained as 'physiological demands for the preservation of a particular kind of life'. Nietzsche holds that each person has a particular psycho-physical constitution, formed by both heredity and culture. Now, 'all animals, including *la bête philosophe* [the philosophical animal], strive instinctively for an optimum combination of favourable conditions which allow them to expend all their energy and achieve their maximum feeling of power'. Putting these points together, there are different 'types' of people, who are drawn to the different types of life that suit

On the Genealogy of Morals, III § 7

them best. Different values, and different interpretations of these values, support different ways of life, and so people are instinctively drawn to particular values and ways of understanding them. On the basis of these interpretations of values, people come to hold particular philosophical views.

§ 2 has given us an illustration of this: philosophers come to hold metaphysical beliefs about a transcendent world, the 'true' and 'good' world, because they cannot believe that truth and goodness could originate in the world of normal experience, which is full of illusion, error and selfishness. Therefore, there 'must' be a pure, spiritual world and a spiritual part of human beings, which is the origin of truth and goodness.

> The main division Nietzsche discusses is between people who are naturally 'masters' and leaders, and those who need to be obedient, 'slaves'.

Philosophy and values

But 'must' there be a transcendent world? Or is this just what the philosopher *wants* to be true? Every great philosophy, claims Nietzsche, is 'the personal confession of its author' (§ 6). The moral aims of a philosophy are the 'seed' from which the whole theory grows. Philosophers pretend that their opinions have been reached by 'cold, pure, divinely unhampered dialectic' when in fact, they are seeking reasons to support their pre-existing commitment to 'a rarefied and abstract version of their heart's desire' (§ 5), namely, that there is a transcendent world, and that good and bad, true and false are opposites.

Consider: many philosophical systems are of doubtful coherence, for example, how *could* there be Forms, and if there were, how *could* we know about them? Or again, in § 11, Nietzsche asks 'how are synthetic a priori judgments possible?' The term 'synthetic a priori' was invented by Kant. According to Nietzsche, Kant says that such judgements are possible, because we have a 'faculty' that makes them possible. What kind of answer is this? Furthermore, no philosopher has ever been proved right (§ 25).

Given the great difficulty of believing either in a transcendent world or in human **cognitive** abilities necessary to know about it, we should look elsewhere for an explanation of why someone would hold those beliefs. We can find an answer in their values.

There is an interesting structural similarity between Nietzsche's argument and Hume's. Both argue that there is no *rational* explanation of many of our beliefs, and so they try to find the source of these beliefs outside or beyond reason. Hume appeals to imagination and the principle of 'Custom'. Nietzsche appeals instead to motivation and THE BEWITCHMENT OF LANGUAGE (p. 205).

> The position that there can be **synthetic** a priori judgements is rationalism, discussed in Unit 1.1 REASON AND EXPERIENCE.

> How does Nietzsche connect metaphysical theories to values?

See NATURE OF BELIEF AND IMAGINATION, p. 19, and THE SCOPE OF MATTERS OF FACT, p. 28.

So Nietzsche argues that philosophy is not driven by a pure 'will to truth' (§ 1), to discover the truth whatever it may be. Instead, a philosophy interprets the world in terms of the philosopher's values. For example, the Stoics argued that we should live 'according to nature' (§ 9). But they interpret nature by their own values, as an embodiment of rationality. They do not see the *senselessness*, the purposelessness, the indifference of nature to our lives.

Nietzsche applies his argument to moral philosophy in § 187.

Philosophers' values: the 'ascetic ideal' and the 'will to truth'

Nietzsche argues that our values support a particular kind of life, one in which we can achieve a maximum feeling of power. If philosophical beliefs rest on values, and values are expressions of power, then philosophical beliefs are also, indirectly, an expression of power. How are philosophers' values supposed to express their 'instincts' and create 'favourable conditions' for philosophers? In fact, Nietzsche only hints at this idea in *Beyond Good and Evil*, but spells it out in his next book, *On the Genealogy of Morals*.

See also NIETZSCHE'S ACCOUNT OF RELIGION, p. 253.

In brief, philosophy requires a lifestyle not of action but of contemplation. And as a way of life, philosophy requires a certain 'ascetism', that is, self-discipline and a refusal to indulge one's bodily desires. People who are constitutionally drawn to a life of contemplation will find it difficult if they are surrounded by a culture of action, of politics and business, and a set of values that supports these activities. They can protect their life of the mind, and justify their ascetism, by arguing that there are transcendent values of the mind – knowledge of the truth and goodness – that are greater than the values of the body and the world of experience and action. This enables them to maximise their feeling of power – over themselves (ascetism) and over others (in the first instance, in getting other people to *respect* their way of life).

On the Genealogy of Morals, III §§ 7–9

We will discuss the precise nature of THE 'WILL TO TRUTH' on p. 213.

We can now interpret § 1. Philosophy is wrong to think that it is an expression of the 'will to truth', as other values come into play. Second, making *the discovery of truth* 'at whatever cost', one's guiding value is itself an expression of the ascetic ideal. It elevates knowledge (mind) over action (body), and expresses a willingness to bear the 'cost' of the truth. The truth can be unpleasant and its discovery arduous. So what is the value of 'will to truth'? Why do we prefer truth to untruth, uncertainty, ignorance? In fact, Nietzsche argues, often we don't, but we *say* that we do, that is, we hold truth to be a value, even if we do not always act according to that value. So what does truth as a *value* do for us?

Nietzsche is immediately aware of the paradox of this question – he wants to know *the truth* about the will to truth! So he is expressing the will to truth in asking the question. In raising the question, the questioner is asking about himself. But the question, Nietzsche says repeatedly, is dangerous. How much are we really willing to risk in looking for an answer? Nietzsche argues that the will to truth originates in a kind of self-deception (§ 2). It presents itself as driven by the value of truth alone (as though this has no relation to anything else), but in fact, it is part of a set of values that seeks to protect conditions in which certain kinds of people, such as philosophers, can live the kind of life that maximises their feeling of power.

> Explain the relationship between the will to truth and asceticism in philosophy.

A brief reflection

What are we to make of Nietzsche's argument? First, are we being encouraged to try to do philosophy *without* imposing our values on the world? Not at all – in fact, this is not possible, says Nietzsche. But we should not lack the courage to see that this is what we are doing. THE NEW PHILOSOPHER (p. 214), the philosophers of the future, will explicitly set out to be the creators of values. Unlike the values of the past that have all concealed their origins, the new values will explicitly and openly express THE WILL TO POWER (p. 224).

Second, is Nietzsche's critique accurate and fair? In many instances, it is not. For instance, it is often over-simplified. But we must remember that Nietzsche is *inviting* us to think of philosophy differently, suspiciously, in relation to the idea that even philosophers are a kind of animal, and there are facts about how any animal is motivated to express its power. He is not trying to prove to us (using traditional philosophical arguments) that philosophy is as he says it is. His rhetoric is part of his method.

So what about his 'factual claim' that all animals try to create favourable conditions in which to express their 'power'? We have seen no support for it yet; we shall discuss it in THE WILL TO POWER (p. 224), and must defer further objections to his analysis of philosophy until then.

> If you find Nietzsche immediately persuasive, ask yourself why.

The 'correct' philosophical questions

The title of the book, *Beyond Good and Evil: Prelude to a Philosophy of the Future*, suggests that the past has been concerned with the wrong question, a concern with what is good and its distinction from what is evil. In § 1, Nietzsche makes the same point with truth – philosophers have asked 'What is true?', but they have not asked what the value of the truth is. They have not questioned their will to truth.

Nor have they questioned their judgement that appearance is less important than truth. Less important in what way, or for what? There is an assumption that what is true will, in some way, be *beneficial* for us. We assume that the true and the good are the same (as in Plato's theory of the Forms). Nietzsche invites us to consider whether what is false could actually be essential, *essential for life*, 'that man could not live without accepting logical fictions' (§ 4), such as the 'I' (see the next section) or the idea of a transcendent world. That 'truth' and 'goodness' are more important than falsehood and deception may itself be a deception that we cannot live without (§ 3). 'Admitting untruth as a condition of life: that means to resist familiar values in a dangerous way; and a philosophy that dares this has already placed itself beyond good and evil' (§ 4). That is, such a philosophy does not approve just of what is good and true; it may also approve of what is false and evil. The standard by which it operates, the life it recommends, lies beyond our usual values.

These are not easy thoughts; they are difficult and distressing. Yet we must come to recognise, says Nietzsche, that hatred, envy, greed and hunger for power are necessary for life (§ 23). To disapprove of them is to disapprove of life. THE ASCETIC IDEAL (p. 253), he will argue, does just this – it disapproves of organic, bodily, instinctual life, and deceptively substitutes for it a life of the 'spirit'. In rejecting the illusions created by the ascetic ideal, we travel beyond morality.

> Explain the importance of Nietzsche's questioning the will to truth.

Key points • • •

- Nietzsche argues that theoretical beliefs can be explained by a person's values, for example, the belief in a transcendent world can be explained in relation to belief about the value of truth.
- Values are best explained as 'physiological demands for the preservation of a particular kind of life'. Everyone strives for conditions in which they can 'achieve their maximum feeling of power'.
- Metaphysical systems, therefore, are not constructed by pure reason, but are guided by the philosopher's values. Philosophy is not driven by a pure 'will to truth'.
- Philosophers are thinkers, and philosophy as a way of life requires asceticism.

To survive in a culture of action, philosophers must argue that there are values that transcend those of the world of experience and action.

- The will to truth is itself an expression of the ascetic ideal. But it rests on a self-deception, because it denies its origins in values that seek to protect a particular way of life. The philosophy of the future will openly express this connection to power.

- We must ask whether falsehood and deception could be valuable, such that we can't live without them. To accept this is to place one's values 'beyond good and evil'.

The bewitchment of language

We said (p. 197) that Nietzsche criticises past philosophers on two grounds. We have looked at the role of motivation; the second ground is the seduction of grammar. Nietzsche is concerned with the subject–predicate structure of language, and with it the notion of a 'substance' (picked out by the grammatical subject) to which we attribute 'properties' (identified by the predicate). This structure leads us into a mistaken metaphysics of 'substances'. In particular, Nietzsche is concerned with the grammar of 'I'. We tend to think that 'I' refers to some thing, for example, the soul. Descartes makes this mistake in his *cogito* – 'I think', he argues, refers to a substance engaged in an activity. But Nietzsche repeats the old objection that this is an illegitimate inference (§ 16) that rests on many unproven assumptions – that *I* am thinking, that some thing is thinking, that thinking is an activity (the result of a cause, namely, I), that an 'I' exists, that we know what it is to think.

For discussion, see **ABSOLUTE CERTAINTY** OF THE *COGITO* AND ITS IMPLICATIONS, **p. 156.**

So the simple sentence 'I think' is misleading. In fact, 'a thought comes when "it" wants to, and not when "I" want it to' (§ 17). Even 'there is thinking' isn't right: 'even this "there" contains an *interpretation* of the process and is not part of the process itself. People are concluding here according to grammatical habit'. But our language does not allow us just to say 'thinking' – this is not a whole sentence. We have to say 'there is thinking'; so grammar constrains our understanding. Furthermore, Kant shows that rather than the 'I' being the basis of thinking, thinking is the basis out of which the appearance of an 'I' is created (§ 54).

Once we recognise that there is no soul in a traditional sense, no 'substance', something constant through change, something unitary and immortal, 'the way is clear for new and refined versions of the hypothesis about the soul' (§ 12), that it is mortal, that it is multiplicity rather than identical over time, even that it is a social construct and a society of drives.

Nietzsche makes a similar argument about the will (§ 19). Because we have this one word 'will', we think that what it refers to must also be one thing. But the act of willing is highly complicated. First, there is an emotion of command, for willing is commanding oneself to do something, and with it a feeling of superiority over that which obeys. Second, there is the expectation that the mere commanding on its own is enough for the action to follow, which increases our sense of power. Third, there is obedience to the command, from which we also derive pleasure. But we ignore the feeling of compulsion, identifying the 'I' with the commanding 'will'.

Nietzsche links the seduction of language to the issue of motivation in § 20, arguing that 'the spell of certain grammatical functions is the spell of *physiological* value judgements'. So even the grammatical structure of language originates in our instincts, different grammars contributing to the creation of favourable conditions for different types of life. So what values are served by these notions of the 'I' and the 'will'? The 'I' relates to the idea that we have a soul, which participates in a transcendent world. It functions in support of THE ASCETIC IDEAL (p. 253). The 'will', and in particular our inherited conception of 'free will', serves a particular moral aim, which we will discuss in FREE WILL AND INTROSPECTION, p. 233.

> This picture is complicated further by our thinking of the will as 'free'. This is discussed in FREE WILL AND INTROSPECTION, p. 233.

> This view rejects the traditional empiricist theory of the origin of ideas in favour of a form of **nativism**, as our physiological constitution is largely **innate** (see DO ALL IDEAS DERIVE FROM SENSE EXPERIENCE?, p. 12).

Key points • • •

- Nietzsche argues that grammar, especially the subject–predicate structure of language, leads us to philosophically mistaken conclusions, in particular a metaphysics of substance.
- The 'I' we take to refer to a soul that can voluntarily engage in 'thinking'. The 'will' we take to be unified (and free), when it is very complex.
- These aspects of grammar support the ascetic ideal, suggesting the existence and value of a transcendent world in which the soul participates.

Truth and interpretation

Perspectivism

In the opening sections of the book, Nietzsche repeatedly refers to 'perspectives'. In the Preface, he says that perspectivity is 'the fundamental condition of all life'; in §§ 2 and 3 he refers to the beliefs in the opposition of values and the value of truth as 'foreground evaluations, temporary perspectives'; in § 11, he refers to the belief in synthetic a priori judgements 'one of the foreground beliefs and appearances that constitute the perspective-optics of life'. What does all this mean?

The term 'perspective' comes from the language of vision. We literally see things from and with a particular perspective. Our eyes are located at a particular point in space, from which some things are visible and others are not, for example, the top of the table, but not its underneath. A scene looks different from different perspectives – from high up, we can see further and things look smaller, from below things 'loom' over us and we cannot see very far.

The idea of perspective has a rich metaphorical life. Important for our purposes, when someone seems to overreact emotionally, we tell them to 'get things in perspective' – what has happened is not as important as they seem to think, they need to see the 'bigger picture' or take the 'longer view'. In emotional overreaction, the immediate experience (which is near) dominates the person. This relates to Nietzsche's talk of 'foreground evaluations' – we take what is near to us (in the foreground) as the standard by which we interpret the world.

Nietzsche talks about 'perspective' when he is relating beliefs to our values (and hence to our instincts). He uses the word 'interpretation' to mean a belief about something as if it is like this or that. An interpretation is an understanding of the world from a particular perspective; and so interpretations, like perspectives, relate back to our values.

So Nietzsche is saying that philosophical beliefs about truth and goodness are part of a *particular perspective* on the world, a short-sighted, distorting perspective. One of its most important distortions is that it denies that it is a perspective (Preface), claiming that its truths are unconditional (§ 4), that it represents the world as it truly is. But philosophers are wrong to think that it is possible to or hold beliefs about the world that are value-free, 'objective', 'disinterested'.

This applies even to sense perception, which we might expect to be *most* responsive to how the world is (§ 192). First, we find it easier, argues Nietzsche,

> In § 2, he talks of 'a perspective from below', though the literal translation is 'a frog's perspective' – which was also slang for 'narrow-minded' (because you can't see far or wide).

to reproduce an image we are familiar with than to remember what is new and different in our sense impression. We are averse to new things, and so already, our experience of the world is dominated by an emotion. Familiar emotions – what we fear or love – will affect what we see. Second, we cannot take in everything – we do not see every leaf on a tree, but out of our visual experience, create for ourselves an image of something approximating the tree. We do the same for everything we experience; our emotions affect this process. Third, whenever a new idea or experience arises, people become over-excited, impatient to develop or experience it. Over time, we become more cautious, see it more for what it is.

We can support Nietzsche's argument by an evolutionary account of human cognition. We can't possibly take in everything around us. We must be selective in order to survive at all. So from the very beginning, our intellects are responsive to our interests, our biological instincts and all that develops from them – our emotions, desires and values. So we do not and cannot experience the world 'as it is', but always selectively, in a way that reflects our values.

> Different perspectives are defined by different *values*; differences in belief are not themselves enough. Two people with different religious beliefs, for instance, may occupy the same perspective if their beliefs reflect the same underlying set of values.

> Explain what Nietzsche means by 'perspective'. Why does he argue that philosophy has had a 'foreground' perspective?

> Nietzsche does *not* say that we *should* interpret nature this way. For discussion, see THE WILL TO POWER, p. 225.

Going further: the laws of nature

Nietzsche uses his perspectivism in some contentious ways. For example, in § 22, he argues that the scientific idea of 'laws of nature' is an expression of the value of equality (something Nietzsche strongly disapproves of). It is an interpretation of nature driven by ideas of democracy and atheism - there is no god, no master, all are 'equal before the law'. It is a ridiculous analogy of natural events with a particular morality, one that thinks of morality as a single set of laws that apply to everyone. We could just as well interpret natural events as the assertion of power claims. That there is an equally good way of interpreting nature shows that the 'laws of nature' approach is an interpretation, from a particular perspective.

We can object that if Nietzsche were right, the scientific idea of laws of nature should have arisen at the same time as ideas of democracy and an increase in atheism. Yet Leonardo da Vinci did much to contribute to the idea that all natural events follow strict laws even as he worked in a very hierarchical culture in which atheism could be severely punished. It wasn't until over 150 years later (around 1650) that ideas of democracy and atheism began to rise.

Nietzsche could challenge this in two ways. First, he could argue that our historical account is wrong, for example, that the idea of democracy was part of John Wycliffe's thought. Wycliffe, who lived in the fourteenth century, attacked the authority of the priests and argued that the Bible should be available to everyone to read in their own native language. He was also interested in natural science. Second, Nietzsche could argue that the connection between democracy, atheism and the scientific idea of laws of nature can be seen in the emergence of all three together *over several hundred years*. Nietzsche's histories are often imprecise in this way, as he is only interested in the big picture.

> Discuss Nietzsche's derivation of the idea of 'laws of nature' from the value of equality.

The paradox of perspectivism

If Nietzsche claims that all our knowledge is from a particular perspective, then his claims about perspectives and his theory of perspectivism must *itself* be from a particular perspective. So is what he says about perspectives objectively true or not? If it is meant to be objectively true, this would be a contradiction of his perspectivism. But if objective knowledge is impossible, then aren't all perspectives *just* perspectives, all equal? Nietzsche denies this as well.

First, he says that some perspectives are *foreground* perspectives, suggesting that others – his own, for example – are better, less distorting perspectives (§ 2). Second, he claims that particular philosophical or moral views are *false*, for example, the belief in the opposition of values (§ 4). Third, Nietzsche is an empiricist – he says that our sense organs can become 'fine, loyal, cautious organs of cognition' (§ 192) while he rejects the possibility of synthetic a priori judgements (§ 11). But how can the senses be a *better* source of beliefs than a priori reason unless some perspectives are better than others?

Nietzsche's view is that perspective cannot be eliminated, that is, values cannot cease to guide our knowledge, and that the attempt to eliminate it completely is misguided. However, some perspectives are less distorting than others. First, a perspective may be aware that it is a perspective. Becoming aware of the perspectival nature of knowledge is itself an improvement in knowledge. Second, we can find a less perspectival perspective by assembling many different perspectives:

On the Genealogy of Morals, III § 12

perspectival 'knowing' [is] the *only* kind of 'knowing'; and the *more* feelings about a matter which we allow to come to expression, the *more* eyes, different eyes through which we are able to view this same matter, the more complete our 'conception' of it, our 'objectivity' will be.

We need to be flexible, not trapped by one set of values or the illusion of value-free knowing, but able to move from one valuational perspective to another, and from these many points of view, assemble our picture of the world.

We may still ask, from what perspective does Nietzsche develop his views, his critique of philosophy, his position 'beyond good and evil'? The answer, roughly, is 'life' – what he means by 'life' and how this could be a value, we discuss in THE WILL TO POWER (p. 224).

> **Discuss the paradox of perspectivism and Nietzsche's solution to it.**

Is truth perspectival?

Perspectivism is a claim about *knowledge*, about our beliefs and representations of the world. But many philosophers have thought that Nietzsche is also a perspectivist about *truth* – there is no truth, only 'truths'. This doesn't follow from what has been said. Certainly Nietzsche says that what people *believe* is true depends on their perspective, as does how they understand the concept and value of truth. But this does not mean that truth itself varies between perspectives. This claim would contradict Nietzsche's claim that certain per-spectives are distorting – how can they be distorting if what is true, from that perspective, depends on that perspective?

Nietzsche's attacks on the *value* of truth are not attacks on the idea that there is any such thing as truth. That appearance may be as valuable as truth does not imply that there is not truth – instead, it presupposes that there could be! Perspectivism claims only that the truth must always be represented from some perspective; there is no *one* way to represent the truth.

However, there are passages in which Nietzsche seems to be a perspectivist about truth, for example, § 43 in which he discusses the 'new philosophers'. Unlike past philosophers, they will not insist that 'their truth' will have to be 'a truth for everyone else'. But Nietzsche then rephrases the point in terms of *judgement*: 'My judgment is *my* judgment: no one else has a right to it so easily.' Nietzsche is saying that new philosophers, unlike past philosophers, will not want everyone to agree with them, to occupy their perspective, to share their values. As we saw at the start (p. 196), Nietzsche thinks his views are not for everyone, but only a select few. We can interpret the phrase 'their truth' to refer to their judgements, and not as a suggestion that what is true is itself dependent on perspectives.

The desire that everyone agrees on the truth is part of the mistaken metaphysical picture that denies perspectivism and wants to represent the 'one' truth just as it is. Once we recognise that there are only many perspectives to be had, whether we think that our perspectives should or could be shared by others is an open question.

We will look further at the new philosophers' relationship to truth in THE WILL TO TRUTH, p. 213.

What is the difference between perspectivism about knowledge and perspectivism about truth?

Going further: truth and appearance

If truth is not perspectival, then is there a 'true world', the world as it really is, independent of how we can know it? Isn't this the philosophical myth – a true world transcending the world of experience – that Nietzsche attacks? Nietzsche discusses the relation between appearance and truth in § 34 – but it is very difficult to understand, and many philosophers think that his views are expressed better in later works.

The argument in § 34 starts from the question of the *value* of truth and appearance: 'It is nothing but a moral prejudice to consider truth more valuable than appearance.' Nietzsche then says that if we wanted to do away with all appearance, leaving just 'the truth', we can't do so coherently. And then, 'why should we be forced to assume that there is an essential difference between "true" and "false" in the first place? Isn't it enough to assume that there are degrees of apparency . . . lighter and darker shadows and hues of appearance'. Does this mean that there are only appearances, no truth except what appears in different perspectives?

In *Twilight of the Idols*, Nietzsche presents a story of the development, through six stages, of philosophical theories about the relation between appearances (how the world appears) and truth (how it is 'in itself'). First, we thought the true world could be known to the good and wise person (Plato). Second, we thought that it was unattainable, but promised, to the good and wise person, for example, in an afterlife (Christianity). Third (Kant), we came to think that we can neither known or achieve the true world, but the thought of its existence was a consolation and the source of our moral obligations. Fourth (later German Idealists), we realised that if we cannot know anything

'How the "True World" Became a Fable'

about the true world, it is neither consoling nor does it give us moral obligations. Fifth, we realise that therefore even the *idea* of a 'true world' has no use – and this seems to be what Nietzsche suggests in § 34. But there is a sixth stage, perhaps present in § 34, but represented more clearly in Nietzsche's later thought – if we abolish the idea of the 'true world', in what sense are appearances just *appearances*? They can only be thought of as appearances if we have something to contrast them with. But in getting rid of the idea of a 'true world', there is no contrast. 'Appearances' are no more 'false' than 'true' – they are all there is.

How does this help? We can suggest that instead of supposing that there is some 'true world' which then appears to us, we must understand 'appearances' as what comes first, logically speaking. We then *interpret* 'appearances' to be the 'appearance' of something. This quickly leads to mistakes, for example, we think in terms of substances and properties. We should resist this interpretation, and understand 'appearances' as ever-changing relations. For example, we can only talk about 'hues' of red in relation to each other – darker or lighter, more or less intense; we cannot talk about a shade of colour 'absolutely'. This should be a model for our understanding of appearances. The world is ever-changing, not some *thing* 'behind' or 'beyond' appearances, that appears differently at different times. We are wrong to talk of a 'true world' beyond appearance.

But this does not mean that 'truth' is relative to *perspectives*. Appearances and perspectives are not equivalent. Perspectives can distort appearances; and so what 'appears' from a particular perspective may be a distorted version of those very appearances. Perspectives that are not distorting (or less distorting) of appearances have a better grasp of what we may call the 'truth' – without meaning to refer to some world beyond appearance.

What is the relationship between 'appearances' and 'truth'?

Going further: the will to truth

Nietzsche is more concerned to analyse the will to truth than to develop a systematic theory of what 'truth' is. The will to truth in philosophy has, so far, understood the 'truth' in terms of the mistaken belief in the opposition of values. It understands the truth as 'unconditional' in two ways. First, it is free of perspective. And so the will to truth, correspondingly, attempts to be free of perspective and values, encouraging the 'objective' detachment that one finds praised in philosophy and science. But this attitude, argues Nietzsche, is an impoverishing of life, which is both emotional and perspectival. Second, the truth is unconditional in being of incomparable worth (it is also identical to the good). So the will to truth aims at the truth 'at any price', rather than placing the value of truth in relation to life. But the will to truth misrepresents itself, because it is not 'pure', but part of a particular system of values, namely, THE ASCETIC IDEAL (p. 253) that demeans life and the world available to us.

By contrast, Nietzsche argues, that a judgement is false may be no objection to it (§ 4); there are other values more important. The truth can be dangerous, a threat to life. New philosophers will place truth, the value of truth and the will to truth in relation to life, and will use them for greater ends. Their will to truth will not be unconditional.

Is Nietzsche suggesting that new philosophers will want to have false beliefs or knowingly believe what is false? Does this even make sense? If you believe something, you believe it to be true. Nietzsche asks 'why do we not prefer untruth?' (§ 1). But does the question make sense? *Can* we prefer untruth if we cannot believe what we know to be false?

The idea of the will to truth is about how we understand the value of truth, that is, how that value guides us in *forming* our beliefs (when we don't yet know what is true or false). While it may be true that we cannot *consciously and deliberately* believe what we know to be false, Nietzsche has argued that what happens consciously when we form beliefs is unconsciously guided by our values. The will to truth serves (or can serve) as part of a *self-deception* - we think we want the truth, and for its own sake, but this desire in fact serves the will to power, to create favourable conditions in which we attain the maximum feeling of power.

Paradoxically, it is the will to truth that leads to this discovery, undermining its own foundations. See NIETZSCHE'S ACCOUNT OF RELIGION, p. 253.

What is 'the will to truth'? Why does Nietzsche argue that it should not be unconditional?

Key points • • •

- Nietzsche argues that our knowledge, beliefs and experience are always part of a particular perspective on the world. Perspectives are determined by a set of values (and these by instincts). Interpretations of the world are made from particular perspectives.
- Even in sense perception, our experience and beliefs are influenced by emotions, such as a desire for familiarity and impatience, and by selectivity. We cannot take in everything, so what we take in is influenced by our interests, our values.
- A more contentious claim relating value to beliefs is that the idea of laws of nature is driven by the values of democracy and the rise of atheism.
- Nietzsche's perspectivism must itself express a perspective. But this doesn't mean that all perspectives are equally acceptable. Some are distortions, and those that deny perspectivism are very distorting. Greater objectivity is gained by being able to assemble different perspectives, not by transcending perspective (which is impossible).
- The values of Nietzsche's perspective are those of 'life'.
- Perspectivism doesn't claim that truth itself is relative to perspective, only that all ways of representing the truth are. New philosophers will not necessarily want everyone to share the same perspective (and so agree on the truth).
- Is 'the truth' transcendent of perspectives? Nietzsche argues that we must abandon the image of the truth as something to contrast with appearances. There are only 'appearances'. However, appearances are not perspectives, but what perspectives are perspectives on.
- An unconditional will to truth, part of the ascetic ideal, misrepresents the truth as unconditional, meaning beyond perspective and of incomparable worth. New philosophers will place the value of truth in relation to life, so their will to truth will not be unconditional.

The new philosopher

Creators of new values

Nietzsche has criticised past philosophers for their belief in the opposition of values, and with it, a belief in a transcendent world which is the source of truth and goodness, and for their ascetic ideal, of which these beliefs are a part. He has said that this ideal is an expression of philosophers' attempt to create favourable conditions in which to achieve their maximum feeling of power. However, their beliefs are false and their ideal demeans this world and our instinctual life. There will be a new kind of philosopher, Nietzsche prophesies (§ 2), one who understands the real origin of values and how values are connected to their opposites, who rejects the ascetic ideal and values 'life' above all.

But for them to do this, the new philosophers need to have not just different *beliefs*. *All* animals seek to create conditions favourable to them – so new philosophers must be a different form of human being, with different instincts and drives, ones that do not express themselves best through the ascetic ideal. The new philosopher is aligned to THE WILL TO POWER (p. 224), and they will create new values that understand and approve of the origin of values in instincts.

The new philosopher will not have an unconditional will to truth (§ 25). They recognise the danger of the truth. They know that just because something makes us happy or even virtuous, this does not make it true; and likewise, that it causes harm, does not make it false (§ 39).

The truth about the origin of values is one such truth. Nietzsche argues that the ascetic ideal provides an answer to *suffering*. The promise of another world that can be attained through virtue or after death helps us cope with the suffering of this life. But there is no such transcendent world. So how can we face the suffering of life? Nietzsche suggests that 'The strength of a person's spirit would then be measured by how much "truth" he could tolerate, or more precisely, to what extent he *needs* to have it diluted, disguised, sweetened, muted, falsified' (§ 39). To go beyond the ascetic ideal, new philosophers will need strong spirits.

On the one hand, then, new philosophers will travel further towards the truth, and so they need to be trained in the truthfulness that characterised the ascetic ideal. On the other hand, the truth is something that the ascetic ideal has disguised, and so they have to travel beyond the ascetic ideal. They must therefore overcome the ascetic ideal, above all, in themselves. But, as Nietzsche notes, to go beyond good and evil (as understood so far) leaves one without an orientation in judgement (§ 23). And so new philosophers will create new values.

Does this make sense? Can anybody 'create' values? Nietzsche argues that we always have, in seeking to create favourable conditions for ourselves – it is just that we were *not aware* that this is what we were doing. Creating values self-consciously is impossible for most people; we have a *need* to receive our values from outside, a need to obey (§ 199). New philosophers, however, will have strength: '*true philosophers are commanders and lawgivers*'.

> See NIETZSCHE'S ACCOUNT OF RELIGION, p. 253.

> **?** Why does Nietzsche say that we must be strong to tolerate the truth?

> We must not make the mistake of thinking of new philosophers as 'scholars' (§ 211). Scholars can survey and summarise values (as Kant and Hegel have done), but the task of the new philosopher is to create values.

The new philosophers' will to truth is will to power (§ 211). The purpose of knowledge is to create new values, and therefore a new perspective and new appearances. Their knowledge is not mere *representation* of the world, it fashions the world.

So what are these new values? We cannot understand Nietzsche's thoughts on this topic without first discussing THE WILL TO POWER (p. 229), so we will return to this question in that section.

> Explain why new philosophers must create new values. Does the idea of creating values make sense?

> There are also 'false' free spirits – see HERD MORALITY AND THE CRITIQUE OF 'MODERN IDEAS', p. 244.

Free spirits and experimenters

New philosophers are not the same as 'free spirits'. They will be free spirits, 'but something more, higher, greater and fundamentally different' (§ 44). Genuine free spirits are people who question and begin to move beyond the ascetic ideal. They can help tear down the old values, but they may not necessarily be able to create new values. They include the 'exceptional' people Nietzsche talks about in § 26, who seek solitude because they are exceptional. But if such a person remains 'tucked away . . . in his fortress . . . he is not made for, not destined for, knowledge'. Only those who are strong enough to come 'down' and 'into' the mass of humanity can become new philosophers.

'[T]hese philosophers of the future might rightfully – perhaps also wrongfully – be described as *experimenters*' (§ 42). The German word also translates as 'tempters', and Nietzsche means the pun in several ways.

First, someone who 'tempts' seduces other people; new philosophers will create new values that others can adopt.

Second, new philosophers will have to undergo and resist many temptations: 'Those of us who are destined to be independent and to command must . . . set ourselves our own tests' (§ 41). And these tests or temptations are designed to help the new philosopher become truly independent, independent enough to create new values. And so any dependency on honours, money, position, the senses, someone loved, a home country, a settled life, on a particular academic discipline (a 'science'), must be overcome. Even dependency on one's own detachment and virtues, or on pity, will have to be sacrificed (§§ 41, 44).

And this is because, third, they are also 'experimenters', and their experiments may well go beyond what conventional morality can allow (§§ 44, 210). They will be harsher than humane people would like and investigate things to the point of cruelty. But, again, these are not experiments designed just to discover truth, but to help create new values that go 'beyond' good and evil.

> Why does Nietzsche call new philosophers 'experimenters'?

Nietzsche further describes new philosophers, and free spirits more generally, in terms of the idea of a 'mask' (§ 40). Masks play several functions.

1. Free spirits must be disguised to conduct their investigations of ordinary people (§ 26), in order to discover the truth about them and so about values, the will to power, the ascetic ideal and so on.
2. Free spirits cannot interact with ordinary, 'lower' people without distress (§ 26) – they see the truth. The mask disguises their distress.
3. Free spirits are repeatedly misunderstood. What people see is not who they really are, but a misinterpretation (§ 40).
4. Free spirits, or at least, new philosophers, cannot be dependent on any of the usual sources of our identity – where we are from, what we do, who we love; Nietzsche describes them in terms that suggest *transience*, always moving from this identity to that without staying with any (§ 44). This last use of the mask relates to his perspectivism: we achieve 'objectivity' by occupying many different perspectives (see p. 210) – so this is what new philosophers will have to do.

> What was Nietzsche like to meet? Genteel, apparently! His public persona was quite different from the scathing, critical tone of his books.

As new philosophers try on their different masks, experimenting with this and that perspective, and in doing so, going beyond conventional morality, so they also leave behind 'foreground' perspectives of all kinds: 'As his intellectual sight and insight grow stronger, the distances, and, as it were, the space surrounding a man increase: his world becomes more profound' (§ 57). From a distance, we gain a more complete perspective, and are not taken in by what is near. Concepts that have meant so much in the history of human thought, such as 'God' and 'sin' may, from the distance new philosophers can achieve, look like children's toys.

> Nietzsche looks at the 'big picture' in his genealogies, in which he covers thousands of years in a few sentences.

The sceptic and the critic

Two of the 'masks' of the new philosopher are those of 'sceptic' and 'critic' (§§ 209–10); but again, they will not be mere sceptics and critics, but go beyond both. What does Nietzsche mean by these terms?

Nietzsche distinguishes between two types of sceptic, connecting each type to their instincts. The first has 'bad nerves' and is constitutionally unable to say 'yes' or 'no' to anything (§ 208). They call their **scepticism** 'objectivity' or 'the scientific method' or (in aesthetics) 'art for art's sake'. It promotes caution,

> Explain Nietzsche's concept of a 'free spirit'. How does it relate to his perspectivism?

> § 208 is not on the syllabus, but necessary for understanding § 209.

'disinterest', a dampening down of all passionate responses, supported by a morality that disapproves of decisive answers. Such sceptics exhibit a lack of will.

The second kind of scepticism does not originate in fear or lack of nerves (§ 209). It is suspicious of easy answers and the refusal to give answers, and will dig deeper for the truth. Such a sceptic will call into question the value of existence itself.

This is one aspect of new philosophers. But they could equally call themselves 'critics' (§ 210). A critic seeks to analyse and define an area of knowledge, to test it for consistency and find its underlying principles. Critics draw the boundaries of what can be known. Kant was a great critic. New philosophers will have the rigour and 'neatness' of critics. But they will be critics 'in body and soul', that is, not just in their thought, but through the way that they live. They apply criticism to themselves, they will experiment with themselves (§ 41). And they will not be just critics for their criticism will serve the creation of new values (§ 211).

By their scepticism and criticism, new philosophers take 'a vivisecting knife to the breast of the *virtues of their age*', uncovering hypocrisy and falsehood (§ 212). In so doing, they reveal 'their knowledge of a *new* human greatness, a new, untrodden path to human aggrandizement', the new, greater type of human being that they will embody and the new values that they will create.

Discuss Nietzsche's account of new philosophers as sceptics and critics.

Eternal return

Untimely Meditations, II § 9

Nietzsche says that no sacrifice is too great to help bring new philosophers into existence (§ 23). What could justify this? The quick answer is that they justify life, even with all its suffering. With them, it is possible to say that it – life, history – is worth it. The goal of humanity, says Nietzsche in an early work, lies in its highest specimens.

Throughout history, human beings have suffered terribly, physically and mentally. For what purpose? We deceive ourselves about this to try to make life bearable. One self-deception is to say that this life is not worth much, that there is a better, greater world, that we suffer because we sin. But there is no transcendent world. This life is it. With no transcendent world, are we left with the judgement that life is worthless, pointless – pessimism?

See NIETZSCHE'S ACCOUNT OF RELIGION, p. 253.

We need a new ideal, one based in this life, not denying it. We need 'the ideal of the most audacious, lively, and world-affirming human being, one who has learned not only to accept and bear that which has been and is, but who also wants to have it over again, *just as it was and is*, throughout all eternity' (§ 56). The ability to say 'Yes' to life is the ultimate mark of someone who is 'higher' and a genuine free spirit.

This idea of 'having it over again . . . throughout all eternity' is the idea of the 'eternal return' of the world and everything that happens. In his unpublished notebooks, Nietzsche toyed with the idea that the world actually *does* repeat itself, that everything that has happened in the past will happen again, that everything that happens in the future has happened in a previous cycle. But he never defended the idea in print. So we should not interpret him as making a metaphysical claim. Instead, Nietzsche presents it as a psychological test: what sort of person could *will* the eternal return of the world?

To will eternal return is different from merely accepting it or resigning oneself to it. It is to want it. Second, in what you will to happen again, you change nothing. So to will eternal return is to will all the wars, genocide, natural disasters, diseases, torture, mental illness and broken hearts that have ever occurred. All events are 'entangled' with each other. So to will the return of any happiness or joy is to will the return of every sorrow. Third, to *will* something is also to accept responsibility for it. You can be held accountable for what you deliberate choose to do. To will eternal return, then, is to be able to accept responsibility for the entirety of human history. New philosophers 'assign value and rank according to how many and how many sorts of things one person could bear, could take upon himself, by how *far* a person could extend his responsibility' (§ 212). To will eternal return is to take responsibility, of a k ind, for everything that happens. New philosophers will take on themselves responsibility for the future of the human race, to make of us something 'higher' (§ 61).

So what would it take to be able to will eternal return? Above all, one needs to resist *pity* for people suffering: 'taking all the pain of the world together, who could dare decide whether the sight of it should *necessarily* seduce and coerce us to feel pity in particular, thus redoubling the pain?' (§ 30) – why should we add more suffering to the suffering we see? 'There are heights of the soul from which vantage point even tragedy ceases to have a tragic effect.' To will eternal return is to have a particular *perspective* on suffering that is able to say 'Yes' to it because it is part of life.

Free spirits express a strong, healthy yearning for life, even as it is. They do not seek to avoid or minimise suffering. *Suffering is necessary for people to achieve greatness*. Free spirits are therefore *grateful* for everything that is past, all the suffering included, because it has made their lives possible. And in them,

> Explain Nietzsche's concept of eternal return.

> We cannot fully understand the idea of eternal return until we have understood Nietzsche's views on pity, suffering and greatness, and for this, we need to understand his criticism of morality (NATURE OF MORALITY, p. 231) and modern ideas (HERD MORALITY AND THE CRITIQUE OF 'MODERN IDEAS', p. 244).

the *joy* of life is deeper and stronger than suffering, even though they suffer terribly because they are deep, insightful people.

See p. 200. 'Types' are discussed at length in NATURE OF MORALITY, p. 231.

We should recall again that Nietzsche does not separate beliefs and life; our beliefs are an expression of our values, and these are an expression of our instincts and our psycho-physiological 'type'. Free spirits, then, do not just 'believe' that life is worth living over and over again, exactly as it is; they are the living embodiment of this affirmation. Their lives *are* the affirmation of life, and in this way, their lives redeem life, they show it is something that can be affirmed as worthwhile. It is, therefore, possible for life to affirm itself in full self-conscious knowledge. Their existence demonstrates why and how.

There is deliberately a 'religious' feel to Nietzsche's thought here, discussed further in ADVANTAGES AND DISADVANTAGES OF RELIGION, p. 256.

New philosophers, then, are the 'goal' of humanity and 'ordinary' people can be only the means to this end. They are an ideal, 'everything that *mankind could be bred to be*', on which free spirits set their hopes (§ 203). Nietzsche means 'breeding' literally, because new philosophers will be a new psycho-physiological type of human being. You can't be trained to become a true philosopher:

> We have to be born to every higher world; put more clearly, we have to be *bred* to it. We have a right to philosophy (taking the word in its finest meaning) only because of our origins – here too, ancestors, 'bloodlines' are decisive. Many generations have to have prepared the ground for the philosopher's development. (§ 213)

Nietzsche can only negate the ascetic ideal, he cannot say what the new values are that new philosophers will create, but they will be ones that do not consider suffering evil. In some of his works, he claims that he says 'yes' to life, but in a letter to a friend, he writes 'I do not wish for life again. How have I borne it? Creatively. What makes me bear the sight of life? The view of the "super-man" [the higher type of human] who affirms life. I have tried to affirm it myself – alas!'

? How does Nietzsche use the idea of eternal return to argue that new philosophers 'redeem life'?

Criticisms

There are many moral objections that we could make to Nietzsche's ideal – that it supposes there are 'higher', and so 'lower', people; that it requires that lower people are sacrificed for the goal of creating 'higher' people; that what is worthwhile about life is demonstrated only in the lives of 'higher' people. However, these objections presuppose moral values, for example, of equality, that Nietzsche rejects; and we have not looked in detail at his arguments for rejecting these values. Moral objections, then, will have to wait until we have discussed his criticism of morality.

See especially pp. 242, 247 and 251.

However, we can question whether the idea of eternal return has the significance Nietzsche gives it. We are being asked to imagine our response to the thought that everything will recur, just as it has. One response is 'So what?' If everything happens again identically, then just as we have no knowledge now of what we did last time, so next time, we will have no knowledge of what we will do this time. We can do nothing to change what happens – so why should we feel any horror at the thought?

But doesn't the prospect of everything recurring make you feel horror, for example, to think that all the suffering that has happened will happen again? Doesn't this seem *worse* than it happening just once? But if eternal return makes things seem *worse*, then we can't will it. To someone who can affirm eternal return, life recurring seems better, not worse. And Nietzsche is not asking us just to imagine how we feel at the prospect of eternal return, as though we were mere observers, he is asking if we can *will* it, if we could take responsibility for it. It is one thing to be aware of suffering, another to will it, even as a necessary means to greatness.

A second objection: suppose that we could affirm eternal return; then what? What difference does that make to our lives? How would we live differently? Nietzsche never discusses what new philosophers *do*. In fact, Nietzsche says that 'It is not the works, it is the *faith* that is decisive here' (§ 287).

We will return to this issue of attitude when discussing Nobility (p. 249), which is part of Nietzsche's ideal.

Third, in his requirement that we say 'yes' to *everything*, Nietzsche retains something of the ascetic ideal. He criticises that ideal for its notion of 'unconditional' truth and goodness. But isn't the 'all-embracing yes' equally unconditional? It is, but Nietzsche argues that we must embrace it all, or not at all, because *everything is entangled*. To think that we can separate the good from the bad, the true from the false, suffering from greatness, is an illusion created by the ascetic ideal.

A fourth objection is perhaps the strongest so far: is the attitude of affirming eternal return coherent? There are several reasons for thinking that it is not:

1. We are invited to imagine the return of all events. But a position from which we can see things happening again and again would be *outside* the cycle of events. From our perspective, as part of the series of events, we experience everything just once, so the perspective embodied in the idea of eternal return is not one available to us (any more than an unconditional perspective on the truth).

2. Developing this, from the perspective of eternal return, one does not wish anything differently. But life itself is not indifference, it is the desire for things to be different (§ 9). It would therefore be practically inconsistent to affirm life but not to want things to be different.

3. Is transforming our attitude to the past from 'this is how it happened' to 'this is how I will it to be' a type of self-deception, perhaps self-aggrandisement? There is no willing the past to be as it is. It has happened, end of story.

4. Does it make sense to talk about taking responsibility for human history? In his book *The Joyful Science* (§ 337), Nietzsche says that if you could experience the history of humanity as your own history, and survive this amount of suffering and grief, you would experience a greater happiness than anyone has ever known, full of a sense of power and love. But what are we to do with this idea? It is not genuinely achievable, it rests on a psychological impossibility. We cannot coherently aspire to it. Why should this ideal of limitless suffering, responsibility and then happiness be relevant to us, who are limited?

> **Is the idea of willing eternal return coherent?**

Fifth, the attitude of affirming eternal return seems to contradict other attitudes Nietzsche expresses and attributes to new philosophers. Their affirmation of eternal return is countered by their revulsion at almost all life they meet! Are they really only saying 'yes' to themselves? The biggest objection, Nietzsche thought, to affirming eternal return is the return of the 'small', 'lower' man – which most men are. But to exclude most human life is an odd expression of the affirmation of all life!

Willing at the very general, abstract level of eternal return glosses over the inhumanity of willing this or that particular event (e.g. the Holocaust). At the particular level, Nietzsche is horrified at what he finds – it seems that we can only say 'yes' if we have the blurred vision of the very distant perspective. But this is also a self-deception, because it hides the fact that Nietzsche values some things *more than others*. The 'yes' is not an equal 'yes' to everything – some things are to be put up with for the sake of other things. But Nietzsche can reply here that this is no objection: the whole point is whether our will for the end – life in its highest form – is strong enough to will the terrible means.

We can, finally, turn Nietzsche's method on himself. What is the origin of his valuing new philosophers? We find it, perhaps, in his idea of states of the soul so 'high' that suffering does not evoke pity (§ 30). Nietzsche's philosophy, we can argue, is an attempt to be or become immune to suffering, to achieve a perspective on life (eternal return) from which nothing would upset, repel or harm him. It is a form of self-protection.

Is this fair? It suggests that Nietzsche seeks to avoid suffering – but while new philosophers may reject pity, they do not seek to avoid suffering. Indeed, they are fierce with themselves in their quest to overcome the ascetic ideal (e.g. §§ 41, 44); and we may say the same of Nietzsche.

Key points • • •

- New philosophers, rejecting the ascetic ideal, will create new values. This means they will have different instincts, expressing the will to power. They are 'commanders and lawgivers'.
- The ascetic ideal provides an answer to suffering. To reject it, and bear the truth about suffering, the new philosopher will need a strong spirit.
- New philosophers are, but are also more than, 'free spirits', who help tear down old values. They are 'experimenters' who resist many temptations in their quest to create new values.
- They need masks – to investigate the truth, to cover their distress, and because they move from one perspective to another to gain greater insight.
- New philosophers are, but are also more than, 'sceptics' and 'critics'. They are the kind of sceptic who refuses easy answers, but also rejects the refusal to give answers. They are critics in 'body and soul', testing the limits of knowledge.
- To transcend the ascetic ideal and affirm the value of life in the strongest way is to be able to will the eternal return of everything, as it has been and will be, without changing anything. We cannot change anything, because everything is entangled. And willing eternal return involves the will to take responsibility for everything that has happened.
- To be able to will eternal return requires one to resist pity, to say 'yes' to suffering because it is part of life and necessary for greatness.
- The new philosophers are the affirmation and redemption of life, showing in their 'yes' that life is worthwhile. They are the 'goal' of humanity.
- We can object that eternal return cannot have the argumentative force Nietzsche gives it. Must we react with horror? What difference does it make to our lives?
- We can also object that it is incoherent: we cannot adopt the perspective from which we could see all events; even if we could, willing nothing

1. Discuss the link between the concepts of the new philosopher and eternal return.
2. Critically discuss the role of eternal return in Nietzsche's attack on the ascetic ideal.

different contradicts the condition of life, which is to want things to be different; and we cannot will or take responsibility for events that are long past, so it involves a false pretence.

- Willing eternal return is also in tension with Nietzsche's revulsion at ordinary human life.

The will to power

The will to power is perhaps the key concept in Nietzsche's philosophy. It is strongly connected to his concept of 'life'. So in § 13, Nietzsche says 'A living being wants above all else to *release* its strength; life itself is the will to power'. And we noted earlier (p. 200) his claim that 'all animals . . . strive instinctively for an optimum combination of favourable conditions which allow them to expend all their energy and achieve their maximum feeling of power'. Each form of life has a particular constitution, with its instincts having different strengths, such that certain conditions will favour its form of life. This brings different types of life into conflict with each other, as each wants different conditions to prevail: 'life itself *in its essence* means appropriating, injuring, overpowering those who are foreign and weaker' (§ 259), though this language suggests that such activity is immoral, when it is simply a function of being alive.

On the Genealogy of Morals, III § 7

And 'life' does not refer just to biological life; the same is true of societies, of classes within society, wherever we find different 'types' of people. The *'original fact* of all history' is that society originates in and is based upon 'exploitation'. History is, then, a history of the forms of life through which the will to power has been expressed, the various moralities, values, social institutions and structures and cultures. The will to power, claims Nietzsche, even underpins philosophical theories (see MOTIVATIONAL ANALYSIS, p. 200).

So what exactly is the will to power? There are three possible interpretations:

1. Metaphysical: that everything that exists is the will to power.
2. Organic: that the will to power is specifically related to all life.
3. Psychological: that it is related to living creatures with a will.

The metaphysical interpretation

Two passages in *Beyond Good and Evil* seem to support the metaphysical interpretation, § 22 and § 36. In § 22, Nietzsche argues that the scientific idea of 'laws of nature' is an interpretation driven by the value of equality. Someone could just as easily 'read out of [nature] the ruthlessly tyrannical and unrelenting assertion of power claims'. But Nietzsche does not say that such a reading would be more *correct* or that we *should* read nature in this way.

In § 36, he raises this question

> Assuming that nothing real is 'given' to us apart from our world of desires and passions . . . may we not . . . ask whether this 'given' also provides a *sufficient* explanation for the so-called mechanistic (or 'material') world . . . as a world with the same level of reality that our emotion has – that is, as a more rudimentary form of the world of emotions . . . – as a *preliminary form* of life?

See PERSPECTIVISM, p. 207.

Nietzsche has argued repeatedly that how we understand what appears depends on our perspective, which embodies our values, which originate in our instincts. We cannot go beyond the reality we experience, grounded in our instincts, to some 'deeper' reality. So can we understand the physical world in analogous terms? The hypothesis to be tested is whether 'all mechanical events, in so far as an energy is active in them, are really the energy of the will'. If so, and if the will is the will to power, then we could say that all energy is the will to power.

But is Nietzsche asserting that this is how we *should* understand the world? Some philosophers have interpreted Nietzsche this way, but there are three good reasons to resist. First, Nietzsche says that the question comes down to 'whether we believe in the causality of the will', then arguing that it is the only form of causality. But he explicitly *rejects* both causality (as real) and the causality of the will. In § 21, he says that '"cause" and "effect" should be used only as pure *concepts*, as conventional fictions for the purpose of description or communication, and *not* for explanation'. If we think the world 'itself' contains causation, which the metaphysical interpretation claims, we project our concepts mistakenly onto it. In §§ 16 and 19, he argues that willing is a highly complex phenomenon, that it depends on what happens outside our consciousness and outside our control. 'Willing' is not something we can identify as the truth about reality.

Second, Nietzsche repeatedly rejects the projection of philosophical theories onto nature (§§ 9, 16, 21, 22). In an earlier work, he explicitly claims that will

Some support is given to this reading by his remark in § 12 – that Boscovich has demonstrated that we should give up the idea of 'atoms' of substance in physics. Boscovich, an eighteenth-century physicist, argued that matter is comprised of force fields. Is Nietzsche suggesting that each force field is essentially a drive to expand its field and so increase its power relative to other force fields?

Human, All Too Human,
II § 5

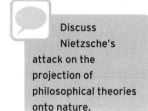

Discuss Nietzsche's attack on the projection of philosophical theories onto nature.

is only to be found in creatures with an intellect and that the idea of will 'has been turned into a metaphor when it is asserted that all things in nature possess will'. It would be very curious for him, therefore, to take his idea of will to power and project it onto nature.

Third, as discussed below, he claims that some forms of life can 'lack' the will to power.

The organic and psychological interpretations

The organic interpretation has a stronger basis in the text – Nietzsche explicitly asserts that life is the will to power (§§ 13, 259). Will to power would then be the force that distinguishes what is living from what is inanimate. But if by 'life' Nietzsche means life in the biological sense, he is still projecting a psychological theory onto nature. And we have just seen that he asserts that only creatures with an intellect possess will – which excludes all forms of life that are not animals. Furthermore, Nietzsche talks of *societies* being 'alive' and exhibiting the will to power (§ 259), which again indicates that 'life' is not meant biologically. So what does he mean by 'life' in this context?

Antichrist, § 6

One passage in particular helps: 'Life itself is . . . the instinct for growth . . . for power: where the will to power is lacking there is decline. It is my contention that all the supreme values of mankind *lack* this will'. The will to power cannot be life in the biological sense if something alive, such as the human race, can lack the will to power. In the sense of 'life' used here, somewhat paradoxically, some forms of life (and some values, such as the ascetic ideal) fail to express or value *life*. This is the sense in which we talk of someone as 'full of life' or as 'rather lifeless'. The psychological interpretation of 'will to power' is therefore best, *bearing in mind* that for Nietzsche psychology is very firmly rooted in physiology, in biology. It also fits with Nietzsche's *use* of the idea of will to power in providing accounts for a wide variety of human behaviour and thought.

The will to power is the basic character of our drives or instincts. The essence of a drive is to assert itself. To do so successfully, to achieve expression, *is* for it to have power. Power is not a *separate* aim of the drives. In asserting itself, each drive comes into competition with others, and with the drives of other individuals. And so drives are always in relations of power to each other.

The will to power is not, therefore, a will to *political* power, although this may be one form it can take. Instead, as we'll see in NOBILITY (p. 249), Nietzsche

See SOCIAL IMPLICATIONS OF NIETZSCHE'S CONCEPT OF NOBLE VALUES, p. 252, for discussion of Nietzsche's views on politics.

understands its greatest expression to be a genuine creativity – of art, of insight, and of course, of new values.

Going further: what does the will to power explain?

Is the will to power meant to explain *all* human behaviour? If so, how can we understand the passage quoted above from *Antichrist* § 6? Does 'lacking' mean 'absent' - so not all actions and values exhibit the will to power? Or does it just mean 'weak'? Nietzsche says that the supreme values of mankind, that is, the ascetic ideal, lack this will; but as we have seen in Motivational analysis (p. 202) and will see in Nietzsche's account of religion (p. 253), he argues at length that the ascetic ideal is an expression of the will to power. A better interpretation is to say that the ascetic ideal does not express the will to power *forcefully*, that in such people as adopt it, the will to power is weak. The will to power manifests itself throughout all human life for Nietzsche, but in differing strengths.

Explain the will to power.

Objection

We can challenge Nietzsche's claim that so much, if not all, of human life – actions, thoughts, values – can be understood in terms of the will to power. First, would we not do better to say that, for example, decadence, despair and passivity are not will to power *at all* (rather than weak forms of it)? But what force combats the will to power, and can even overcome it? Nietzsche leaves us with a very incomplete understanding here. Second, can we accept that all love and thought are expressions of will to power? Even if they are, are they to be understood as *nothing more*?

But does Nietzsche want to claim they are 'nothing more' than the will to power? Or only that the will to power is one very powerful and much overlooked factor in human behaviour? I suggest that Nietzsche approves of those understandings and expressions – of love, of thought – that fit with and express the will to power, without necessarily concluding that they are nothing but the will to power.

We can also wonder whether there is a *destructive* drive in human beings that cannot be understood as the will to power so much as the 'will to nothingness', what Freud called 'the death instinct' in *Beyond the Pleasure Principle*.

Will to power, values and new philosophers

Nietzsche understands the new philosophers as the greatest and purest expression of the will to power.

1. To say 'yes' to life is to say 'yes' to the will to power. Affirming eternal return is an expression of just how strongly they want to live. To understand why Nietzsche makes the will to power the basis of the new values they will create, one has to remember the sense of joy that comes from exercising power. This is not necessarily power over other people, but any successful attempt to overcome obstacles and suffering to achieve something genuinely creative.
2. The new philosophers recognise the will to power for what it is and its place in human life; they are also the will to power recognising and affirming itself. Their whole lives, thought, values are a channel for the will to power; they are its embodiment.
3. They are commanders with a strong will, by contrast with the mentality of obedience that characterises all ordinary people.
4. They will conduct experiments in breeding that will make the will to power in the human race stronger.

We can object that Nietzsche moves from a factual claim – that the instinctual life of human beings is the will to power – to evaluative claims about the new philosophers. But what is natural is not *necessarily* what is good, or again, we cannot infer from how things are to how things should be. Just because life is the will to power does not make the will to power a standard of what should be valued.

Nietzsche's argument occurs in the context of his rejection of a transcendent source of goodness. We create values. So without life, valuing is not possible. Therefore, any values that deny or impoverish our living undermine their own foundations. We must, therefore, take the affirmation of life to be the basis of all values; and that means the will to power is the evaluative standard we should endorse.

But this argument uses 'life' with two meanings. The sense in which Nietzsche approves of 'life' is life as the strong expression of the will to power. But the sense of 'life' that is necessary for valuing is simply a matter of being alive. People with a 'weak' will to power still have values. In fact, the forms of life Nietzsche calls weak are doing very well at staying alive (§ 199). The 'higher'

This is known as the naturalistic **fallacy**, discussed in MORAL TRUTH AS BASED ON NATURAL FACTS, p. 221.

form of life he praises is *not* what makes valuing possible. So we can coherently ask why we should value it over what he calls the 'lower' forms.

Until we have discussed the values and virtues of the higher and lower forms, we cannot settle the issue. So we must defer the objection until we have discussed the NATURE OF MORALITY (p. 231).

> **Discuss Nietzsche's defence of the will to power as the basis for new values.**

Going further: the will to power, physiology and psychology

Nietzsche emphasises that we cannot be 'great' simply through aspiration or education: 'There is no way to efface from a person's soul what his ancestors best and most regularly like to do . . . It is simply impossible that a person would *not* have his parents' and forefathers' qualities and preferences in his body' (§ 264). However, this quotation reveals Nietzsche's poor understanding of evolution (evolution was itself poorly understood at the time Nietzsche wrote). He subscribes to a form of Lamarckism, the theory that the characteristics an organism acquires in its lifetime, for example, certain preferences, can be passed on to its offspring. We now know this to be false. You inherit traits from your parents via genes, and the genetic code is not altered by their behaviour. So you do not carry your ancestors' preferences in your 'body'.

But Nietzsche doesn't distinguish biological inheritance (via the genes) from social inheritance (e.g. he sometimes refers to 'races', sometimes to 'classes', sometimes just to 'types') – and there *is* a strong tendency for people to have the same values and preferences as their parents (see also § 194). He is concerned with the idea of inheritance in general, not biological inheritance specifically. His mistake, perhaps, is to connect the psychological aspect of inheritance too closely to the physiological.

However, this forms an objection. If there is a gap between genetics (physiology) and psychology, then the 'will to power' is not as connected to 'bloodlines' as Nietzsche claims. Social circumstances, rather than biological history, will be far more important for strengthening someone's will. We therefore need to reconsider his claim that we are each a 'psycho-physiological type'. If psychological types, for example, having a strong or weak will, having the instinct for commanding or obeying, are not based in physiology, then we need to reinterpret many of his analyses and criticisms of people with weak will. For example, sceptics are not sceptics because they suffer from a physiological complaint of 'bad nerves' (§ 208).

Furthermore, if a strong will to power is not based in a healthy physiology, a weak will in a sickly physiology, then Nietzsche's claims about life itself being the will to power must be reconsidered. It seems his views on the will to power are not reflections of what is 'necessary' for (physiological) life itself, but *value* judgements that we can question.

This is too quick. Suppose the 'vitality' Nietzsche values is a psychological vitality, not a physiological one. As human beings, we are not concerned with, nor do we value, mere physiological life. A human life is a *psychological* life – to lose our minds is to lose everything, we may think. If Nietzsche can defend the idea of psychological types, perhaps he can meet these objections. For example, in § 200, he speaks of the degeneration that occurs when the 'races' are mixed. But his concern is that such a person embodies contradictory values, and so feels in conflict with himself. As a result, his idea of happiness will be tranquillity. A stronger person, he continues, will exercise his will to power to make something productive of the tension within him. So while Nietzsche bases his remarks in 'race', his concern is psychological throughout. We can read the story of mixed 'races' in terms of mixed value systems instead.

> Discuss and evaluate Nietzsche's concept of the will to power.

Key points • • •

- History is the history of various expressions of the will to power.
- The metaphysical interpretation of the will to power is that everything, including physical forces, expresses the will to power. However, while Nietzsche raises this hypothesis, he never endorses it; and he explicitly rejects its key premises.
- In *Human, All too Human*, Nietzsche claims that only something with an intellect can have a will. The will to power is best interpreted psychologically, as restricted to those forms of life with a will.
- The essence of a drive is to assert itself; its power is indicated by its success. Nietzsche is not claiming that any drive explicitly aims at 'power' itself.

- It is unclear both whether Nietzsche thinks all, or just a great deal, of human behaviour can be explained as the will to power; and whether he thinks all motivation and intellectual activity are nothing more than expressions of the will to power.

- The new philosophers are the strongest and purest expression of the will to power, in their affirmation of life, their explicit recognition of it as the basis of values, their creation of values, and their development of the human race.

- We can object that Nietzsche has not argued *why* we should accept the will to power as the basis of values. One answer is that it is life, and so what makes any values possible. But this seems false, as there are forms of life that express the will to power only weakly.

- Nietzsche misunderstands biological inheritance, thinking that we inherit, for example, preferences, physiologically. However, at a psychological and social level, his claims may be true, as many people's preferences resemble those of people around them.

- This means that we must read Nietzsche's connection between the will to power and 'life' as referring to psychological life.

II. NATURE OF MORALITY

Morality and human nature

Nietzsche gives an account of morality in non-moral psychological terms. As we have seen, he interprets moral values – and the history of their development – in terms of THE WILL TO POWER (p. 224). We have therefore already begun the discussion of the connection between morality and human nature. In this section, we introduce Nietzsche's ideas on morality, returning to the connection with human nature at the end.

The 'attack' on 'morality'

THE ATTACK
It is easy to misinterpret Nietzsche as rejecting everything about conventional morality. But he says:

It goes without saying that I do not deny – unless I am a fool – that many actions called immoral ought to be avoided and resisted, or that many called moral ought to be done and encouraged – but I think that the one should be encouraged and the other avoided *for other reasons than hitherto*. We have to *learn to think differently* – in order at last, perhaps very late on, to attain even more: *to feel differently*.

Daybreak, § 103

So the extent to which his attack will lead to different ways of acting is unclear; his concern is with the *psychology* of morality.

Nietzsche has also been misinterpreted as attacking all values, which would be a form of nihilism. But he calls this 'the sign of a despairing, weary soul' (§ 10), refers to his new ideal as a morality (§ 202), and speaks of the duties of free spirits and the new philosophers (§§ 212, 226).

What Nietzsche finds objectionable about conventional morality is that our existing values weaken the will to power in human beings. They are therefore a threat to human greatness. The moral ideal is a person who is not great, but a 'herd animal', who seeks security and comfort and wishes to avoid danger and suffering. Nietzsche's aim is to free those who can be great from the mistake of trying to live according to this morality.

And it is puzzling: isn't what is valuable what is great, exceptional, an expression of strength and success? So how did traits such as meekness, humility, self-denial, modesty, pity and compassion for the weak become *values*? This is the question that Nietzsche wants to answer with his 'natural history'.

? **Why does Nietzsche attack conventional morality?**

ON 'MORALITY'

There are many particular existing moral systems – Kantian, utilitarian, Christian, and the moral systems of other religions; but Nietzsche spends little or no time defining their differences. He attacks any morality that supports values that harm the 'higher' type of person and benefits the 'herd'. He also attacks any morality that presupposes free will (§ 21), or the idea that we can know the truth about ourselves through introspection (§§ 16–19), or the similarity of people (§ 198). But he also links these together, explaining the theoretical beliefs in terms of the moral values, and values in terms of favouring the conditions that enable one's type to express its power.

See MOTIVATIONAL ANALYSIS, p. 200.

So what does Nietzsche mean by 'morality', the morality he means to attack? There are four ways we could try to categorise it:

1. By its values, for example, equality, devaluation of the body, pity, self-lessness.

2. By its origins, in particular motives, especially '*ressentiment*'.
3. By its claim that it should apply to all.
4. By its empirical and metaphysical assumptions, for example, about freedom, the self, guilt.

We discuss these last two points below, and will return to the first two in MASTER SLAVE MORALITY (p. 239).

Particularity of moral systems

If there were universal moral values, they would be the same for everybody, and all that a history of morality could do is tell us how we came to discover them and why people didn't discover them sooner. A 'history' of morality would then be like a history of science. Scientific truths themselves don't have a history, for example, the Earth has always been round (since it existed at all) – so there is no history to this fact. But we can tell the history of how people came to believe that the Earth is round, when previously they didn't believe this. But a history of morality is not like this – we can tell the story of how values themselves changed.

    Not everyone accepts this. Many philosophers argue that there are universal moral principles, for example, that morality is founded upon pure reason, or that it rests upon happiness, and that we can know this. Nietzsche rejects this, as it assumes that there is no natural history of morality. In fact, this claim to universality is a specific feature of the morality we have inherited – it assumes that what is good and right for one person is good and right for everyone (§ 198). It does not recognise that there are different *types* of people, that what is good for one type is not good for another. But it matters who the person is (§ 221), for example, whether they are a leader or a follower. Nietzsche is particularly concerned with this distinction, which we discuss below (p. 239).

What is the difference between a history of science and a history of morality?

See KANT'S ATTEMPT TO PROVIDE A RATIONAL GROUNDING FOR A DEONTOLOGICAL ETHICS, p. 258, and ACT UTILITARIANISM, p. 248.

Free will and introspection

Nietzsche argues that each person has a fixed psycho-physical constitution, and that their values, their beliefs, and so their lives are an expression of this. A person's constitution circumscribes what they can do and become, relative to their circumstances. The will, then, has its origin in unconscious physiological forces. A 'thought comes when "it" wants to not when "I" want it to' (§ 17), and 'in every act of will there is a commanding thought' (§ 19) – so an act of will has its origins in something else. And in general, whatever we are conscious of in ourselves is an effect of something we are not conscious of, for example, the facts about our psycho-physiological constitution. Introspection, then, cannot lead to self-knowledge (§§ 16, 34).

And yet conventional morality requires that we make moral judgements on the basis of people's *motives*; it presupposes that we can know, in ourselves or others, which motives caused an action. Even when we have clearly formed an intention, it is not (just) this that brings about the actual action we perform, but any number of other factors – habit, laziness, some passing emotion, fear or love, and so on.

The idea that the will is 'free' is the idea that there are no causes of an act of will (other than the will itself) – the person can will or not will. There is no course of events that leads to just this act of will. The will is its own cause, a '*causa sui*'. But this 'is the best internal contradiction ever devised' (§ 21). Our experience of willing does not *have* to lead to this idea; so we should ask what *purpose* it serves. One purpose is to defend our belief in ourselves and our right to praise (§ 21).

Another purpose, more apparent in Nietzsche's *On the Genealogy of Morals*, Essay I, is that we can and should *hold people to blame* for what is in their power. At the point of action, they could have chosen differently, we think, so we can blame them for wrongdoing. The idea of free will also relates to the idea that values – purely and on their own – could be the basis for an act of will. The will is not conditioned by anything of this world. The 'moral law' can determine the will itself. This locates moral values outside the normal world of causes, in a transcendent world.

But Nietzsche's attack on free will does not imply that the will is 'unfree' in the way that is meant by determinists. Whenever someone talks of being caused to act, this serves the purpose of denying any responsibility and reveals self-contempt and a weak will. Free spirits experience free will and necessity *as equivalent* – real creative freedom, for example, in art, comes from following 'thousand-fold laws', a sense of necessity – it must be just like this, not like that (§§ 188, 213). We make a mistake when we oppose freedom and necessity in the will.

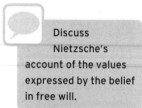

Discuss Nietzsche's account of the values expressed by the belief in free will.

See **Determinism defined**, p. 351, and **Good art is moving or captures a mood or feeling**, p. 286.

Going further: morality and evolution

Nietzsche tells several stories about how pity, self-denial and so on became values, how 'herd morality' came to dominate. One is from the perspective of the 'masters'; one is from the perspective of the 'slaves'. But a third explanation draws on the role of evolution in forming human nature. The three stories should be seen as complementary, together building up the whole picture.

In § 199, Nietzsche writes that 'for as long as there have been humans, there have also been . . . a great many followers in proportion to the small number of commanders . . . obedience has until now been bred and practised best and longest among humans'. He continues later, 'the herd instinct of obedience is inherited best, and at the cost of the skill in commanding'. In evolution, what does not reproduce well does not survive in future generations. What enables a person to get on well with many other people will favour most individuals and their reproductive success – but these will be 'herd' instincts and values, because by definition, the majority are the 'herd'. What is exceptional, what is great, is rare. So evolution opposes greatness and favours what is common. The kind of 'commanders' the herd favours are tame, modest, hard-working and public-spirited, commanders who actually *serve* the herd rather than commanding them.

Nietzsche develops the point in § 268: to communicate with and understand other people, we have to share experiences with them. What thoughts and feelings words immediately bring to mind reflects our values. So people of different types will have difficulty understanding each other. People who are commanders will be hard for other people, the 'herd', to understand. And so they rarely procreate. If we are to breed new philosophers, and new philosophers are to breed the human race to become greater, we will have to draw on 'enormous counterforces' since we are in conflict with the natural forces of evolution.

However, the constraint placed on the will to power by 'herd' morality has been creative; it is 'the means by which the European spirit was bred to be strong, ruthlessly curious, and beautifully nimble' (§ 188). This tension drives free spirits to overcome the ascetic ideal and prepare the conditions for new philosophers.

See NIETZSCHE'S 'HISTORY' OF MORALITY, p. 236, and MASTER SLAVE MORALITY, p. 239.

How has evolution favoured the 'herd'?

Key points • • •

- In his attack on conventional morality, Nietzsche is more interested in getting us to think and feel differently than to act differently.
- His main objection is that conventional morality weakens the will to power and threatens human greatness.
- Nietzsche attacks any morality that has particular values, origins in particular motives, claims universality, or makes particular assumptions, for example, about free will.
- Nietzsche argues that morality has changed over time. It is not universal, and what is good for one person is not so for another.
- Every act of will, he argues, originates outside consciousness. This undermines the idea that we can judge people's actions by their motives and the idea of 'free will', which serves the purpose of holding people to blame.
- However, Nietzsche does not argue that the will is not free. Free will and necessity are equivalent.
- Evolution has favoured the herd, for those who can get on well with others will reproduce best. To understand others, we must share their values. So true leaders will not reproduce well.

Nietzsche's 'history' of morality

One of Nietzsche's primary concerns in providing a history of morality is to understand how certain values (pity, selflessness, etc.), which he associates with 'herd' morality, became values. 'Morality', both its scope and its psychology (e.g. conscience, guilt), is a product of historical development. We can't understand a moral value or psychological state unless we use history, because that value or state frequently often inherits several different meanings from different times in the past. Through understanding its history, we can distinguish the different meanings and different feelings, and see how and why they changed over time. In turn, this helps us to understand that *there are alternatives* to these values and states.

In §§ 257, 258 and 262, Nietzsche gives us one such history. Every 'higher' or noble culture began with barbarians, 'predatory' humans who conquered either the 'more well-behaved, peaceable' ones or 'crumbling cultures'. They establish an 'aristocratic' class, based in ideas of a natural hierarchy between people, who dominated by their stronger will to power. This class is the origin of ideas of 'NOBILITY' (p. 249).

The aristocratic class – Nietzsche has in mind the aristocratic societies of ancient Rome and Greece – faced challenging conditions, wars with other societies, the threat of revolt by those oppressed. These conditions made for strong, unified people with a harsh and intolerant set of values. Such a class has no qualms about using 'lower' human beings for its own ends; this is itself understood as 'justice' (§ 265) and 'natural'. The whole of society is understood to exist for their sake, for the sake of what is great and noble.

Over time, conditions change, and life for the aristocrats becomes easy. So the attachment to discipline, both self-discipline and severe punishment, fades away as it is no longer necessary. Individuals emerge as individuals, varied from one another, rather than expressions of class values. They assert their individual wills and values, and both good and bad develop new forms. The old unity of values, of 'instincts', is broken, leading to a sense of decay and misunderstanding. This new danger is located not in enemies or slaves, but among neighbours and even in oneself. The great, strong and harsh will has dissipated and become corrupt. The new danger is met with a new morality, one based on fear of the individual. What remains, and what makes sense, is the 'mediocre', a morality that encourages people to be the same.

This is one way, Nietzsche says, that values associated with greatness were replaced by values that favoured the majority, the 'herd'. We can identify the story of 'decline' with several points in history: first, changes in ancient Greek societies, between 800BC (the time of Homer's tales of war) and 250BC, after which the Greek empire was slowly eclipsed by the rise of the Roman empire; second, changes in the Roman empire between 400BC and AD300 (when the emperor Constantine converted to Christianity); and once more, in changes in European societies between the Middle Ages and the modern period (e.g. Nietzsche refers to the French Revolution).

> Discuss whether Nietzsche's account of 'decline' is a valid interpretation of historical change in one of these three periods.

What is noble today is not identical to its origins in these aristocratic societies. The very earliest nobles, descendents of the barbarians, are fairly boring in their approach to life and their indifference to suffering. By contrast, Nietzsche repeatedly praises the creativity that the constraints of 'herd' morality has produced (§§ 46, 59, 188). It is not until the will to power turns back against the self, seeks to exercise power over its own instincts, as in the ascetic ideal, that things get interesting. Second, the aristocrats' greatness was that of a united class, and the independence of free spirits and new philosophers was not recognisable then. However, there are continuities between noble aristocracies of the past and 'nobility' today.

> See NIETZSCHE'S ACCOUNT OF RELIGION, p. 253.

> Explain how a strong-willed aristocracy could have given way to a morality of mediocrity.

Key points • • •

- Nietzsche uses history to explain how 'herd' values became values.
- According to one version, barbarians establish an aristocracy with a harsh morality. Life becomes easier, discipline unnecessary and individuality tolerated. The old morality crumbles, and a sense of corruption arises. Fear of one's neighbour, even oneself, promotes a morality of mediocrity.
- What nobility is does not remain the same, and Nietzsche argues that the growth of herd morality has produced a creativity not previously possible.

The three stages of morality

In § 32, Nietzsche talks about the different stages that morality has gone through. Depending on how we divide up his account, we can get three or five stages.

1. 'Pre-moral': in the first stage, of human pre-history, the value of an action depended entirely on its consequences. Motives were considered unimportant.
2. 'Moral':

    a) In the next stage (or part-stage), morality begins as the origins of an action became important. In order to be a morally good person, one needed to 'look 'inwards'.

    b) But then a terrible mistake, still with us today: the 'origin' and value of an action was equated with the person's *intention*, that is, what the person consciously decided.

> For Nietzsche's criticisms of conscious intention, see FREE WILL AND INTROSPECTION, p. 233.

3. 'Extra-moral':

    a) The next stage, in the near future, will identify the value of an action not by what the person intended, which is superficial and misleading, but by what was not intentional (e.g. an 'unintended' consequence or the manner in which the action is done), which we can relate to what brought about the action that was not part of the intention.

    b) Finally, we will move beyond good and evil and new philosophers create new values.

Many remarks suggest that the master morality of the aristocrats accepted 2a, while the shift to 2b corresponds with the rise in slave morality, with the breakdown of the unity of the instincts and the resulting concern with the danger 'in oneself'. With these changes, identifying the *particular* thought or motive becomes important, and the illusion that we can identify particular motives in this way as the causes of actions is encouraged.

Explain and discuss Nietzsche's three stages of morality in relation to his history of philosophy in §§ 257, 258 and 262.

Key point • • •

• Nietzsche divides the history of morality into 'pre-moral', 'moral' and 'extra-moral' stages. The first identifies the value of an action with its consequences, the second with its origin, then specifically its intention. The third returns to the origin of action outside intention, and finally to the creation of new values.

Master slave morality

§ 260 describes the fundamental division between the moralities of the 'herd' and of 'higher' people. While the contrast is stark, Nietzsche says, at the outset,

> I would add at once that in all higher and complex cultures, there are also apparent attempts to mediate between the two moralities, and even more often a confusion of the two and a mutual misunderstanding . . . even in the same person.

So his descriptions are 'idealised', while identifying the diverse origins of our actual morality.

See p. 199 on genealogy.

Master morality

In a master or noble morality, 'good' picks out exalted and proud states of mind, and it therefore refers to *people*, not actions, in the first instance. 'Bad' means 'lowly', 'despicable', and refers to people who are petty, cowardly or concerned with what is useful, rather than what is grand or great. (Notice that none of this depends on the idea of free will.) Good–bad identifies a hierarchy of people, the noble masters or aristocracy and the common people. The noble person only recognises moral duties towards their equals; how they treat people below them is not a matter of morality at all. The good, noble person has a sense of 'fullness' – of power, wealth, ability and so on. From the 'overflowing' of these qualities, not from pity, they will help other people, including people below them.

Noble people experience themselves as the origin of value, deciding what is good or not. 'Good' originates in self-affirmation, a celebration of one's own greatness and power. They don't need others to say they are good. They revere themselves, and have a devotion to whatever is great. But this is not self-indulgence: any signs of weakness are despised, and harshness and severity are respected.

A noble morality is a morality of gratitude and vengeance. Friendship involves mutual respect and a rejection of over-familiarity, while enemies are necessary, in order to vent feelings of envy, aggression and arrogance.

All these qualities mean that the good person rightly evokes fear in those who are not their equal and a respectful distance in those who are.

See Nobility, p. 249, for further discussion.

Outline, in your own words, the main features of a 'master' morality.

Slave morality

Slave morality *begins with the rejection of master morality*. It does not and cannot stand on its own. The traits of the noble person are *evil* (not 'bad'), and what is good is their absence. Its focus is the relief of suffering – whatever is useful or opposes oppression is morally good. So pity, altruism and a lack of interest in oneself are good. In opposing the noble morality, it also encourages humility and patience. It questions the apparent happiness of the noble person, rejects hierarchy and argues that morality is the same for all.

But it is pessimistic about the human condition, doubting the goodness of this life, and so it sees people as weak and pitiful. So it must look to the future and believe in 'progress', in things getting better. It lacks respect for the past, for traditions and ancestors. Finally, when slave morality dominates, there is a tendency for 'good' people and 'good' actions to be thought of as 'stupid' or simple-minded.

See Herd morality and the critique of 'modern ideas', p. 244, for further discussion.

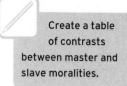

Create a table of contrasts between master and slave moralities.

The 'slave revolt'

If societies in Europe began with a noble morality, at some point, slave morality became dominant. How and when did this revolution in values occur? Nietzsche's third historical account, this one from the perspective of the slaves, identifies the Jewish prophets as the origin (§ 195). It was they, he says, who 'fused "rich", "godless", "evil", "violent", "sensuous" into one entity, and were the first to mint the word "world" as a curse word'. Worldly success (what was 'good') indicates moral failure (is now 'evil'). But the Jewish prophets were only the beginning – it is Christianity which carried forward the revolt.

What drove this 'revaluation of values'? In § 46, Nietzsche says the slave's 'manifold *hidden* suffering rages against that noble sensibility which seems to *deny* suffering'. The Roman rulers seemed, and valued being, free-spirited (re-interpret: wicked), self-confident (decadent), care-free (lazy), tolerant (unruly). They viewed slaves with contempt, pity and disdain, causing hatred that could not be expressed directly. And so it turned into what Nietzsche calls elsewhere *ressentiment*, a kind of resentment. In someone with a slave mentality, the feeling grows as no action is taken. Instead of a political revolt, revenge took the form of a moral revolt. The pent-up feelings of resentment were expressed through *blame*, an idea that has little place in a noble morality.

A slave morality therefore centres on the question of blame, and not just for actions, but also for being who and how one is. This requires the idea that one could act or be different (see Free will and introspection, p. 233), and makes guilt (for not being or doing 'better') the heart of morality. Guilt causes suffering, but the slave has known only suffering, tyranny, being commanded – so morality becomes unconditional commands, for example, of a God (§§ 194–5).

Ressentiment is a *reactive* rather than *creative* attitude towards the world, focusing on others, rather than oneself. It tends to produce self-deception – the slave morality must cover its origins carefully, not least because it disapproves of the very motives, of envy, hatred and *ressentiment*, that drive it. The sacrifice that morality requires is seen not as tyranny or revenge, but as an act of love. In contrast to the simplicity of the original nobles (p. 237), it was through *ressentiment*, Nietzsche says, that 'the human soul became deep', and certain kinds of cultural expression became possible, for example, in response to the deep guilt people felt about themselves.

While it is important that - *at its origins* - real class differences between these groups and the Greek and Roman aristocracy existed, as usual, Nietzsche is more interested in the psychological story. There is nothing specifically Jewish about a slave morality, and Nietzsche is uninterested in the differences between Jew, Christian and slave in this account.

This account is not complete until Nietzsche's account of religion, p. 253.

Explain the priests' and slaves' revaluation of values.

Outline the main features of 'slave' morality in relation to the revaluation of values.

Discussion

Can we take Nietzsche's histories of morality seriously? He provides us with no references, no scholarly support or detailed analysis for his claims. Some philosophers argue that his claims are just random facts, impressions and anecdotes. But recently, philosophers have shown that Nietzsche read and relied on the best historical scholarship of his time. Still, can we believe that what explains the triumph of Christianity in the Roman Empire is *ressentiment*? Of course not – not on its own. There are other economic, social and political factors. But Nietzsche does not need to deny this, even though he shows no interest in these other factors.

Nietzsche invites us to reflect on what he says. Henry Staten expresses the challenge well:

> What are we to say about this overwhelming spectacle of cruelty, stupidity, and suffering? What stance is there for us to adopt with respect to history, what judgment can we pass on it? Is it all a big mistake? Christianity attempted to recuperate the suffering of history by projecting a divine plan that assigns it a reason in the here and now and a recompense later, but liberalism is too humane to endorse this explanation. There is no explanation, only the brute fact. But the brute fact we are left with is even harder to stomach than the old explanation. So Left liberalism packages it in a new narrative, a moral narrative according to which all those lives ground up in the machinery of history are assigned an intelligible role as victims of oppression and injustice . . . Against the awesome 'Thus it was' of history we set the overawing majesty of 'Thus it *ought* to have been'.

Nietzsche's Voice,
pp. 78–9

We try to make sense of suffering throughout history by appeal to morality. Morality turns suffering into injustice, and then we have someone to blame. We find this reassuring; but how truthful is this response and how much confidence can we place in the values we appeal to? Nietzsche argues that the condemnation of suffering is in tension with greatness, as discussed in ETERNAL RETURN (p. 218).

A different objection: Nietzsche commits a 'genetic fallacy' in attacking conventional morality by looking at its origins. Just because morality originated in the ressentiment of slaves does not mean that we should reject morality. The origins of an idea don't determine whether that idea is true, false, good or bad. Compare: Coleridge composed the poem 'Kubla Khan' while he was under the influence of opium; this doesn't tell us anything about whether the poem is good or bad.

Nietzsche can reply that this misunderstands his use of genealogy. First, our intuitions about values are formed by history, so we can only understand them by historical investigation. Any other approach will appeal to moral intuitions without understanding their (historical) nature. (Traditional ways of doing moral philosophy cannot succeed.)

Second, Nietzsche does not mean to identify just the past origins of morality. Both master and slave moralities continue, evolved and mixed up, in us *today*. The motives present at the origin of slave morality *continue* to motivate morality today. We discuss this in the next section.

See ORIGINS AND OPPOSITES, p. 199.

Critically discuss Nietzsche's account of the slave revolt against master morality.

Key points • • •

- Nietzsche identifies two basic types of morality, master and slave, which are mixed in all complex cultures.
- The master morality contrasts good (= great) and bad (= lowly), and applies them to a 'natural' hierarchy of nobility versus commoners. Moral relations hold only between noble people.
- The good person overflows with a sense of power and ability, the origin of a sense of 'good', and may help others from this sense. They are devoted to what is great and are harsh with weakness, thereby evoking fear or respectful distance.
- The slave morality equates what is 'good' according to the master morality with evil. What is good alleviates suffering, for example, altruism and pity. In this, it expresses pessimism about life, which leads to a belief in progress.
- The revaluation of values, from master to slave, began with the Jewish prophets, but continued with Christianity. It was driven by *ressentiment*, rage at the masters' insensitivity to suffering, which was expressed by blame.
- Slave morality centres on guilt, and produces self-deception, for example, about its own origins. But through its complexity, the soul and culture became more profound.
- In telling this story, Nietzsche drew on historical scholarship, but shows no interest in other factors that led to the 'slave revolt'.
- Genealogy does not say, simply, that we can judge morality by its origins. It aims to uncover the continuing meaning of morality today.

Herd morality and the critique of 'modern ideas'

Nietzsche objects to herd morality because it values what does not have value. It is in the interests of lower, not higher men. If each person's values help establish favourable conditions for themselves, then the triumph of herd morality will lead to the continuation of herd-like people. It is therefore not something for the human race as a whole to live by.

On the Genealogy of Morals, I § 14

Herd morality is a development of the original slave morality which inherits most of its content, including a reinterpretation of various traits: impotence becomes goodness of heart, craven fear becomes humility, submission becomes 'obedience', cowardice and being forced to wait become patience, the inability to take revenge becomes forgiveness, the desire for revenge becomes a desire for justice, a hatred of one's enemy becomes a hatred of injustice. Happiness is opposed to suffering; pity versus indifference to suffering; peacefulness versus danger; altruism versus self-love; equality versus inequality; communal utility versus endangering such utility; ridding oneself of instincts versus enjoyment of instinctual satisfaction; well-being of the soul versus well-being of the body.

This morality values what has no intrinsic value, and very often endangers what is of much greater value, namely, human greatness. Greatness requires suffering, danger, self-love, inequality, it goes against what is in the interests of people in general and is an expression of instinctual energy. 'Well-being' in herd morality limits human beings, promoting people who are modest, submissive and conforming. And so it *opposes* the development of higher people, it slanders their will to power and labels them evil. Belief in its values limits people who could become higher people, leading them to self-doubt and self-loathing (§ 269).

Nietzsche calls this morality both clever (or shrewd) and stupid (§ 198). It contains and controls powerful instinctual emotions and drives. This is shrewd because these are dangerous to a herd person, who does not have a strong enough will to control their own emotions or stand up to others. But it is stupid, because it is based on misunderstanding and fear and opposes the development of higher people. The deep fear of other people also undermines herd morality's own values. Fear means there can be no genuine neighbourly love (§ 201). We do not and cannot *practise* altruism, but our moral values require us to believe in it.

See p. 248.

As herd morality has developed, it seems to have lost that element that belonged to THE ASCETIC IDEAL (p. 253). It becomes a form of UTILITARIANISM, aimed at happiness in this world, rather than redemption in the next. But with the loss of the ascetic ideal, there is nothing to inspire people to try to become better, greater, by overcoming their weaknesses or finding creative, powerful responses to their *ressentiment*. Nietzsche *praises* Christianity for the greatness in art and architecture, for the depths of the soul, it produced. Without the ascetic ideal, we lose this, and morality is no longer a form of self-overcoming, and people become 'smaller', less great.

Above all, herd morality has led to the degeneration of the human race (§ 62). We are not a species of animal that has fully developed into what it can be, because we keep alive 'a surplus of deformed, sick, degenerating, frail' people, which *'ought to perish'*. Christianity has bred a mediocre, sickly, good-natured animal.

Why does Nietzsche attack 'herd morality'?

Democracy and pity

By 'modern ideas', Nietzsche means what we might call 'secular humanism'. 'Modern ideas' include the values of democracy and equality, a work ethic, a morality that opposes suffering, and beliefs in science and positivism (the view that philosophy should limit itself to what is 'given' in experience and the study of scientific methodology). Nietzsche criticises these values and argues that they originate in religion, even though most people of 'modern ideas' claim to be 'atheists'.

Democracy is founded on the value of equality – that all people are equal and so should have an equal say in how society is run. Yet the idea of equality should be more contentious than it has become. Samuel Johnson said 'So far is it from being true that men are naturally equal, that no two people can be half an hour together, but one shall acquire an evident superiority over the other'. If inequality is so easily established, what does our belief in equality rest upon?

Boswell, *Life of Johnson*, Vol. 1, p. 318

Equality and democracy are instincts of 'the herd' (§ 202), values that favour the unexceptional and mediocre. They do not recognise and respect the exceptional. In this, democrats, anarchists and socialists, even if they are atheists, uphold the values of Christianity. They all want a 'free' society of equals, that is, a society of an autonomous herd, and believe the community will save humanity. The elimination of suffering is the foundation of their morality, which they think of as objective. They cannot recognise its perspectival nature.

When Nietzsche condemns pity, he is not suggesting we should be heartless. He isn't talking about refusing to give food to someone hungry. He opposes pity as the basis of morality, because pity seeks to eliminate suffering, which is the origin of greatness. First, pity wrongly preserves the weak and prevents people from becoming stronger through suffering. Second, pity demeans both the person who is shown pity and the person who shows it. The pitied person is shown to lack power, and their self-respect will be undermined; so pity brings them more suffering. The person who shows pity suffers for the suffering of the other person – again, doubling suffering. And they show a lack of self-respect, as pity asserts a false equality, that 'you and I' suffer together. Third, human beings inevitably suffer, so pity's attempt to alleviate all suffering sets itself against life. Finally, pity sees *individuals* as valuable, but, Nietzsche has argued, the goal of humankind lies in its highest specimens (see p. 218). Nietzsche's pity does not focus on 'social welfare', but on how the human race as a whole has been reduced, prevented from greatness, by values of a morality of pity (§ 225).

Work ethic, atheism and false 'free spirits'

Another 'modern idea' is the work ethic (work is morally good and makes us better people). This destroys time for self-examination and reflection. Because a religious life requires this time (§ 58) (as does the new philosophy), the work ethic contributes to atheism. Believers in 'modern ideas' are liable to feel superior to religion, but they completely fail to understand it. They don't understand whether they should treat it as work or leisure, their minds have become so narrow in its categories of understanding. But they seek to be 'tolerant', while actually avoiding the pain of real tolerance. They fail to show the proper reverence for what is of real value, feeling as if they have the right to investigate, touch, everything; they lack shame (§ 263). Nietzsche, even as he attacks religion, has enormous regard for it, so he has no respect for people who reject religion thoughtlessly.

Thinkers who 'freed' themselves from the dogmas of religion and advocated a secular humanism thought of themselves as 'free spirits' – turning over past conceptions of right and wrong, advocating a new basis for society. But Nietzsche argues that they are merely continuing the work of religion under a new guise (§ 44), supporting the further domination of 'herd' values and undermining the conditions necessary for human greatness. By contrast, the new philosophers see that humankind is degenerating; they see 'the fate that lies hidden in the stupid innocence and blissful confidence of "modern ideas"' (§ 203).

1. How are democracy and pity expressions of 'herd' morality?
2. Discuss Nietzsche's attack on pity.

See WHAT IS TOLERANCE?, p. 236.

How do religious values outlive religious belief?

Science and positivism

Nietzsche does not criticise science, but scientism, a faith in science as the ultimate source of knowledge and solutions to the problems of life and suffering. Science does not genuinely *explain* the world (§ 14), but only describes it. This is accepted and applauded by positivism as all we can do. We are convinced by science because it agrees with the popular idea that we can only clearly know about what we can see and touch. But while Nietzsche agrees, he argues that we must treat the evidence of our senses cautiously, as all our experience is shot through with our values. Believers in science and positivism fail to recognise this; as with their morality, they think that scientific knowledge is unconditional and objective. For example, they do not recognise the connection between the scientific idea of 'laws of nature' and their commitment to the values of democracy and equality (§ 22; see p. 208).

See Perspectivism, p. 207.

And so science cannot replace philosophy for two reasons. First, it is philosophy that establishes the truth of perspectivism; the perspective of science is a foreground perspective that fails to acknowledge itself as a perspective. Second, science incorporates values but cannot create or dictate values. This is the job of the new philosophers. Science, then, is a tool in the service of new philosophers. Believers in 'modern ideas' elevate science above its proper position.

> What does Nietzsche mean by 'modern ideas'? Discuss his rejection of them.

> This is not an application of Darwinian evolution, because what counts as a 'failure' for Nietzsche is a 'success' in Darwinian terms. In evolutionary theory, success is a matter of reproduction; but it is the herd who have managed to reproduce most successfully, while higher people are rare.

Going further: discussion

We see in § 62 an explicit statement of what Nietzsche's rejection of herd morality requires, and therefore the task faced by the new philosopher in raising the human race to a higher level: many people must be allowed to die, as 'failed' human beings.

But why should we reject herd morality and accept the value Nietzsche gives to will to power? One answer we considered (p. 228) was that life is the will to power, and without life, nothing can be valued – valuing life is valuing the ground of all values. But 'weak' forms of life, the herd, are still life, and even dominate life. So we can coherently value life, and the herd, without valuing the will to power as Nietzsche does.

However, given Nietzsche's criticisms of conventional morality, do we want to value herd values? But suppose we reject these, and even adopt some noble values, this does not mean that people who are herd animals *have no value* except as a means to creating higher people. *This* conclusion requires Nietzsche's claim (given in ETERNAL RETURN, p. 218) that the goal of humanity lies in its highest specimens.

In ETERNAL RETURN (p. 218), we noted the inconsistency of willing eternal return while feeling contempt for almost everyone who has lived. To will eternal return, we must find value in the 'herd', for example, that they are alive and will continue living. Life, in this broader sense, is valuable, *even if* Nietzsche's narrower sense of life as the vitality that expresses will to power is a valuable development of life.

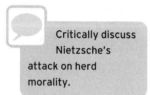

Critically discuss Nietzsche's attack on herd morality.

Key points • • •

- Herd morality is a development of slave morality, reinterpreting negative traits as positive, and opposing suffering, inequality, instinctual satisfaction and self-love.
- By attempting to eliminate suffering, it undermines greatness, which needs suffering to develop. And the fear of others undermines its own value of altruism.
- As it has developed, herd morality has lost the ascetic ideal, which encouraged people to become great and creative, so it has led to degeneration.
- 'Modern ideas' of equality and democracy are part of herd morality, continuing the values of Christianity even as people reject the existence of God.
- Nietzsche argues that pity wrongly preserves the weak, demeans people and doubles their suffering, opposes life and wrongly values individuals.
- Believers in modern ideas don't understand religion. Their work ethic encourages a superficial atheism, while their values are Christian in origin and lead to degeneration.
- Science cannot replace philosophy. Only philosophy establishes perspectivism (scientism wrongly understands science as objective) and can establish new values.
- Even if we accept many of Nietzsche's criticisms of herd morality, we need not accept that 'herd' people have no value except in relation to 'higher'

people. To will eternal return consistently, we must find value in everyone's lives.

Nobility

Just as herd morality is a development out of slave morality, so the morality of nobility has developed from master morality, and it finds its ideal form in the new philosophers. We said that the noble person has a sense of themselves as determining what is good and bad, and new philosophers will create values. The noble person feels full of greatness and power, the new philosophers express the will to power in its purest form and are full of joy in the affirmation of life. The noble person despises what is weak; the new philosopher ranks people by how much truth and suffering they can bear. Both are independent and are not moved by the suffering of common people.

See MASTER MORALITY, p. 239, and THE NEW PHILOSOPHER, p. 214.

The best sign of a high rank, Nietzsche says, is an instinct for *rank* (§ 263), not only among human beings, and a sense of what is great. *Every* elevation of human beings has been and will be achieved by hierarchical societies (§ 257). Nobility involves a 'grand attitude' (e.g. the perspective of eternal return) and a longing for 'expansive inner states', not a sense of being caught up in oneself, but a continual 'self-overcoming'. This shouldn't be understood in the usual moral or spiritual terms, for example, overcoming one's selfishness or transcending human desires. It isn't guided by fixed values, but involves the creation of new values, which requires the self-overcoming of all that is too weak to sustain such originality.

So what kind of person is the noble or higher person? In Nietzsche's discussions in §§ 259–70, some of his remarks on nobility are inspired by past aristocratic *classes*, but for the present and future, Nietzsche finds nobility in *individuals* (of a certain 'type'). In other writings, his examples included Goethe, Beethoven and himself. There are five important character traits:

1. The noble man is solitary, independent and deals with others as means to his ends (§§ 26, 212, 273).
2. He is driven by his work, having unified his personality to focus on his project, and seeks responsibilities.
3. He is essentially 'healthy', knowing what is good for him and choosing that.
4. He wills his life unconditionally, and perhaps can will eternal return as well.
5. He has reverence for himself, honouring himself as powerful, and exercising

power over himself in setting and striving for his own values. This sense of reverence extends also to the past (§§ 260, 287) – there is no assumption that what is new is better.

The higher man is most likely someone involved in artistic or creative work (see also § 188), which precisely requires solitude, an obsessiveness about one's projects, an indifference to others' opinions, a certainty about oneself and a respect for the tradition one has inherited.

The noble person's sense of self-worth has several consequences. First, they can't understand vanity (§ 261): why would anyone 'try to elicit a good opinion of themselves that they themselves do not hold . . . and then . . . nevertheless *believe* this good opinion'? They start from a good opinion of themselves, independently of what others think, and then demand that their worth is recognised by others. The common person, by contrast, starts from what others think in forming their opinion of themselves (just as a slave's worth is bestowed by the master's opinion). Second, they are egotistical in believing that others must sacrifice themselves, as only right (§ 265). This shouldn't be narrowly interpreted as selfishness, because they take responsibility for the whole human race in their projects. Third, they respect and revere other noble people, because they see something of themselves in them (§ 265). Finally, noble people don't 'look up' – it is very unlikely, therefore, that the noble person will believe in God. As discussed in NIETZSCHE'S ACCOUNT OF RELIGION (p. 253), Nietzsche thinks the idea of God – at least a perfect, moralistic God who judges us, and before whom everyone is equal – belongs with slave morality, not nobility.

To be noble, one's response to suffering, in *oneself* as much as in others, must *not* be to alleviate it, but to use it in becoming greater still. The noble person suffers greatly but is unwilling to cease their commitment to being great. Nor will they invite pity. So they will not try to display their suffering, but will hide it behind a mask, for example, a mask that treats all suffering casually (§ 216). The terrible suffering of the higher person, and the herd morality that encourages the alleviation of suffering, means they often come to ruin (§ 269). They need to forget what they know about life and themselves, their contempt and revulsion; and so they become seduced by flattery and lose their nobility to become someone 'great', revered by the herd.

A noble person has mastered themselves. Integrating their will to subdue any part that does not fall into line with their project as one expression of their will to power. And in other works, Nietzsche identifies this act of 'self-creation' as central to becoming a higher person.

Nietzsche comments that this desire to value oneself, originally rare, has become more common – an example of the mixing of different value systems.

On masks, see FREE SPIRITS AND EXPERIMENTERS, p. 216.

Explain the values of nobility in relation to the will to power.

Discussion

Some of Nietzsche's ideas of nobility do not seem very radical. A sense of one's goodness independent of others' opinions, a willingness to take responsibility, and an ability to tolerate and use suffering in the quest to make something of oneself and one's life, all express a strong, positive, healthy personality. But can we coherently endorse just these values while ignoring the egoism and inegalitarianism Nietzsche argues goes with them? If someone pursues greatness in their life, how will they react to the lack of anything great or distinctive in others? Nobility is not compatible with an inability to face the truth about human beings.

But recall that Nietzsche is not attempting to defend values for *everybody* to adopt. He wants to free higher people from living by the standards (of equality, modesty, mediocrity) of the 'herd'. Conversely, it would be most inappropriate for herd people to attempt to be noble. To falsely believe one is full of power and goodness is self-deception. Nobility is not compatible with an inability to face the truth about oneself.

Nietzsche's positive vision is not as compelling as his critical analysis of conventional morality, as his inegalitarianism and exclusive focus on greatness is not the only alternative. In many of his remarks, Nietzsche gives familiar values a new, life-affirming interpretation and foundation (e.g. neighbourly love not based on fear, generosity not based on selflessness, etc.). We noted (p. 231) that Nietzsche allows that many acts considered moral should still be done, and immoral ones avoided, but for different reasons. If these are the 'new values' the new philosophers are to create, then their project is not as radical as it seems. This is something we can take from Nietzsche, though not what Nietzsche intended, as it ignores the essential inegalitarianism of his philosophy.

> Explain and discuss Nietzsche's 'noble' values.

Key points • • •

- Noble morality is a development of master morality, and expressed in the new philosophers. Both the noble person and new philosopher feel full of power, affirm life, create values and despise what is weak.
- Nobility involves a keen sense of 'greatness' and continual self-overcoming to achieve it.
- Nietzsche is inspired by the aristocracy of the past, but applies the idea of nobility now to individuals – solitary, driven by work, choosing what is good

for themselves, willing their lives unconditionally and revering their own power.

- Noble people value themselves, so don't understand the attempt to discover one's value in the eyes of others. They are egotistical, don't 'look up' to anyone, and suffer greatly, but use suffering for self-development and shun pity.
- Some of these values express a strong, healthy personality, and Nietzsche presents life-affirming interpretations of familiar values. But his rejection of equality is more difficult to defend.

Social implications of Nietzsche's concept of noble values

Nietzsche is frequently critical of hierarchical societies because they often privilege the *priests*, not those who are truly 'higher'.

Thus Spake Zarathustra, I § 11

See p. 267.

? What social implications does Nietzsche's criticism of conventional morality have?

Nietzsche has *very little* to say about the political and social implications of his theory of noble values. While the values *originated* in a hierarchical society, Nietzsche does not advocate a return to a politics of social class. For higher people to flourish, they must be free enough from conventional morality to pursue their projects of greatness. But this 'freedom' is primarily psychological, not something secured by political arrangements. Nietzsche writes 'Only where the state ends, there begins the human being who is not superfluous.' The noble person now is *solitary*. Nietzsche is concerned that higher people are being undermined by moral *beliefs* more than actual practices, and so it is beliefs he seeks to change.

But perhaps certain social arrangements contribute to mediocrity, an inability to autonomously find value in oneself, and an unwillingness to suffer in order to develop oneself as a person. Herbert Marcuse criticised technology-based capitalism in just these terms – it undermines an inner critical dimension of ourselves and any sense of a 'higher' culture as genuinely 'higher'. It turns us into consumers and all things of great value into something to be consumed. We can argue, further, that these social arrangements are reflections of 'herd morality' and 'modern ideas'.

We can also connect noble values to the grand projects of new philosophers. New philosophers are *commanders* who will seek to breed a higher form of human being (§ 203), guided at first by noble values. How this will be possible, how it will come about, Nietzsche doesn't know – it is for the new philosophers to forge the way. In the hands of new philosophers noble values become a political, not just a personal, vision.

Key points • • •

- Nietzsche's main concern is with freeing the psychology of higher people, not changing moral practices in society as a whole. But we may argue that certain social arrangements will promote mediocrity, while others will promote nobility.
- The new philosophers, however, will eventually undertake the task of raising humanity to a higher form, a project that will have political implications.

III. RELIGIOUS BELIEF

Nietzsche's account of religion; self-denial and sacrifice

The ascetic ideal

'From the beginning, Christian faith has meant a sacrifice: the sacrifice of freedom, pride, spiritual self-confidence; it has meant subjugation and self-derision, self-mutilation' (§ 46). Nietzsche's account of religious belief is closely linked with his account of slave morality and THE 'SLAVE REVOLT' (p. 241). Prior to the revolt, pagan gods were based on the qualities that the aristocratic class saw and valued in themselves. With the revolt, God became reinterpreted as the opposite of human beings' animal nature. Goodness came from a transcendent spiritual world. Whatever was of the natural world, especially our bodies and 'their' instinctual desires, was sinful (§ 47), and something to feel guilt about. So Christian faith required a sacrifice of our animal instincts and wills. Before God, we are guilty *in our very nature*.

> Nietzsche is concerned primarily with Christianity, though he thinks that other religions equally display the ascetic ideal described here, for example, §§ 61, and 195.

This is the ascetic ideal from which slave morality originated. It denies the value of our (animal) life as it is, and looks for redemption in a transcendent realm. It rejects bodily desires and experiences and praises a life of the 'spirit'. In this, it complicates the spirit, setting our wills against themselves. There is what we naturally want, and opposed to this is the ideal of transcending what we want. So the ascetic ideal spurs people on to become better, more developed spiritually. It transforms the energy of their bodily desires into spiritual desires (§ 47), and the constant sense of guilt and failure drives ever greater attempts at 'making amends' for who one is, which can be expressed in cultural achievements and spiritual depth.

See WORK ETHIC, ATHEISM AND FALSE 'FREE SPIRITS', p. 246.

The original force and demands of Christianity have faded, thinks Nietzsche. Religious belief today is 'naïve and quarrelsome'; at least the original Christian faith deserves respect, something that believers in modern ideas are unlikely to understand (§ 58).

Is Nietzsche's interpretation of religious belief fair? For instance, what about the meaning of the Incarnation? This doctrine – that God became human – is usually interpreted as a *validation* of human nature, as a good gift from God. Nietzsche can ask in reply how successfully this message has actually got through. How much Christian teaching has celebrated the body in contrast with that which has denigrated it? Even if there are strands of Christian thought that challenge his analysis, *historically* most religions have incorporated an ideal of a spiritual life that transcends and denigrates the body.

Discuss the role of the ascetic ideal in religious belief.

The will to power in religion

The ascetic ideal is paradoxical for Nietzsche. It seems to oppose life and the will itself; and yet *all* values are an expression of the will to power. How could it have been adopted at all, and how could it have become so widespread? Answering these questions will complete the natural history of morals.

The spread of the ascetic ideal (in the West) originates in the slave revolt, which Nietzsche says began with the Jewish prophets (see p. 241) and continued with Christianity. It was not, then, slaves but priests (and saints) who first held the ascetic ideal. This is only suggested in *Beyond Good and Evil*, but developed at length in *On the Genealogy of Morals*, Essay III.

The priests do not have the direct, expressive will to power as the aristocrats. They resent the power of the aristocrats and the respect they have gained, but they cannot express this directly. So they teach that aristocratic values are evil and decadent, and praise a life of poverty and self-denial, the opposite of the aristocratic ideal. They develop the idea of God to support this revaluation. God will punish evil-doers (the aristocrats) and reward the good (the slaves). They create a standard by which the nobles are inferior to themselves and the common people. So they use the ascetic ideal to gain power as teachers, and therefore leaders, of the people. Nietzsche connects this account to Christianity's gaining power in the Roman Empire, although the 'priest' type exists everywhere, he says.

But why should people listening to the priests accept this revaluation? What is the appeal?

The aristocrats: the ancient aristocrats were amazed by the phenomenon of the saint, respecting the self-discipline involved in self-denial: 'in it they recognized anew and were able to honour their own strength' (§ 51). They made the mistake of thinking that the 'monstrous denial' required by the ascetic ideal could not be for nothing, and so became susceptible to the saint's values.

The common people: the praised life of poverty and self-denial is the common person's life. They suffer physically, but also mentally, through the *ressentiment* they feel towards the aristocrats. But what is worst is the thought that their suffering is *meaningless*. The ascetic ideal gives meaning to their suffering, providing two outlets for their *ressentiment*: first, that the aristocrats can be blamed (an imaginary form of revenge), but second and more centrally, that they are themselves the cause of their suffering. The ascetic ideal condemns the body, our instincts, our sensuous desires; yet we are animals with these desires. Our suffering is our punishment for being what we are, for not successfully transcending the body and the world, for not living up to the ascetic ideal. This makes suffering meaningful, and therefore bearable. Furthermore, the idea of a transcendent world after this one provides hope. And so the common people adopt the ascetic ideal.

Common people have only a weak will to power that struggles to maintain itself in the face of so much suffering. The denial of the will to power, the denial of this bodily life in favour of a spiritual life in a transcendent world, is a way in which their will and their lives succeed in maintaining themselves. So the ascetic ideal is an expression of their will to power.

Nietzsche repeatedly notes that the ascetic ideal cannot be honest with itself (e.g. § 2) and acknowledge its historical or psychological origins, because it disapproves of the motives it is founded upon. Yet more direct assertions of will to power continue to slip out in the actions of people supposedly acting 'morally':

> In helpful and benevolent people one nearly always finds a clumsy cunning that first rearranges the person who is to be helped so that, for example, he 'deserves' their help, needs *their* help in particular, and will prove to be deeply grateful, dependent, subservient for all their help. With fantasies such as these they control the needy like a piece of property. (§ 194)

And how Nietzsche continues the passage illustrates his account of the priests:

> no father disputes his right to be allowed to subjugate his child to *his* concepts and judgments . . . And like fathers, so teachers, classes, priests,

Explain in detail how the denial of the will to power can be an expression of the will to power.

and princes still see in every new person an immediate opportunity for a new possession.

Key points • • •

- The ascetic ideal originates in the revaluation of aristocratic values, and in Christianity, requires the sacrifice of one's animal nature and pride. It opposes the instinctual life we want with a spiritual life we should want, thereby becoming a driving force in the development of the spirit and cultural achievements.
- We can object that Nietzsche's interpretation of Christianity is one-sided. But he can respond that his interest is with the message that has been historically dominant.
- The ascetic ideal expresses the will to power of the priests, who use it to wrest power away from the aristocrats by becoming teachers of the new ideal. The aristocrats respect the self-overcoming involved.
- Common people are attracted by its ability to make sense of their suffering, and its adoption becomes a means for preserving their lives, so it expresses their will to power as well.
- The will to power in the ascetic ideal slips out in the fantasies involved in moral action and teaching.

Advantages and disadvantages of religion, the future use of religion

The first advantage of religion is that it gives people's suffering and their lives meaning, and so enables them to continue to live. We can tell how sick of life someone is, Nietzsche says, by how they want the image of life distorted, falsified, 'transcendentalized' (§ 59). Religious people have a terrible fear that life is meaningless.

See Herd morality and the critique of 'modern ideas', p. 245.

But enabling 'weak' people to live is also the first and main disadvantage of religion. Christianity has kept alive what ought to have perished, and so humanity has become degenerate. We have come to hate life, the will to power, strength, whatever is of the 'world'. And so, a second disadvantage, the development of higher people has been undermined, because their traits are slandered as evil.

But Nietzsche repeatedly praises what the ascetic ideal has made possible, in terms of art and in deepening the soul. Art makes human life bearable by making it beautiful, even as it falsifies it. And so Nietzsche calls religious people the highest artists (§ 59). They falsify the image of life the most, but make something more beautiful out of human beings. This is a second advantage of religion. It allows us to bear the sight of ourselves (§ 61).

A related, third advantage is that the ascetic ideal calls upon people to strive to better themselves. As discussed on p. 245, Nietzsche is concerned that herd morality after the ascetic ideal will lead to us becoming even 'smaller'.

A fourth advantage is that the ascetic ideal is the source of the unconditional will to truth. While Nietzsche condemns this, he says that it is because of the unconditional will to truth that we have been able to discover the origins of the ascetic ideal and undermine it, together with moral values and the idea of God itself. In early times, people sacrificed people to God; then they sacrificed their strongest instincts; and now the same ideal has led them to sacrificing God, so that all hope and comfort is gone (§ 55). The development of atheism in the West is the result of the commitment to truth 'at any price'. But giving up belief in God means that we must, in consistency, also give up the morality that has gone with it. That morality is founded on a belief in a transcendent realm; without this, it lacks foundation. The unconditional will to truth leads us, eventually, beyond good and evil.

See PHILOSOPHERS' VALUES, p. 202.

The fifth advantage leads on to a discussion of the future use of religion by new philosophers, and helps us understand the religious tone of Nietzsche's account of eternal return. This advantage is illustrated not by Christianity, but by pagan Greek religion: 'The astonishing thing about the ancient Greeks' religiosity is the tremendous wealth of gratitude pouring forth from it: only a very noble kind of person can face nature and life like *this*!' (§ 49). We noted (p. 218) that affirming eternal return required a great sense of affirmation of life, which we can now say would naturally lead to and express itself in gratitude for life.

New philosophers will use religion in their grand projects of turning humanity into a higher kind of being (§ 61), adopting a role similar to that of 'priests'. First, religion can be used as a way of overcoming obstacles. It can be used in selecting what kind of people go on to reproduce (presumably by labelling them as valuable or 'chosen'). It is a bond that ties subjects to their rulers, as subjects give up their judgements of right and wrong to their rulers. It protects the more contemplative philosophers against the cruder political authority of others, supporting their authority as derived from a different, higher source. Its practices also protect the 'purity' of their souls.

See PHILOSOPHERS'
VALUES, p. 202.

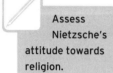

**Assess
Nietzsche's
attitude towards
religion.**

Second, religion can also be used as a training in leadership. Religion provides guidance and the opportunity for exercising authority over others. It encourages self-development, a chance to test one's self-control and solitude – not only for the new philosophers but for the people they are breeding to become higher. New philosophers will also not use the ascetic ideal but *ascetism* in their self-transformation. The ancient philosophers used ascetism to be able to pursue their goal of doing philosophy single-mindedly, and all higher people must have some ascetism to transform themselves and achieve their goals.

Finally, to common people 'who exist to serve and be generally useful', and who are therefore needed to support the project, religion also offers contentment, an acceptance of how things are.

Key points • • •

- Nietzsche identifies five advantages to religion:

  1. It gives suffering meaning.
  2. It falsifies human life, so allowing us to bear it.
  3. It motivates people to develop spiritually.
  4. Its unconditional will to truth has led to atheism and its own demise.
  5. It supports a sense of gratitude for life.

- He also identifies two disadvantages to religion:

  1. It keeps alive people who ought to die, leading to the degeneration of the human race.
  2. It slanders the traits of higher people, undermining their development.

- Religion will be used by new philosophers to overcome obstacles, train themselves in leadership and self-overcoming, and keep common people content.

PREPARING FOR THE EXAM

6

To get good exam results, you need to have a good sense of what the exam will be like and what the examiners are looking for, and to revise in a way that will help you prepare to answer the questions well. This probably sounds obvious, but in fact, many students do not think about the exam itself, only about what questions might come up. There is a big difference. This chapter will provide you with some guidance on how to approach your exams in a way that will help get you the best results you can. It is divided into three sections: revision, understanding the question and exam technique. Before continuing to read this chapter, it is worth looking back at the Introduction to see how exam questions are structured and what the Assessment Objectives are (p. 3).

Throughout the chapter, I will highlight revision points and exam tips. You can find these collected together at the end of the chapter.

Revision: knowing what the examiners are looking for

There are lots of memory tricks for learning information for exams. This chapter isn't about those. Revision isn't just about learning information; it's also about learning how to use that information well in the exam. Being able to do this is a question not of memory, but of directed revision and concentration in the exam. If you've been doing the exercises throughout this book, then you have been putting into practice the advice I give below.

It may sound obvious, but in order to know how best to answer the exam questions, you need to think about how they are marked. The examiners mark your answers according to three principles, known as 'Assessment Objectives' (AOs). These are listed in the Introduction, on p. 3.

You can use these AOs to help guide your revision. AO1 (Knowledge and understanding) leads straight to the first revision point:

> R1: Learn the arguments. Who said what? What terms and concepts did they use? How did they defend their positions?

This, you may think, is challenging enough! But this isn't enough. In displaying your knowledge, you need to show what is *relevant* to the question being asked. Knowing what is relevant is a special kind of knowledge, which involves thinking carefully about what you know about the theories in relation to the question asked. The best way to learn what is relevant is to practise answering questions, either exam questions or questions you make up for yourself or a friend. Try to make up questions that are similar to the exam questions, for example, that use quotations or that use words such as 'assess' and 'critically discuss'. Practising answering different questions on the same topic helps keep your knowledge flexible, because you have to think of just the right bit of information that will answer the question.

> R2: Practise applying your knowledge by answering questions about it. The best questions to practise with are past exam questions, but you can also make up questions for yourself.

AO2 (Interpretation and analysis) means that your knowledge needs to be developed in a particular way. In philosophy, there is no easy, straightforward answer to 'What did he mean when he said. . .'. So in knowing and understanding arguments and issues, you need to be able to *interpret* them and defend your interpretation.

> R3: Revise those aspects of the issue that are hard to understand. Practise arguing that they *can* be understood in more than one way, and why they *should* be understood to have the meaning you give them.

One aspect of interpretation is knowing what is relevant and what is not to the view you are discussing. From this point, what point follows next? Or again, what would be a relevant example? You can either remember good examples you have read, or create your own. In either case, you should know precisely what point the example is making. An irrelevant example demonstrates that you don't really know what you are talking about.

> R4: Prepare examples beforehand, rather than try to invent them in the exam. If you can use your own, that's great (you'll get extra marks if they are good). But they must be short and they must make the right point – so try them out on your friends and teachers first.

But this is only half of AO2. When interpreting someone, you also need to show what his arguments are and how they are supposed to work. This means being able to *analyse* an issue, finding its main claims and main arguments, and then breaking down the arguments into premises and conclusions, and showing how the conclusion is supposed to follow from the premises.

> R5: Spend time identifying the main claims and arguments involved in each issue you have studied, putting arguments in your own words, stating clearly what the conclusion is and what the premises are. Point out or show how the reasoning is supposed to work.

What of AO3? How do you revise for 'assessment and evaluation'? This AO tests you on how well you can relate and compare arguments, how well you build an argument, deal with objections and come to a supported conclusion. The best way to prepare for it is to spend time *thinking* about the arguments and issues. Thinking is quite different from knowing about. You might know Descartes' arguments for substance dualism, but you may never have stopped to really work out whether you think they are any good.

AO3 encourages you to do two things. One is to question what the argument actually shows – do the premises support the conclusion or some other point of view? The second is to relate a particular argument to other arguments and viewpoints on the issue, and in particular to reflect on whether the objections to an argument undermine it. Work through the arguments so that you understand for yourself the pros and cons of each viewpoint. As a minimum, be able to argue both for and against a particular view.

> R6: Think reflectively about the arguments and issues. Practise arguing for and against a particular view. Think about the place and importance of the arguments for the issue as a whole.

You need to be able to construct arguments, not just report them. This means that what you write should also take the form of premises and conclusion. The premises will be your judgements as you go along, in response to this view or that objection. These judgements need to add up to a conclusion. You shouldn't end your essay with a totally different point of view from the one your evaluations in the essay support. In other words, do the judgements you reach reflect the arguments you have presented?

This doesn't mean that you have to find one point of view on the issue and defend it. But if you can't come to a firm conclusion about which viewpoint is right, try to come to a firm conclusion about why the different points each seem right in their own way, and why it is difficult to choose. Philosophy is not about knowing the 'right answers', it is about understanding why an answer *might* be right and why it is difficult to know.

> R7: Think about how your judgements on the various arguments you have studied add up. Do they lead to one conclusion, one point of view being right? Or do you think arguments for and against one position are closely balanced?

These first seven revision points relate to taking in and understanding information. There are two more points that will help you organise the information, learn it better and prepare you for answering exam questions.

A good way of organising your information is to create answer outlines or web-diagrams for particular issues. For example, from Unit 4.1 Hume, you could create an outline or web-diagram for cause and effect. Think about the essential points, and organise them, perhaps like this:

1. According to Hume, what is the idea of a cause?
2. How do we acquire this idea – from what sorts of experiences?
3. What are the roles of 'constant conjunction' and 'Custom' in Hume's analysis?
4. What objections are there to Hume's analysis of cause?
5. How do we know what causes what?
6. What is the idea of 'necessary connection'? Where does the idea come from?
7. What objections are there to Hume's analysis of necessary connection?
8. What are Hume's two definitions of cause? Are they equivalent?

With an outline like this, you should be able to answer any question that comes up on cause and effect.

> R8: Create structured outlines or web-diagrams for particular issues. Try to cover all the main points.

Finally, once you've organised your notes into an outline or web-diagram, time yourself writing exam answers. Start by using your outline, relying on your memory to fill in the details. Then practise by memorising the outline as well, and doing it as though it were an actual exam. You might be surprised at how quickly the time goes by. You'll find that you need to be very focused – but this is what the examiners are looking for: answers that are thoughtful but to the point.

> R9: Practise writing timed answers. Use your notes at first, but then practise without them.

There is one more thing important to revision that I haven't yet talked about, which is how the structure of the questions and how the marks are awarded can help you to decide what to focus on. This is what we'll look at next.

Understanding the question: giving the examiners what they want

The key to doing well in an exam is understanding the question. I don't just mean understanding the *topic* of the question, such as 'liberty' or 'miracles'. Of course, this is very important. But you also need to understand what the question is asking you to *do*. And this is related to the three Assessment Objectives discussed above.

In the exam, there is a difference between the compulsory question and the two essay questions. Notice the difference in 'key words'. The key to understanding what the question is asking, and so to getting a good mark, is to take notice of the key words.

Question structure and marks

The compulsory question uses words such as 'outline', 'illustrate', 'explain'. This question, worth 15 marks, tests just AO1 (8 marks) and AO2 (7 marks). There are no marks available for AO3 (assessment and evaluation), so don't spend any time *evaluating* the philosophical point of view under discussion.

By contrast, the essay questions use key words such as 'assess', 'discuss', 'explore', 'examine'. All three Assessment Objectives are applied to your essay with particular emphasis on AO3 (AO1: 10 marks; AO2: 11 marks; AO3: 24 marks; total = 45 marks). You therefore need to demonstrate knowledge, and analysis, and evaluation. Usually, evaluation is the most demanding – and it is worth noting that it is also the one that receives most marks. So no matter how clearly you describe the theories and arguments, you cannot get a good mark for the question if you do not also evaluate them.

Don't think that you need to divide your essay into parts, first demonstrating knowledge, then analysis, then evaluation. If you concentrate on making your answer evaluative, you will usually demonstrate knowledge and analysis as you go along. The reason for this is that a good evaluative answer to a question provides an *argument* for a conclusion. But for an argument to be good, it needs to clearly display an understanding of the topic, as well as analysis of each issue or point as it is discussed. It needs to start by explaining what is under discussion (what issue or theory), and then explain and illustrate points as they are made, to support the conclusion that this answer to the question is the best one.

Exam technique: getting the best result you can

Exams are very exciting, whether in a good way or a bad way! It can be helpful, therefore, to take your time at the beginning, not to rush into your answers, but to plan your way. The tips I give below are roughly in the order that you might apply them when taking the exam. You might be surprised at the number of things it can be worth doing before you write anything at all.

If you have studied just one text in Unit 4, you have no choice with the shorter compulsory question, and a choice of two questions for the longer essay. If you have studied more than one text, you need to decide carefully which question to answer, and this means reading the whole of each question before making your decision. You might find that although you know the answer to the compulsory question, you aren't sure about the essay questions. If you don't read the whole question first, you could end up wishing you had answered another question.

> E1. If you've studied more than one text, read through all the relevant questions before starting your answer. This will help you to decide which question you can answer best overall, taking into account all the parts.

Once you've decided which question to do, you need to think how long to spend on each part. Here the marks available for each part should be your guide. You have 90 minutes for the exam, and there are 60 marks available. That means you should spend around 22 minutes on the compulsory question, and 68 minutes on the essay. But this isn't exact, and you may want to spend more time on the essay question, which will require more planning.

Before you start to write your answer, read the question again very closely. Notice the precise phrasing of the question. Because an exam is exciting (good or bad), many people have a tendency to notice only what the question is about, for example, the Forms or God. They don't notice the rest of the words in the question. But the question is never 'so tell me everything you know about God'! *Every word counts*. Your answer should relate not just to the issue in general, but to the *specific words* of the question.

> E2. Before starting your answer, read the question again very closely. Take note of every word.

You are now ready to start answering the question. But many people find it is worth organising their thoughts first. What are you going to say, in what order? Arguments require that you present ideas in a logical order. If you've memorised an outline or a web-diagram, quickly write it out at the beginning so that you note down all the points. It is very easy to forget something or go off on a tangent once you are stuck into the arguments. Having an outline or web-diagram to work from will help you keep your answer relevant and structured. It will also remind you how much you still want to cover, so it can help you pace yourself better. However, you might discover, as you develop your answer, that parts of the outline or diagram are irrelevant or just don't fit. Don't worry – the outline is only there as a guide.

> E3. Before you start your answer, it can be worth writing out your outline or web-diagram first. This can help remind you of the key points you want to make, and the order in which you want to make them.

Finding and using a good example is very important. Good examples are concise and relevant, and support your argument. But you need to explain why they support your argument. An example is an illustration, not an argument.

> E4. Keep your examples short and make sure they support the point you want to make. Always explain how they support your point.

Because philosophy is about the logical relationship of ideas, there are a number of rules of thumb about presentation. Here are four important ones.

> E5. Four rules of thumb:
>
> 1. Don't use a 'technical term', such as 'the greatest happiness principle' or 'the cosmological argument', without saying what it means.
> 2. Describe a theory before evaluating it. (If you have described it in answer to a previous part, you don't need to describe it again.)

> 3. Keep related ideas together. If you have a thought later on, add a footnote indicating where in the answer you want it to be read.
> 4. Don't state the conclusion to an argument before you've discussed the argument, especially if you are going to present objections to that conclusion. You can state what the argument hopes to show, but don't state it *as* a conclusion.

It is worth noting that evaluation is more than just presenting objections and responses side by side. Get the objections and the theory to 'talk' to each other, and try to come to some conclusion about which side is stronger. Furthermore, one good discussion is worth more than many weak or superficial points, so choose two or three of the *most powerful* relevant objections, and discuss those in depth.

> E6. Make sure your discussion is not just reporting a sequence of points of view, but presents objections and replies, and tries to reach a particular conclusion.

Finally, it is very easy to forget something, or say it in an unclear way. Leave time to check your answer at the end. You might find you can add a sentence here or there to connect two ideas together more clearly, or that some word is left undefined. These little things can make a big difference to the mark.

> E7. Leave time to check your answer at the end. You may want to add a helpful sentence here and there.

Revision tips

R1: Learn the arguments. Who said what? What terms and concepts did they use? How did they defend their positions?

R2: Practise applying your knowledge by answering questions about it. The best questions to practise with are past exam questions, but you can also make up questions for yourself.

R3: Revise those aspects of the issue that are hard to understand. Practise arguing that they *can* be understood in more than one way, and why they *should* be understood to have the meaning you give them.

R4: Prepare examples beforehand, rather than try to invent them in the exam. If you can use your own, that's great (you'll get extra marks if they are good). But they must be short and they must make the right point – so try them out on your friends and teachers first.

R5: Spend time identifying the main claims and arguments involved in each issue you have studied, putting arguments in your own words, stating clearly what the conclusion is and what the premisses are. Point out or show how the reasoning is supposed to work.

R6: Think reflectively about the arguments and issues. Practise arguing for and against a particular view. Think about the place and importance of the arguments for the issue as a whole.

R7: Think about how your judgements on the various arguments you have studied add up. Do they lead to one conclusion, one point of view being right? Or do you think arguments for and against one position are closely balanced?

R8: Create structured outlines or web-diagrams for particular issues. Try to cover all the main points.

R9: Practise writing timed answers. Use your notes at first, but then practise without them.

Exam tips

E1. If you've studied more than one text, read through all the relevant questions before starting your answer. This will help you to decide which question you can answer best overall, taking into account all the parts.

E2. Before starting your answer, read the question again very closely. Take note of every word.

E3. Before you start your answer, it can be worth writing out your outline or web-diagram first. This can help remind you of the key points you want to make, and the order in which you want to make them.

E4. Keep your examples short and make sure they support the point you want to make. Always explain how they support your point.

E5. Four rules of thumb:

1. Don't use a 'technical term', such as 'the greatest happiness principle' or 'the cosmological argument', without saying what it means.
2. Describe a theory before evaluating it. (If you have described it in answer to a previous part, you don't need to describe it again.)
3. Keep related ideas together. If you have a thought later on, add a footnote indicating where in the answer you want it to be read.
4. Don't state the conclusion to an argument before you've discussed the argument, especially if you are going to present objections to that conclusion. You can state what the argument hopes to show, but don't state it *as* a conclusion.

E6. Make sure your discussion is not just reporting a sequence of points of view, but presents objections and replies, and tries to reach a particular conclusion.

E7. Leave time to check your answer at the end. You may want to add a helpful sentence here and there.

GLOSSARY

a posteriori – Knowledge of propositions that can only be known to be true or false through sense experience.

a priori – Knowledge of propositions that do not require (sense) experience to be known to be true or false.

analytic – An analytic proposition is true (or false) in virtue of the meanings of the words. For instance, 'a bachelor is an unmarried man' is analytically true, while 'a square has three sides' is analytically false.

argument – A reasoned inference from one set of claims – the premises – to another claim – the conclusion.

cognitivism – The theory that knowledge of some specific type of claim is possible, for example, moral cognitivism claims that there is moral knowledge.

conditional – A proposition that takes the form of 'if. . ., then. . .'.

contingent – A proposition that could be either true or false, a state of affairs that may or may not hold, depending on how the world actually is.

counterfactual – a conditional statement, in which the first clause picks out a state of affairs that is contrary to fact, for example, 'if the water hadn't spilled, the table would be dry', which implies that the water *did* spill.

deduction – An argument whose conclusion is *logically entailed* by its premises, that is, if the premises are true, the conclusion *cannot* be false.

dualism – The metaphysical theory that there are two distinct types of substance (mind and body); or, as property dualism, that there are two distinct types of property (usually physical properties and properties of consciousness).

empirical – Relating to or deriving from experience, especially sense experience, but also including experimental scientific investigation.

empiricism – The theory that there can be no a priori knowledge of synthetic propositions about the world (outside my mind), that is, all a priori knowledge is of analytic propositions, while all knowledge of synthetic propositions must be checked against sense experience.

epistemology – The study ('-ology') of knowledge ('episteme') and related concepts, including belief, justification, certainty. It looks at the possibility and sources of knowledge.

fallacy – A pattern of poor reasoning. A fallacious argument or theory is one that is mistaken in some way.

induction – An argument whose conclusion is *supported* by its premises, but is not logically entailed by them, that is, if the premises are true, the conclusion may be false, but this is unlikely (relative to the premises); one form of inductive argument is inference to the best explanation, that is, the conclusion presents the 'best explanation' for why the premises are true.

innate – Knowledge or ideas that are in some way present 'from birth' or cannot be derived from experience.

metaphysics – The branch of philosophy that enquires about the fundamental nature of reality.

nativism – the theory that there are innate ideas, concepts or knowledge.

necessary – A proposition that *must* be true (or if false, it must be false), a state of affairs that *must* hold.

proposition – A declarative statement (or more accurately, what is claimed by a declarative statement), such as 'mice are mammals'; propositions can go after 'that' in 'I believe that. . .' and 'I know that. . .'.

rationalism – The theory that there can be a priori knowledge of synthetic propositions about the world (outside my mind); this knowledge is innate or gained by reason without reliance on sense experience.

scepticism – The view that our usual justifications for claiming our beliefs amount to knowledge are inadequate, so we do not in fact have knowledge.

sense-data (singular **sense-datum**) – In perception, mental images or representations of what is perceived, 'bits' of experience; if they exist, they are the immediate objects of perception.

synthetic – A proposition that is not analytic, but true or false depending on how the world is.

veridical – A proposition that is true or an experience that represents the world as it actually is.

INDEX

eBooks – at www.eBookstore.tandf.co.uk

A library at your fingertips!

eBooks are electronic versions of printed books. You can store them on your PC/laptop or browse them online.

They have advantages for anyone needing rapid access to a wide variety of published, copyright information.

eBooks can help your research by enabling you to bookmark chapters, annotate text and use instant searches to find specific words or phrases. Several eBook files would fit on even a small laptop or PDA.

NEW: Save money by eSubscribing: cheap, online access to any eBook for as long as you need it.

Annual subscription packages

We now offer special low-cost bulk subscriptions to packages of eBooks in certain subject areas. These are available to libraries or to individuals.

For more information please contact webmaster.ebooks@tandf.co.uk

We're continually developing the eBook concept, so keep up to date by visiting the website.

www.eBookstore.tandf.co.uk